Leader's Guide

by
Fiona Vidal-White

CHURCH PUBLISHING
an imprint of
Church Publishing Incorporated, New York

Copyright © 2006 by Church Publishing Incorporated

ISBN-13: 978-0-89869-501-4
ISBN-10: 0-89869-501-5

Church Publishing Incorporated
445 Fifth Avenue
New York, NY 10016
www.churchpublishing.org

5 4 3 2 1

This book is dedicated to

My first choir mistresses
Mrs. Winifred Bonas and Miss Llywella Harris
who introduced me to excellence
in choral repertoire and singing

and

The Rev. Dr. John Hooker:

When in our music God is glorified,
And adoration leaves no room for pride,
It is as though the whole creation cried:
Alleluia! Alleluia! Alleluia!

How often, making music, we have found
A new dimension in the world of sound,
As worship moved us to a more profound
Alleluia! Alleluia! Alleluia!
#140

Contents

Author's Preface

When I first started this work, I somehow believed that it was about removing what I knew from my mind and depositing it on the paper (much like Professor Dumbledore and his Pensieve in Harry Potter). In the last four years I have discovered that the beginning was only a seed, and I have grown enormously and learned prodigiously throughout the process. Many, many people have helped me along the way, and I owe them my grateful thanks and praise.

I met John Hooker as a student in one of his classes at the Episcopal Divinity School, and from that moment on I decided I want to learn from him to the end of my days. John has the gift of convincing me that what I do and say has lasting worth, and I thank him from the bottom of my heart. He is also the person who, when I intended to write a guide to children's music only, kept saying, "This hymnal is so needed!" until I realized the Holy Spirit was speaking. John's gifts to me and to the Episcopal Church are boundless.

Having Marilyn Haskel as an editor has been something between a profound blessing and an absolute necessity. This being my first book, I had no idea what editors do, and now I know that without Marilyn I am nothing. Her vision, breadth of knowledge, humor, and rigor have guided me all the way.

Marilyn Haskel introduced me to Caroline Fairless, director of *Children at Worship, Congregations in Bloom*, soon after I began. It was Caroline's vision of the role of children in worship that helped me see that the implications of what I was doing were far greater than just musical. Caroline has helped me struggle, has listened to me when I felt ready to give up, and has given me opportunities to work with her and for her. I am also delighted to have her husband and colleague, Jim Sims, as a friend. He has taught me so much about being a musician, church musician, minister, servant — and told me some really bad jokes. May the three of us work together often.

Thanks also to the people of the Church of St. Andrew's, Wellesley, Massachusetts, who were my laboratory for the beginning of these ideas, especially the Reverend Addison Hall; Director of Religious Education Deborah Aylesworth; and Music Director Harry Kelton; and to Daniel Viggiani for his generous help with my non-existent Spanish. Most importantly, to my children's choirs 1996–2000: thank you for everything you taught me about teaching children church music.

Thanks to many people in the Diocese of Massachusetts who have answered my endless questions, especially Pat Michaels, Mark Engelhardt, and the Reverend Kim Hardy.

I also want to acknowledge the huge influence that the work of John Bell and the Wild Goose Resource Group has had on me as a worshiper and a church musician. May our paths converge one day.

To my parents-in-law who are old hands in publishing matters — thank you for all your support. To my sister Stephanie, wise counsel, advisor on group process, and hard-nosed businesswoman — thank you for your listening and your advice. To my parents, Paddy and the Reverend Mark Vidal-Hall — sometimes it takes a while to see all that your parents have taught you. Having a father who was, for more than thirty years, a vicar who always honored young people and pushed the limits of a sometimes limited church, and a mother who is both a musician and Christian educator, has made me who I am, and molded what I can do. For all these blessings, thanks. To my children, Aidan and Zoë — there have been many times when I have had to work, work, work. I hope this book will make church a place you want to be and give you all it has given me since my childhood.

And to my husband, Jeremy, who has contributed with continual grace, conversation and advice, technical help, looking after the children, cooking meals, and all the responsibilities a spouse has to take on during a project like this — with the added complication that as an atheist, he has learned way more than he bargained for — thank you for being my help-meet. I will always need you as my guide and my light.

Fiona Vidal-White
Feast of St. Nicholas 2005

COME AND GATHER ROUND

Says Jesus, "Come and gather round.
I want to teach my friends
some truths about the love I bring
the love that never ends.
Look to the child, here in your midst,
who has so much and more to say
of what it means to follow me,
to come and walk my way."

Christ speaks to us, who, growing old,
get burdened down with care;
while caution reigns, we seldom see
God's presence everywhere.
He points to gifts that children bring —
the will to risk, the trust to dare,
through which, no matter where we are,
we'll find God always there.

When was it that we first forgot
that questions helped us grow,
or lost the openness to ask
and learn what we don't know?
Christ points to gifts that children bring,
the searching heart and lively mind
which let God's kingdom grow in those
who seek until they find.

Lord Jesus, we have gathered round
to hear you teach your friends
the truths about the love you bring,
that love which never ends.
We look to children in our midst
for they have much and more to say
and join with them to follow you,
to live and walk your way.

Words: Leith Fisher
From *Common Ground*
© Panel on Worship,
The Church of Scotland
Used by permission.

Introduction

This leader's guide is designed to help directors of Christian education, teachers, church musicians, liturgists, and clergy use *My Heart Sings Out* in the best possible way for all-age worship in church, church school, children's chapel, religious schools, and vacation Bible schools.

One of the foundational assumptions of this collection of music is that music for worship must be accessible to all. People want and need to worship God, and singing helps make that possible. Another assumption is that all can join in singing a melody, and many can learn to sing harmony.

For some people, singing in harmony, particularly the relatively simple pieces in this collection, will be quite easy and very satisfying. For others it will be difficult—an entry into a world fraught with anxiety. Even though there are excellent school music teachers who strive to teach both the talented and the musically challenged, music can be a subject in which those with talent thrive and those without are left by the wayside, particularly in secondary education and beyond. The musically abandoned then have no experience from which to draw in church, perhaps the only remaining place where communal singing is practiced today.

Some people avoid singing altogether because they have taken to heart a perceived model of church music lifted wholesale from the world of secular classical music where the quality of what one does — one's excellence — is measured against the great classical music of sacred composers such as Tallis, Byrd, Purcell, Bach, Handel, and Mozart. It is difficult not to feel like an "also-ran" when compared to that exacting standard.

Such a comparison does not stand up to theological scrutiny. Harold Best tackles this subject in "Personal Excellence, Success, and Competition," chapter 5 in his book *Music through the Eyes of Faith* (HarperSanFrancisco, 1993). He uses the letter to the Philippians, in which Paul writes, "I keep striving [in some translations, "pressing on"] to win the prize....[I] forget what is behind me to reach what is ahead. So I run straight towards the goal in order to win the prize, which is God's call through Christ Jesus to the life above." From this Best draws a definition of excellence for Christians: "Excellence is the process — note that word, process — of becoming better than I once was." This does not mean rejecting one's earlier achievements or interests, but focusing on the process rather than the product, for God has given us the wonderful gift of being able to learn and to create. For a church musician, this might mean both improving one's keyboard skills and gaining a better understanding of rock-based contemporary Christian music. For a member of the congregation it might mean either learning to sing a congregational song in parts or joining the choir to sing the best choral music that a particular choir can achieve.

Best then asks the question, "Can one music be better than another?" and answers, "...better-than-ness may not be hierarchical but functional." In musical terms this means that a Bach cantata and a Taizé chorus are not compared in terms of "quality" but in terms of their relevance for a particular service of worship. If, for example, the service is one of mourning, listening to Bach might be just as healing as singing Taizé. If the liturgy is a family service, the Taizé might be more appropriate. In a service of carols or a Lenten Tenebrae service, Bach might be more appropriate.

If Christian educators, musicians, and liturgists seek to provide meaningful opportunities for the community to praise and worship God, then singing needs to be accessible to all who are in the process of striving for excellence and celebrating their intrinsic goodness at what ever skill level they may have. Everyone must be included. In God's sight, our music is incomplete and out of tune if we relegate some to the back row and forbid them to sing.

To Directors of Christian Education

The recent trend has been for churches to create a monthly all-age or family worship service in which children are more consciously included. *My Heart Sings Out* is intended to be the primary source of music for such services. Because the planning for these services is often included in the director of Christian education's job description, this leader's guide is particularly aimed toward the person who oversees not only worship, but also teachers and the education of children.

In the commentary on each song guidelines are given suggesting possible liturgical uses, the connections to lectionary readings, and teaching ideas based on the text. Since not all have musical training, general musical suggestions have been included.

To Church Musicians

Many church musicians in the Episcopal church have been brought up in the "English Cathedral Tradition" (as, of course, I was myself). This repertoire brings with it certain assumptions about the role and purpose of church music:

- It is primarily composed by Europeans in the Western classical tradition.

- It spans a period from 1500 to the present day, with a heavy focus on the nineteenth century.

- It is complex and challenging to perform, and musicians work at it to offer God the best results of skill and talent.

- It is mostly performed by "specialists," the organist and choir members, on behalf of the congregation. The congregation is also led in the singing of hymns with the accompaniment of the organ and choir.

This model has provided a massive selection of music, from which churches and musicians continue to draw.

Worship and theology have greatly changed in the last hundred years, not to mention the changes in the world, and so must our selection and use of music in worship. *My Heart Sings Out* and its leader's guide propose a new model of church music particularly for a majority of parish churches. The two primary goals of this model are these:

- to match music to the liturgical and scriptural themes of the Sunday service;
- to include all, particularly the children in the pew who have so far been excluded from complete participation in worship by musical choices that are made.

The first goal, of course, is key to good worship planning. The second goal is perhaps a new and more challenging one, bringing scrutiny to preconceived notions of who worships and how.

In this multicultural church and world, it is imperative to include songs of many cultures, particularly if our own congregation is predominantly Anglo. Music helps share the faith experiences of people all around the world and encourages a dominant culture to express its own faith in new and different ways.

The music in this collection includes a wide range of forms from traditional strophic hymns (see glossary) to cyclical choruses, but all has been chosen because the theology is sound, and the sound is glorious! There is also a large body of music that should be sung unaccompanied in harmony. While it may seem a daunting task to take on the musical training of the congregation as well as the choir, it will prove to be a transforming experience for all involved. For those who have been working with the goals of this book and consider them second nature, may you find here much of the music from different collections that is already familiar in your planning and as an educational resource to help train future leaders.

To Clergy

Those who serve a large church with both a director of Christian education and a church music director may have only one task — to pass this book on to them. Those who serve a small church with a tiny budget will find much-needed music and information in this book that fulfills the desire to help children worship with everyone else on Sunday even if there is no organist. There is music here for every event from Sunday worship to Wednesday youth group or the Saturday potluck. The vestry might even sing a chorus or two before beginning their meeting. This leader's guide will introduce the theology of music and worship to those who are called to be music, worship, and education leaders in the church.

How to Use This Book

The book is arranged in three large sections: "Service Music," which contains selections for specific places in the liturgy as well as more general texts for praise, gathering, prayer, and leaving; "The Church Year," which includes hymns and songs for Advent through All Saints; and "Other Themes," which present topics such as baptism, healing, and peace.

The opening three chapters provide basic information and skill-development guidelines for selecting music not only from this book, but in general; for teaching and leading music with an all-age congregation; and for planning worship that considers what children find easy and what challenges them.

An explanation about each sectional heading precedes the selections under that heading throughout the book. These contain teaching points or liturgical suggestions that will help shape worship for children. Each song is printed in full with an occasional new arrangement or instrumental accompaniment. Each selection is also accompanied by the following information:

- *Age Group:* Suggests the age group most likely to find the song accessible. For a full explanation of these codes, see chapter 3, "Worship Planning," page 17.

- *Essential Accompaniment:* Suggests whether a song should be accompanied or not and, if so, which instruments are best in order of priority.

- *Liturgical Use:* Suggests placement of the song within the Sunday liturgy or at other events that include worship. The suggestion "Liturgy of the Word" means that the particular hymn or song would work well between readings either to respond to or support the texts. The suggestion "congregational prelude" opens the possibility of using the pre-service gathering time to sing favorite selections or learn songs to be used in the liturgy.

- *Lectionary:* Notes specific occasions or seasons in the church year when the song may be used or when its scripture-based text is appointed in the lectionary.

- *Learning:* Contains information and teaching points about the text or music; may be scriptural, historical, or biographical.

- *Performance:* Gives tips on how to prepare the song with the congregation or choir and ways of performing it in the context of liturgy.

- *Question:* Suggests questions that may be asked of children in a teaching environment. This practice is patterned after the *Godly Play* curriculum in which lessons are followed by "wondering questions." Open-ended questions give children a chance to express their own theological ideas and begin to form their theological vocabulary. Questions are intended to be open and non-judgmental. Allow children to answer them however they want, especially, when appropriate, in different media such as writing, art, music, dance, and play. Affirm children's right to form their own language and ideas about God.

Pronunciation guides are included for selections printed in two languages. The text is given in regular type and the pronunciation is given underneath in italics. The system used is consistent and simple. The goal is to encourage non-native speakers to become familiar with the sounds. Native speakers may be helpful in clarifying the finer points of pronunciation where this simple method falls short.

Instruments typical of the culture of the music are often suggested, but other more readily available instruments may be used to approximate the sound described. The goal is to engage children physically in playing instruments or aurally in hearing their sounds.

Certain words in the text are typeset with SMALL CAPITAL LETTERS. This indicates that the words are included in the glossary. Be sure to explore the indexes at the back of the book, which will help with planning an event or worship.

Notes on Spanish pronunciation

Language is best taught aurally, so any system to give instruction in print only will fall short of the desired sound. However, the goal in this volume is to provide some help for those who do not know Spanish but find themselves in the ever-growing parts of the country where Spanish is a major second language or who have begun to embrace world cultures as a way of understanding those different from their own. The following should be helpful in deciphering the pronunciation system used in this volume:

- The vowel sounds for "a" and "e" in this pronunciation system have been simplified for ease of learning. Refinements, if desired, may be obtained from a good Spanish dictionary or from a native speaker. In Spanish "te" is pronounced "teh" to rhyme with the English vowel in "bet" and not "tay" which in English combines two sounds: "eh" closing to "ee," a hybrid sound known as a diphthong. The same is true for the "o" vowel which in Spanish does not close to an "oo" sound as occurs when pronouncing the letter "O" in English. The Spanish word "Oremos" is pronounced "Oh-reh-mohs" with the "oh" not closing to "oo."

- Elided syllables and double vowels are, perhaps, the most challenging for non-Spanish speakers. In the pronunciation guides in this book the vowel (of a double vowel) that is sounded the most is capitalized such as "tahm-beeEHN" (también). In elided syllables such as "que_a" both vowels ("keh" and "ah") are pronounced but run together. Occasionally, the pronunciation of elided vowels contains a capitalized vowel. This is done to assist singing the word to the notated rhythm which may not match rhythmic emphasis in the spoken text. When elided syllables create a melded sound, an attempt has been made to suggest a similar sound. For example in "como_el" the two elided syllables combine "moh" and "ehl" sounds, but the elision is pronounced "coh-mwehl." Occasionally the melded sound is close to an English word, so that is used. For example "canto_y" is pronounced "cahn-toy" since the English word "toy" is a diphthong combining the vowels "oh" and "ee."

- Syllables that have a marked accent in Spanish are stressed. In the pronunciation guide that syllable appears in bold typeface.

- The letter "d" in the middle of a word has a softer sound than in English. Instead of putting the tongue at the front of the hard palate, move it forward to the back of the teeth when saying the "d," creating a sound between "d" and "th."

- The double "l" in Spanish is pronounced as "lli" in the English "million or as "y" in "yes."

- A single "r" is flipped and a double "rr" is rolled.

- The pronunciations described above may differ in various geographic areas. Anticipate that Mexicans, South Americans, Puerto Ricans, Latin Americans, etc. may all pronounce some of the same words quite differently. This should not present problems in singing as a congregation. Each should sing in their familiar style.

Thanks to Gus Chrysson for his help in devising the pronunciation guide used in this volume.

PLEASE NOTE

The layout of this book affords a minimum of page turns for the accompanist and allows the musician/teacher to see each song clearly with any additional instrumental parts in close proximity. Because of this, some pages will seem to have an unnecessarily generous amount of empty space.

Chapter One

Selecting Church Music for Children

The criteria that have been used for selecting the music for this collection, appropriate for both children and adults, may be used as guidelines when choosing music from other sources. Consideration of children's needs has not often been part of the music selection equation. Some churches have the occasional "Children's Sunday," when the church school and the children's choir sing all the music, but at other times children are expected to keep up as best they can when the worshiping community sings.

In the twentieth century, The Hymnal 1940 reserved a section with the heading "Hymns for Children," and The Hymnal 1982 included an index of materials suitable for use with children in "Resources for Service Planning." Christian educators have long advocated that the church see children as full members of Christ's body who are musically and spiritually awake. Rather than being banished to basements and boiler rooms, children are more and more included in the liturgy and life of the growing parish. This requires the regular and sensitive evaluation of music that will be readily accessible to them.

Music

The primary criterion for choosing the hymns, songs, and acclamations in this collection is simplicity. Included are a few of the best hymns written in a particularly simple style and language, such as #49 "From hand to hand" and #107 "We are all children of the Lord," which appeal to the youngest children. These are intended for use in a setting with few adults, such as in church school or at a children-only chapel service. Such songs are less successful in a liturgy that fully engages both adults and children and will be left behind as children mature in their faith and in their ability to read words and music.

The simplest songs are folk songs or those with a melody that consists of repeated phrases or patterns alternating with a new varied phrase; i.e., overall forms such as AABA and ABACA. A melodic SEQUENCE also helps make a song memorable and easy to sing. Such melodies are often found in the authentic folk or folk-like tunes from various cultures and are represented by the following selections:

From the American folk tradition:

#52   All who hunger gather gladly

#7   Glory to God from *Missa Appalachia*

From the African American tradition:

#87   I want Jesus to walk with me

#10   I thank you, Jesus

From the Hispanic-Latin tradition:

#4   Dios está aquí (Mexico)

#53   Let us now depart in your peace (New Mexico)

#79   Sent by the Lord (Nicaragua)

Cyclical songs are those intended to be sung repeatedly as an aid to prayer and focus on worship. Such songs come from many cultures, particularly those with a strong oral tradition or those where printed music is less prevalent. Some examples:

#2   Uyai mose (Africa)

#31   Mungu ni mwema (Congo)

#18   Halle, halle, hallelujah! (Caribbean)

#34   Amen, siyakudumisa (South Africa)

#47   Behold, I make all things new (Scotland)

#58   Christ is coming (United States)

#61   Prepare the way of the Lord (TAIZÉ Community)

Melodies that move by scale step or by intervals that are primary to the key structure are also simple to sing. The important intervals for young children are the fifth, the octave, and the fourth. An example is #62 "Stay awake, be ready."

Another mark of simplicity is a melody that is based on arpeggios or on a PENTATONIC SCALE. An arpeggio is the "scaffold" of our Western music, for example, the first, third, fifth, and eighth degrees of the DIATONIC scale. Melodies utilizing such patterns are easy to learn and reinforce an understanding of musical structure. An example is #33 "Day by day," in which the arpeggio is outlined in the first two measures.

A PENTATONIC melody has only five pitches: the first, second, fourth, fifth, and sixth degrees of the DIATONIC scale. Pentatonic melodies appear again and again in traditional music from cultures as far apart as Scotland and China. Examples in this collection are #55 "May the Lord, mighty God" and #52 "All who hunger gather gladly."

The second criterion for selecting music for this collection is that a less simple song had to be inherently memorable. A working assumption was that these songs would be successfully sung unaccompanied even though they might have an accompaniment. This assumption eliminated hymns or songs with complex key changes requiring an accompaniment to be fully satisfying to sing. Many selections with refrains were chosen so that even the youngest child could join in.

Children's voices are pitched above the comfort zone of most untrained adult singers so they are naturally more at ease with higher notes. The greatest violation of children's abilities by adults is to expect them to sing music that is too low. The songs found here generally fall within the range middle C to E ten notes above, with occasional pitches outside those boundaries. This range should be comfortable for both children and adults.

As the teacher of these songs, you must be able to sing each one perfectly before you can easily teach it. Learners need to hear the words and music sung correctly with each repetition even if they are readers. Teaching without the aid of the printed page is the most effective.

Age appropriateness

The hymns and songs in this collection are each coded for the most appropriate age level:

A pre-readers   C readers
B early readers D teens

Folk and cyclical songs, described above, can be sung successfully by all pre- and early readers. Categories C and D require fluent readers who can manage lines of both text and music. Music coded in these last two categories must be thoroughly analyzed to determine the best teaching method for the varied adult and child singers.

Musical form

Both music and poetic texts have rules and forms. A well-matched text and tune may have similar patterns and forms. By using a simple scheme for analysis, learners can understand the "map" or overall shape of a melody, its repeated elements, and the origin of developed musical ideas. The following method for analyzing music is used in this guide:

- The initial melodic phrase is labeled "A," and subsequent new phrases are given the next alphabet letter: B, C, etc.

- If a melodic phrase repeats, it is give the same letter as the original statement. If a melodic phrase is derived from ideas of an earlier one but does not quote it exactly, it will be labeled as the second version of whichever phrase is its origin: A2, B2, etc.

- A pattern of musical intervals that is repeated exactly, but beginning on a higher or lower pitch, is called a SEQUENCE.

The musical map for #51 "Gentle Jesus, risen Lord" looks like this:

A   Gentle Jesus, risen Lord,

B   we come to your table (*This line is a repeated response.*)

A   with our hearts so full of joy,

B   we come to your table. (*The music of the first two lines is repeated in the second two.*)

C   We come, we come,

B   we come to your table.

C   We come, we come,

B   we come to your table. (*These last two lines are a repeat of the above.*)

Teaching this form helps the singers understand the simplicity of this song. It is readily apparent that "B" is the most repeated musical phrase (textually as well in this case) so teach that phrase first alone. Sing the entire song, inviting the learners to join you on the B phrase. Because the part marked "Refrain" uses the same words for each verse, teach part C next. Repeat the entire song, inviting the learners to join you on the B phrase and the refrain. Listen for accuracy and correct as needed. The learners will know the melody of part A by now, having heard it several times. All that remains is for the early readers to learn the text of part A. Pre-readers can sing parts B and C, memorizing part A with repetition.

The musical map for #50 "Let us talents and tongues employ" looks like this:

A   Let us talents and tongues employ,

B   reaching out with a shout of joy:

A   bread is broken, wine is poured

B2   Christ is spoken and seen and heard: (*This phrase is changed slightly to return to the keynote C.*)

C   (refrain) Jesus lives again, earth can breathe again, pass the word around, loaves abound: (*The refrain is made up of a* SEQUENCE.)

As you analyze melodies this way, you will begin to see some common patterns such as AABA, ABACA as mentioned above.

Words

The primary criterion for choosing the texts in this collection, as with the music, was simplicity. Elements of form, familiarity, repetition, theology, language, and biblical themes and stories were also important considerations.

As with the tune, the song will be easiest to learn if there is a clear structure and a repeated pattern. The phrases can be labeled in the same way as the music. Here is the text "map" of two examples:

#47 "Behold, I make all things new"

    A Behold, behold, I make all things new,

    B beginning with you and starting from today.

    A Behold, behold, I make all things new,

    C my promise is true, for I am Christ the way.

Also note the rhyming pattern: the two A lines "rhyme" (since they are identical), and so do the B and C lines.

#87 "I want Jesus to walk with me"

Verse 1

    A I want Jesus   **B** to walk with me; *(echo)*

    A I want Jesus   **B** to walk with me;

    C All along my pilgrim journey,

    A2 Lord, I want Jesus **B** to walk with me.

    (Since this last line remains unchanged each verse,
    it then becomes a kind of refrain.)

Verse 2

    D In my trials,   **B2** Lord, walk with me *(slight variant)*

    D In my trials,   **B2** Lord, walk with me

    E When the shades of life are falling,

    A2 Lord, I want Jesus **B** to walk with me.

This shape is very common in African American music. Since slaves were forbidden to read and write, songs included a common response alternating with changing phrases that were improvised by the song leader.

The familiar texts that children hear each Sunday in church are important learning tools and will become lifelong touchstones for worship. The music associated with these repeated texts will immediately spring to mind when the words are heard: Glory to God (Gloria in excelsis), Lord, have mercy (Kyrie eleison), Holy God (Trisagion), Holy, holy, holy Lord (Sanctus and Benedictus), Lamb of God (Agnus Dei), and acclamations such as Alleluia. These ancient words, called the ORDINARY and sung week by week, are key elements of our liturgical heritage.

Songs that are settings of familiar prayer texts, such as #33 "Day by day," #56 "May the Lord bless us," and #41 "Our Father in heaven" are important texts for children to rely on for daily prayer, bedtime, or when comfort is needed. She who sings, prays twice — and learns twice.

Never forget that a hymn is the text, not the music. These words communicate theological concepts. You must be able to explain the unfamiliar words and the theological concepts they convey in language understandable to the age group who will sing the song.

The education director, teachers, music director, and clergy person should agree on how each liturgical season is to be taught to children. For example, particular care is needed during Lent, when a variety of themes could be the focus: will it be the desire to make a right relationship with God and God's desire to forgive, rather than penitence and denial?

Archaic language obscures the meaning of the text and should be avoided. Careful attention must be given to language that excludes any group, that is gender specific, or that may be interpreted as racist. Children are very aware of these issues as they are addressed at home, in church, and at school. Our own stereotypes must be examined and challenged as we teach the next generations. We need to emphasize that God loves all people because all are created in the image of God.

Look for texts that focus on:

Scripture and Prayer Book — the stories of the Hebrew Bible and the New Testament; familiar prayers and psalms

God's Love — the goodness of humanity and the love and acceptance of God

Creation and the Environment — the goodness of all God's creation and our need to be good stewards of it

Inclusiveness — the inclusion of all Christians at the communion table and in all aspects of ministry

Diversity — the different faces of God as seen in a variety of cultures, genders, races, and forms (as in metaphors of rushing wind, fire, an eagle, etc.)

The Eucharist — the transforming power of the Eucharist, which brings us together as a family to learn, pray, worship, and share in a ritual meal that is both a remembering of the past events and the renewing of our relationship with Jesus Christ.

Mission — the journey from the communion table out into the world: the knowledge that Christians must worship and serve

God's abiding presence — the knowledge that God is with us in sorrow and grief as well as joy; trust that God is with us whatever happens in our lives.

The Holy Spirit — through the power of the Holy Spirit we gain strength to act as Jesus acted, even when we feel the situation is beyond our personal or human resources. The Holy Spirit also fills us with the joyful knowledge that Jesus is with us and loves us at all times.

Chapter Two

Music Leadership Skills

The Cantor

The instructions in this guide assume that someone will act as a song leader or a CANTOR to assist in learning and leading these songs. To encourage people to use their voices in God's praise, someone must stand in clear view using his or her voice to model, encourage, and teach.

The tradition of cantor began in the synagogue and continues to this day. The role was re-created in the Roman Catholic Church as Catholics embraced a flood of new music born out of the reforms following Vatican II, and it is becoming more prevalent in other denominations as well.

The cantor's role is to lead and nurture the singing congregation, often without accompaniment. The cantor should act not as expert, but as "one in our midst." The difference between being a professional soloist and being a facilitator and encourager is one that requires humility, grace, and finely honed skills of leadership rather than self-importance. A cantor must love the sound of congregational singing and assure the congregation of God's joy in this central part of the communal act of worship, whether perfection is attained or not. Cantors must also do all they can to make the congregation comfortable in a process that is quite rare today — singing together in public.

A cantor needs the following qualifications:

- a call to do this ministry — which may first appear as a call from the pastor, choir director, or director of religious education
- a call to nurture in others the ministry of worshiping God in song
- a good sense of pitch
- a good sense of pulse and rhythm
- a pleasant voice, not necessarily "trained" and not intimidating to the congregation
- good diction so that the pronunciation of words is clear
- good communication skills
- a desire to facilitate rather than perform
- a desire to encourage, to assist, to draw all in, to rejoice with those who find it easy to sing, and to commiserate with those who find it hard
- grace

For those who need confidence!

Some will be trained in music leadership; some will have the role thrust upon them. Those with limited musical experience might find the following points particularly useful:

- First and foremost, remember that your desire to do this ministry is a *vocation*, a call from God. God does not judge our shortcomings and gives us whatever we feel we do not have when we do God's will. A pre-performance prayer really helps.

- Begin your personal preparation for this vocation by reflecting on your singing experience. If, for example, you can sing a song in tune to your child at bedtime, you can be a cantor. What you need is the confidence for doing so in front of a group. Remember that children are an uncritical audience, partly because they're much more interested in themselves than you!

- If you do make a mistake, say, "I'll just do that again for you," without drawing attention to yourself or the mistake. We have all at some point made mistakes that still make us blush. Remember — the group's memory of an event is shaped by your reaction to it. If a group has given you responsibility for something, they want and expect you to maintain that responsibility. If you maintain the sense of being in control while making a joke and clearly correcting the problem, others will not notice the mistake. If you give up responsibility by becoming flustered, giggling, or looking around helplessly for someone to save you, the group will become embarrassed on your behalf. You are in control, even when you goof!

- Confidence can be communicated by maintaining eye contact at all times.

- Your most important task is to know the music yourself. Prepare each song by singing it constantly, writing down the words, checking the pitch of the beginning of each line, at the end of the next line, and the relationship to the following line. Choose music you are confident you know completely. Singing just two or three new songs in a season or semester is still a real addition to your worship or church school program.

Teaching Methods

Melody

When learning to sing a melody, most people hear the human voice better than they hear other TIMBRES. Children can match a human voice easier than the sound of an instrument. Using voices alone encourages vocal independence and develops better listening skills. Use the following procedure to teach a melody:

- Begin by singing the whole song, asking children to be quiet, listen, and really "soak up" the music.

- Next, sing a phrase at a time and have all repeat it, giving a beginning pitch and clearly indicating TEMPO. Judging how much to teach at a time is always tricky.

Be ready to break the phrase in half if singers struggle or add more if they sing it easily without a problem.

- Point out the form, calling attention to repeated phrases: "Now we simply repeat what we just sang." "This phrase has different words, but the same tune." "You see we sing the Alleluia at the end of each line."
- Always give sincere praise for good work.
- Correct any mistakes immediately, without implying fault. "Let's just do that line one more time—listen carefully."
- In a classroom situation, point out melodic patterns. "Now we roll down the hill note by note." "Now we jump up in a pattern called an arpeggio." "Now we leap up an octave." "Do you see how we just repeated the melody but began on a different note?"
- As soon as possible, sing the entire song. Risk rushing this process a little bit, because it can be helpful to go faster than singers think possible, thus breaking through some of their fear of failure and anxiety. Once they have sung the song through, they will realize with surprise what they have achieved and sing even better the next time.
- Once all the words and notes are correct, don't forget to talk about the meaning of the words, the phrasing, and other details that help the transition from the learning exercise to expressive, spirit-filled hymn singing.

Harmony

Since there will be a wide range of singing abilities in a congregation, an "entry level" must be found for everyone to welcome them into the new world of singing in harmony.

Aim to give a foretaste of the heavenly kingdom, not a reminder of the first bad singing experience! Everyone can participate in part-singing, but it takes time to build both ability and confidence. The first entry level is the drone. This is a single note, repeated continuously, often in the bass. For example in #15, a Russian Orthodox Kyrie eleison, rather than singing the printed part, have basses sing only the TONIC and DOMINANT degrees of the scale: an E on a long "hommmmm" sound on "Kyrie eleison," then B on the "Christe eleison," returning to the E on the final "Kyrie eleison."

Parts often run in parallel lines, as the soprano and alto do in this same piece. Once the soprano/melody is learned, add the alto, explaining that it moves parallel to the soprano beginning a third below. Some people cannot hold their own part while hearing another; keep them on the melody and let them physically move away from the others while practicing. Encourage people to sing parts in the octave suitable to their voice.

General guidelines for teaching harmony are these:

- As with teaching a melody, you must know every note and every word of every harmony part before you begin teaching.

- Place children in the melody group initially. If there are older children who have experience singing harmony, assign them to the alto.
- Make it clear that anyone may sing any part if so moved. More able adults or teens should be asked to help lead a harmony part that needs more support.
- Teach all the parts to all the people first. Let them sing in whatever range is comfortable. This approach encourages those who have not discovered their ability to sing a harmony part.
- Ask all the women to sing both soprano and alto. Then ask all the men to sing the tenor and bass parts.
- Plan the order of steps to work on individual parts. Remember:
  - The soprano is almost always the melody line so it should be taught first.
  - If the bass is simple, such as a single drone, or if it moves from TONIC to DOMINANT and/or SUBDOMINANT, teach that next. Then combine soprano and bass.
  - Soprano and alto, or soprano and tenor, are often paired in parallel harmonies and should be taught one after the other and sung together.
  - If it hasn't already been included, add the bass part last.
  - There will be pairs of parts which do *not* sound good together because of a missing note in the chord or a dissonance not resolved in the chord. Make sure you don't pair them in rehearsal!
- As with teaching a melody, call attention to the musical form and repeated phrases. Make sure you are clear where a part repeats and where it deviates for a few notes.
- Once a song is fully learned, repeat it several times to give people time to experience the joy of singing together. This may be the first time some have ever experienced singing in parts, and it will be exhilarating for them.
- Explain the theological importance of what the singers are doing: we bring ourselves and our voices, however great or small, to join together in praise of God to make something much greater and more mystical than we could imagine. When we sing, we sing with "angels and archangels, and all the company of heaven."

Using hand gestures to indicate pitch

The technique of using hand gestures to help non-readers follow the shape of a melody takes a little work to learn, but it is one of the key elements in the success of many cantors.

While singing the melody of the song, use one hand to "mark" the pitch in the air in front of the body. The other hand can be free for small conducting gestures. The hand should be held flat, palm down, fingers pointing to the side. Keep the elbow lifted away from the body but relaxed. In preparing a song, notice the range of pitches—where the lowest note is and where the highest is. Also notice if the song starts on the lowest pitch or somewhere else, and where it finishes. The hand should "mark" each pitch by indicating the level of the note up or down as if moving on the rungs of a ladder. The range of hand signals should begin about chest level and finish no higher than the head. If the song has a "sol do" (5–1) beginning, make the first "mark" below the chest level. Find a note in the melody that is the bedrock, the note the melody keeps returning to. This will probably be the TONIC ("do" or the keynote) — but it might not be. Make sure that you know exactly *where* you are marking that note, so its importance is clearly seen.

Practice in front of a mirror. Sing scales, octaves, and arpeggios, moving the hand to indicate steps, jumps, and leaps and making sure that the space between marks is fairly consistent. Repeated notes need repeated marks in the same place.

Practice special gestures that indicate slightly unexpected movements. Each person will need to develop a personal style of gestures that work. Consistently use particular gestures and singers will come to understand them, so be inventive!

The benefits of learning this technique are numerous:

- It is another tool to help with the preparation necessary to teach the congregation well.

- With gestures a cantor takes on some of the responsibility for singing accurately.

- It relieves singers from relying entirely on their memory, which most people do not trust.

- It is a great help particularly for those who have high anxiety about music and singing, especially those who were told in their youth that they couldn't sing or that they should "go stand in the back and mouth the words."

- People learn in different ways, and this visual, physical cue is a great addition to aural and academic cues.

- Martin How, who has worked tirelessly for the Royal School of Church Music, once said, "Whenever I teach a group of young singers for the first time, I tell them, 'This is the basic principle of sight reading: when the notes go up, your voice goes up. When the notes go down, your voice goes down. When the notes stay still, your voice stays still." Hand gestures help singers realize that this is indeed the core of singing melody — not some great mystery open only to those who have given it years of study.

Instilling leadership qualities in children

If there is the opportunity for working with a children's choir, it can be an instrument for helping teach new music. The word "choir" is used in a broad sense. There might not be the resources for a choir that meets weekly and has constant attendance. But a group of children who are able to meet only before church or once a month can be excellent leaders of the congregational parts of worship.

Children have many gifts to offer this ministry of music. A congregation may be reluctant to learn new music. Children, by contrast, are constantly in a learning environment, taking naturally to new material. If the choice of music is appropriate,

they will sing it with enthusiasm and communicate that to the adults, who will respond in kind.

Children long to be respected as whole human beings. If they are asked to be leaders and are genuinely respected for the gifts they bring (not merely admired because they are "cute"), they will take their role seriously. Adults will learn that children are inspired both by *being* leaders and by *being seen as* leaders.

Remind child choristers that they, too, are ministers. They are helping people sing God's praises, just as the preacher helps everyone better understand God's word, or the eucharistic minister helps administer the sacrament at communion. Set a high standard of behavior for them, expecting them to demonstrate good behavior in the pew, to follow the service, and to join in responses in addition to leading the singing. They will always rise to the standard set.

If there are children who have a particular gift for singing who would like to share it, encourage them to become cantors. On the next page Below you will find an introduction to the role of CANTOR for young people that can be reproduced. Many musically talented children can satisfy all the requirements. Tell them that since they have the appropriate gifts, they are welcome to act as leaders in the same way as adults. Simplify hand gestures needed to cue the congregation. Invest time in preparing all the details of the words and music with the children, making sure they can be easily seen in church. Encouraging children who are ready to take on leadership roles is an important ministry of nurture and begins the process of creating a lifelong legacy of service.

SO YOU WANT TO BE A CANTOR!

The tradition of cantor began in the Jewish synagogue and continues to this day. A cantor is considered part of the worship leadership team, which includes the clergy, acolytes, eucharistic ministers, the altar guild, and other musicians. In the 1960s, the Roman Catholic Church wanted to encourage its congregations to participate more actively in worship. It began teaching a lot of new music, re-creating the role of cantor to help people learn it.

Being a cantor is a vocation, that is, a kind of job that one is inclined to do and is particularly well suited for. In our Christian faith, we believe that people are called by God to do different jobs in the church and the world. Some people are lucky enough to literally hear God speaking to them, as in the stories of the Hebrew Bible; others hear that call through encouragement from their teachers, church leaders, or friends. If you believe that you are "called" to do a job for God, remember that the Holy Spirit will always be with you, helping you do it to the best of your ability. Knowing this makes it a little easier when you are nervous!

What you need to be a good cantor:

- a call to this ministry
- a call to help other people sing well when they worship God
- a willingness to rejoice with those who do well, and to be patient, sympathetic, and helpful to those who find singing difficult
- a good sense of pitch
- a good sense of pulse and rhythm
- a pleasant and confident singing voice
- good diction so that words are understood
- confident public leadership

There are two parts to being a cantor: teaching and leading.

Teaching the congregation a new song

If the congregation is to sing a new song, the cantor will teach it to them, either before or during the liturgy, or at a separate rehearsal. If you are new to this ministry, begin by teaching a simple song. Examples include CALL AND RESPONSE songs and simple rounds. In a call and response song the cantor sings a phrase and the congregation responds by repeating it, as in, for example, #1 "Come, Holy Spirit" and #11 "Glory to God." Two simple rounds may be found at #9 "Gloria, gloria" and #61 "Prepare the way of the Lord." Always prepare for teaching by learning the song completely yourself. In preparing music know the song well — not to get it right but so you cannot get it wrong.

Ask your teacher to help you learn how to teach words and melody easily by using the methods described in "Teaching Methods" in *My Heart Sings Out Leader's Guide*.

Leading the congregation in song

Sometimes music is divided between the congregation and the cantor, particularly in a psalm like #101 "Sing, O people." As cantor, you will sing the psalm verses on your own and encourage the congregation to join you on the refrain. To help the congregation feel secure the cantor sings the refrain once at the beginning, and then everyone repeats it. The cantor sings the verse, cueing the congregation to sing where indicated. Always cue the congregation when it is their turn to sing by reaching out both hands to them, just a beat or two ahead of their entry.

Confidence in all things!

First and foremost, know and believe that you have been called by God to do this work. With God we are able to do far more than we could on our own. There are many stories in the Bible of folk who did not think they could do the job God gave them, for example, Moses, Jonah, and David. Have faith and believe that this *is* your calling and then it will be. Psalm 71:5 says "For you are my hope, O Lord God, my confidence since I was young." Confidence is an attitude. Believe it or not, many people, adults included, are afraid of singing! Once you stand in front of them, you are not a young person teaching adults; rather, you are a leader teaching a congregation. Your job as cantor is to build trust and help the reluctant singers gain confidence in their ability to raise their voices in song. A pre-performance prayer either privately or with other worship leaders really helps.

If you do make a mistake when demonstrating, simply say, "I'll just do that again for you," and with a confidence you might not feel repeat the phrase correctly.

Congratulations on taking this first step in your ministry. May God bless your work and give you strength in all things.

Chapter Three

Worship Planning

Two goals are vital when planning music for worship with children and adults.

1. **The music should enhance and clarify the action and meaning of each part of the Eucharist.**

These are the essential parts of the Eucharist; they should be understood theologically and translated when making musical choices:

- We come together as community and experience the joy, the mystery, and the adoration of God's presence.

- We learn about God through readings and are helped to think about our response through the sermon.

- We offer God our prayers of praise and thanks, petition, confession, and new intention.

- We share in communion, which is a gift from God — a feast and an act of unity with God and Christians everywhere.

- We are sent out from our joyful feast refreshed and inspired, with renewed intention to do God's will in the world.

2. **The music should be a vital part of the unified theme of the service, which is determined by the Sunday lectionary or feast day.**

In planning liturgy to include children a single theme is infinitely better than several. This isn't always easy because the various readings may not match perfectly, or one reading may have several meanings. Children need clarity. Work with the worship team or the clergy person to distill a theme from the readings.

Once the theme is chosen, read, pray, and meditate on the particular reading most important to that theme. What do you learn on first reading? What questions do you find yourself asking? Which characters do you find yourself identifying with? What is the most important message in this reading? Would children agree with your answers? Learn to look at the readings with a child's eyes, and ask for children's opinions.

Once a clear direction has been decided, then choose the music. This book includes several choices of music for the ORDINARY of the Eucharist, that is, the parts of the service that are unchanging and often sung:

- Gloria in excelsis (Glory to God) or other song of praise

- Kyrie eleison (Lord, have mercy) or Trisagion (Holy God)

- Sanctus with Benedictus (Holy, holy, holy Lord)

- Agnus Dei (Lamb of God) or other fraction anthem

Each setting is suitable for different resources and conveys a different mood and understanding of its text. The indexes in this book will also help you to find songs to match scripture, themes, lectionary dates, and various occasions in the life of a parish. Even so, develop your own instincts and learn to recall songs that reflect both an understanding of the Eucharist and a particular Sunday or seasonal theme well. Be sure to keep notes about each song and evaluate how well it worked. Having a theme will allow other materials or media such as dance, visual arts, or drama to come together to serve a common message regardless of historical period or style.

The music that is planned should be:

- already familiar

    or

- easy to learn during the service

    or

- previously learned

    and

- in a musical style that is appropriate for the congregation's identity and resources — or even stretches their assumptions a little.

A balance of elements is essential:

- Beginning and ending hymns should be familiar to all, often joyful, and should bring the community together.

- Only one or two pieces in each service should be new, especially if they are challenging musically or theologically. New selections should be sung for several subsequent Sundays if possible.

- Longer hymns and shorter choruses should be balanced depending on the type of liturgy. Congregations that are accustomed to choruses used mostly as prayer or reading responses will find it challenging if such songs replace traditional hymns.

- Congregational song should balance solo, choir, or instrumental pieces.

- A broad spectrum of music from different periods and styles should be planned. This has been standard Anglican practice for hundreds of years. Enjoy the variety of music available, keeping a clear focus on the theme for the day.

Children have many gifts that make it easy to teach them new music:

- Children's work is learning new things; children can memorize quickly and learn new music easily.

- Children love to help, serve, and participate if they are treated with full respect.

- Children are able to learn in different ways, from listening, reading, and repeating to being interactive and learning through movement.

Children also have some challenges:

- reading words consistently before ages seven or eight
- reading a hymnal with the layout of the words and music before ages eight or nine
- maintaining attention to the spoken or written word
- redirecting boredom if they are unable to participate

How to incorporate music into liturgy:

In this leader's guide, songs have been categorized into four major age-suitable divisions:

All   Can be sung by everyone; easily memorized by young children

A*   Especially suited for children aged two to five

B   Simple words and music, easily memorized by pre-readers

B*   Especially suited for children age six up to fluent readers; for use in church school or children's chapel

C   Hymns with a refrain that can be memorized by Group B and easily learned by readers

C*   Especially suited to a gathering where more sophisticated hymns are needed and children are present such as at baptism, confirmation, or major festivals.

D   Strophic hymns suitable for teens and adults

D*   Music and textual themes especially suited to teenagers.

These groups are cumulative. A song in Group A can be sung by everybody. A song in Group B can be sung by everybody except Group A, and so on. Some categories are marked with an asterisk, which means that they are particularly suited for the age group indicated; for example a song marked A* is one that little children will especially enjoy.

Each age category offers unique possibilities for incorporation into the liturgy as described below. For help in finding age-specific selections see the Age Level Index (page 280).

All   Can be sung by everyone; little children can memorize this

These songs and hymns offer a way to easily include the youngest children in worship. This may mean inserting music into the liturgy where you may not have done so before. Or it may mean choosing simpler music to replace some hymns. Because these songs are simple, they may be memorized and sung during physical movement from one place to another, such as going to communion. Alleluias can be used before the Gospel reading. Short, simple pieces are often called "cyclical" because they are to be repeated several times. Many are particularly useful when meditative prayer is desired. Songs in this category may be used:

- before the opening of the service, as preparation
- as a response to each reading
- as a response to each prayer petition
- as prayer itself
- during the Gospel procession or as a response to the Gospel
- during communion

B   Simple words and music, easily memorized by pre-readers

Perhaps the most important group to draw into worship is the elementary school children. They have the interest and concentration to begin understanding what is going on around them and can remain in church throughout the service. Songs in category B are simple enough for this group to learn, although almost all have been selected from "adult" music collections. There are a few songs in this category that are most effective for children only, even though they may be used occasionally for the whole congregation. It is important to expect adults to tolerate and even participate in singing these songs occasionally; however, they are most useful in a children's chapel or in church school. They will also be successful when used as anthems sung by a children's choir.

C   Hymns with a refrain that can be memorized by Group B and easily learned by readers

This category includes hymns that are used on a particular feast day, such as Easter or Pentecost, or when visitors are welcomed for baptism or confirmation. This collection includes hymns with refrains, those that express new ideas well, and several that address a topic previously neglected.

This hymnal is in no way intended to supplant the amazing riches of our hymn tradition. Hymns such as "Lift high the cross" or those for the parish patron saint are essential for a child's repertoire. Such hymns are more easily learned by the youngest if they also include a refrain or repeated phrase.

D   Strophic hymns suitable for teens and adults

These songs are almost all written in the traditional STROPHIC hymn form even though many have been written within the last twenty years when some congregational music is THROUGH-COMPOSED. The strophic hymn form continues to flourish because it can convey profound theological ideas in beautiful poetry with an economy of words. It is important for children and adults to learn strophic hymns as well as the new forms of music. The texts in this category were chosen to appeal to teenagers and young adults and include themes for mission, peace and justice, confirmation, and Rite 13. Specific to this category are texts that describe the struggle to do and be all that God asks in a world that sometimes rewards very different values.

Entering and Gathering

In *Commentary on the American Prayer Book* (HarperSanFrancisco, 1995) Marion Hatchett notes that until the fourth or fifth century, worship probably began with a greeting from the celebrant and continued immediately with the readings.

As buildings became larger and Christianity became the official religion, the ceremony of formal procession was borrowed from court, the clergy bearing the Gospels accompanied by candles and incense. The entrance rite was gradually expanded with psalms, hymns and CANTICLES, litanies and blessings. While it is less formal today, a procession is still the customary way worship begins in many churches — even though there is no provision for it in The Book of Common Prayer. Special days, such as Ash Wednesday, Palm Sunday, and baptism have their own entrance rites.

The usual Entrance Rite is as follows (italics indicate optional elements):

Hymn, psalm, or anthem

Opening acclamation (a greeting between presider and congregation)

Collect for purity

Gloria in excelsis or some other hymn of praise

    OR in Lent and Advent the Kyrie or Trisagion

Collect of the Day

The less familiar an activity, the more important this ritual of entering becomes. The early Christians lived a life steeped in Christian activities of which worship in a church was merely a continuation. For many Christians today, religious life consists of church on Sunday morning and perhaps up to two or three hours of worship, education, or service at other times in the week. The Entrance Rite is important to bring people together as a worshiping community. The practice, common in some other denominations, of learning and singing songs of praise at the beginning of worship is a good way to help make this transition. While singing is in itself an activity that fosters fellowship, singing songs that focus the mind on worship and communion with God helps bring together the Body of Christ.

👥 All

♪ bells, rain stick

✝ Opening of worship or meetings; preparation and response for prayer; healing services; times of repentance, confusion, or loss. Quiet and contemplative in mood.

📖 Day of Pentecost

🔑 The word *maranatha* appears in 1 Corinthians 16:22. Paul joined together two words in Jesus' language of Aramaic, *Marana tha,* meaning, "the teacher comes," which we now interpret as "Christ is coming!" Maranatha became a codeword to the early Christians who used it as a greeting, and a word of assurance.

This song is in CALL AND RESPONSE form. To teach the song, the CANTOR should sing the phrase first each time and the congregation should repeat it. The cantor may hum the first note of the repeated phrase early to give the congregation the pitch. Make sure that the energy of the singing leads the vocal line to the important word "Spirit." The sibilant "S" of Spirit should precede the beat so that the plosive "p" falls precisely on the beat.

🎶 The song is quiet and contemplative in mood. Once the entire song is learned, the cantor part may be sung by one group within the congregation and the answer by another, for example, men and women, adults and children, the two sides of the church, or the back and front of the church. If the song is used as the congregation moves from nave to SANCTUARY, the back group could begin the song as they move forward with the front group answering them.

? *How do you imagine the Holy Spirit? When do you feel the Holy Spirit in church? In your life?*

Come, Holy Spirit

Cantor

Come, Ho - ly Spi - rit.

Come, Ho - ly Spi - rit,

Come, Ho - ly Spi - rit.

Come, Ho - ly Spi - rit.

Ma - ra - na - tha!

Ma - ra - na - tha!

Come, Lord, come.

Come, Lord, come.

* *When repeated, hold this note through beginning cantor part.*

All

♪ A CAPPELLA, except for instruments mentioned in Performance

This song can be used for any gathering activity, such as at the opening of the service or to move people from one place to another, such as for baptism or Eucharist. It could be used for almost any response as long as the season is not penitential.

📖 General; Rogation Days

The part marked *Women* is the main melody and may be sung alone. If you have sufficient singers, add the top notes of the part marked *Men*. Next add the drone bass part (long repeated note on the word "Ahom"), which is the simplest. Finally add a small group, such as your junior choir or a capable soloist, on the descant part marked "CANTOR." If all other parts are singing in English, consider singing this topmost part in the alternative language.

Add drums, maracas, or gourds with seeds in them, or a shekere or axatse (gourd with netted beads on the outside) to this song from Zimbabwe. Use a mixture of simple rhythms such as

♩ ♩   or   ♩ ♩ ♩ ♩   or   ♫ ♫ ♫ ♫ .

Movement is always part of African music. Encourage your singers and percussion players to move as the music calls them to. A basic movement is a rocking or swaying motion that consists of a STEP and a TOUCH occurring on the quarter note beats of each measure. Begin on the left foot (1) L-Step, (2) R-Touch, (3) R-Step, (4) L-Touch. The steps are more like shifting one's weight to that foot than an actual step.

Pronunciation

U - ya - i   mo - se
oo - yah - ee   moh - seh

ti - na - ma - te   Mwa - ri   zvi - no
tee - nah - ma - teh   Mwah - ree   zvee - noh

? *How do we learn the songs of our church? Which songs do we know already?*

Uyai mose *Come all you people*

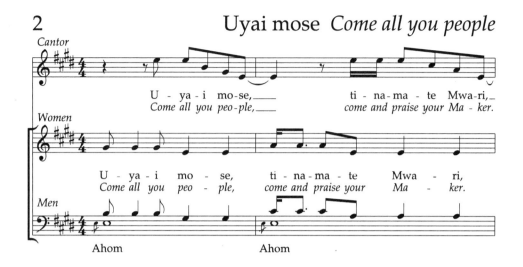

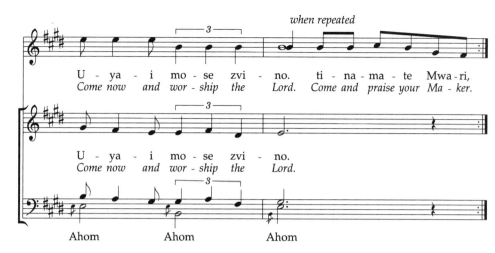

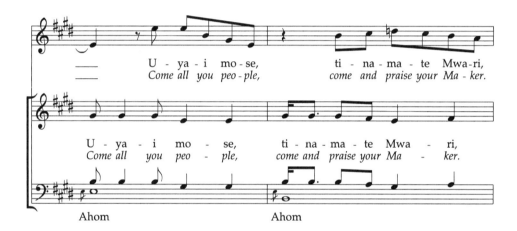

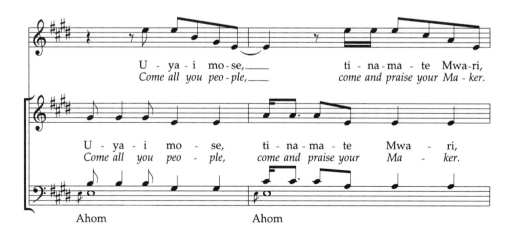

Words and Music: Alexander Gondo; arr. John L. Bell (b. 1949) © 1995 WGRG The Iona Community (Scotland) (admin. GIA Publications, Inc., 7404 S. Mason Ave., Chicago, IL 60638 [www.giamusic.com].) All rights reserved. Used by permission. *You must contact GIA Publications, Inc. to reproduce this selection.*

Come into God's presence

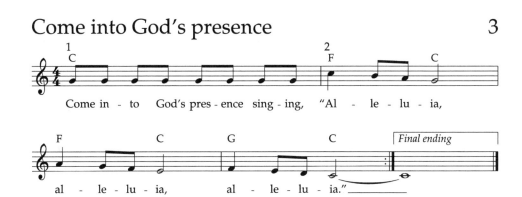

Additional verses may be added: Come into God's presence singing, "Worthy the Lamb . . ." Come into God's presence singing, "We love you so . . ." Come into God's presence singing, "Glory to God . . ." Come into God's presence singing, "Jesus is Lord . . ."

Words and Music: Anon., arr. Betty Carr Pulkingham (b. 1928) © 1990 Celebration, PO Box 309, Aliquippa, PA 15001 [www.communityofcelebration.com]. All rights reserved. Used by permission. *You must contact Celebration to reproduce this selection.*

All, A*

♫ A CAPPELLA

✠ Opening of worship; preparation for prayer; moving into the worship space

📖 Any Sunday other than in Lent or Advent

🔑 The word "Alleluia" is very ancient and comes from the Hebrew, *Hallelu Yah*, meaning "Praise God!" It is a word of spontaneous thanks and praise to God. Some churches make a ceremony of putting away their alleluias for Lent in the form of banners and rediscovering them on Easter. This song could be used for procession when you rediscover your alleluias at the Easter Vigil or on Easter Day.

The musical structure of this song is very simple. After the repeated notes of the initial phrase, the alleluias are sung in a descending SEQUENCE pattern through a C major scale. To teach this the leader could indicate pitch changes by hand movements. See chapter 2, "Music Leadership Skills" (page 13) for an explanation.

𝄞 Use physical movement to highlight the action of moving from everyday life into the place of worship: join hands and walk in a line to your place of worship as you sing. Older children may lead two lines to encircle the worship space, each moving in opposite directions. This song may be sung as a round with the second part beginning when the first part reaches the number "2" above the staff.

? *What do you think is the difference between thanks and praise? What would you like to thank and praise God for today?*

All

Guitar, piano, or strings

Opening of worship, particularly in a non-traditional setting such as a camp or house communion; healing services

Season of Pentecost; Rogation Days

This song celebrates the beauty of the world, and the certainty of the blessings that God has given us. The musical style perfectly reflects this song's simple message. The music should move in a relaxed two beats per measure with the eighth notes in the second line setting the TEMPO. Do not allow the tempo to drag.

Introduce this song by clapping the rhythm or singing it on a neutral syllable such as "loo" and then adding the words. Probably the greatest difficulty for non-Spanish speakers is elisions, fitting two syllables to one note, such as in the second line of words: co-mo_el ai-re. The syllable "mo" is combined with the syllable "el" and sung as "mwehl."

For an accompaniment by stringed instruments, the cello should play the bass line; one violin should play the upper notes of the piano accompaniment; the second violin should play the lower notes in the piano accompaniment. When there are not two notes in the treble piano accompaniment, both violins should play together.

Pronunciation

Dios   es - tá a - quí,
Dyohs ehs - **tah** *ah -* **kee**

tan cier - to co - mo_el ai - re que tes - pi - ro,
tahn seeEHR - toh coh - mwehl AHee - reh keh tehs - pee -roh,

tan cier - to co - mo la ma - ña - na se le - van - ta,
tahn seeEHR - toh coh - moh lah mah - nyah - nah seh leh – vahn -tah,

tan cier - to co - mo que le
tahn seeEHR -toh coh - moh keh leh

can - to_y me pue - de o - ír.
cahn - toy   meh pweh – deh oh – **eer.**

?   *What could I do to help me think of God and God's blessings every morning?*

Dios está aquí *God is here today*

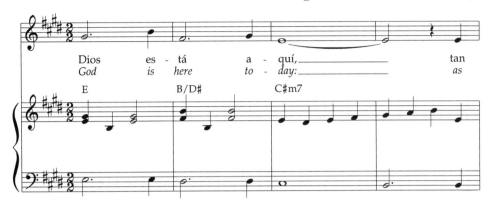

Dios es-tá a-quí,_____ tan
God is here to-day:_____ as

cier-to co-mo que le can-to y me pue-de o-ír._____
cer-tain when I sing you'll hear my song._____

Words and Music: Mexican, tr. C. Michael Hawn, 1998; arr. C. Michael Hawn and Arturo Gonzáles, 1999
© 1999 Choristers Guild, 2834 W. Kingsley Rd., Garland, TX 75041-2498 [www.choristersguild.org].
All rights reserved. Used by permission.

cier-to co-mo el ai-re que res-pi-ro,_____ tan
cer-tain as the air I breathe,_____ as

cier-to co-mo la ma-ña-na se le-van-ta, tan
cer-tain as the morn-ing sun that ris - es, as

Glory to God
and Songs of Praise

The Gloria is one of three or four familiar pieces of service music children should be able to sing week to week: Glory to God; Lord, have mercy or Holy God; Holy, holy, holy Lord; and Lamb of God. Choose one that can be sung by everyone in the congregation. Historically the Gloria was sung in the daily morning office as early as the fourth century. In the eleventh and twelfth centuries it became customary on Sundays and other feast days. The early forms of the Gloria were designed for the congregation.

The challenge for including children in singing the Gloria is that the full text is long and not easy to set to music because it is in free, not poetic, meter. This book includes various solutions to this problem. The Glory to God found at #5 has a congregational refrain alternating with the full text sung by choir or CANTOR. Once the congregation is comfortable with the refrain, they will begin to learn the rest of the CANTICLE with repetition week to week. The two settings at #6 and #7 are constructed of simple repeated musical phrases to make the learning easier. The Gloria, gloria at #9 has an OSTINATO refrain in Latin for the congregation with a cantor singing the text of the full Gloria.

There are alternatives to singing the Gloria. The RUBRICS in The Book of Common Prayer, page 356, say, "...the following hymn [Glory to God] *or some other song of praise*" can be sung at this point in the opening rite. Several suitable hymns of praise are therefore included, such as a shortened form of the Gloria text (#11) and alternative texts (#8 and #10). Other general praise hymns could also be used, such as #133 and #134.

C, C*

Piano or organ

If the Gloria is not used as the hymn of praise at the beginning of the service, it may be used on occasion in place of a hymn elsewhere in the liturgy.

Anytime other than Advent or Lent

This Glory to God uses a verse/refrain form, which allows the congregation to memorize a repeated refrain while a choir or CANTOR sings the full Gloria text. The refrain is marked with an * in the printed music. It is particularly suitable for an all-age congregation when the occasion calls for the complete CANTICLE text.

The TEMPO should not be too fast and should swing broadly — the triplets in the accompaniment should have room to breathe. Once the congregation has learned the refrain, point out that the melody of the verses remains fairly similar throughout and may be easily learned by the congregation as well.

Adding the rhythmic interest of a clapping pattern:

throughout the refrain would especially engage children.

? *Are we "in the glory of God the Father"?*

Glory to God

Glo - ry to God _____ in _ the high - est, and _ peace to God's peo - ple on earth. _____

to God's peo - ple on earth. _____

Lord _____ God, heav - en - ly King, al - might - y God and Fa - ther, we wor - ship you, we give you thanks, we _____

5

world: have____ mer - cy on____ us; you are

seat - ed at the right hand of the Fa - ther: re -

ceive our____ prayer._____

Glo - ry to God_____ in__ the high -

est, and____ peace to God's peo - ple on

earth._____ to God's peo - ple on earth._____

5

For you a - lone are the Ho - ly One, you a - lone are the Lord, you a-

lone are the Most High, Je - sus Christ, with the Ho - ly Spir-it, in the

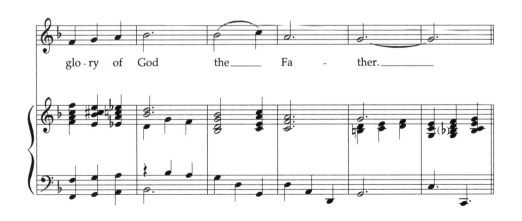

glo - ry of God the___ Fa - ther.___

Glo - ry to God___ in___ the high - est.

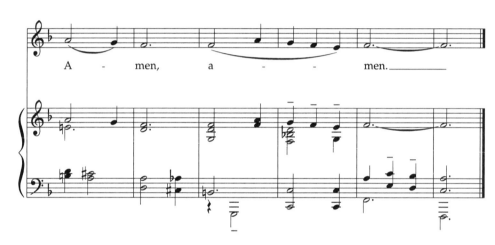

A - men, a - - men.___

* The congregation may sing only this repeated section when a cantor or choir sings the full text.

Words: from The Book of Common Prayer (1979) of the Episcopal Church USA.
Music: James Capers (b. 1948), from *Liturgy of Joy*, arr. Michael Hassell (b. 1952) © 1993
Augsburg Fortress, PO Box 1209, Minneapolis, MN 55440-1209 [www.augsburgfortress.org].
All rights reserved. Used by permission.

✝ D

♪ Piano or organ

✠ If the Gloria is not used as the hymn of praise at the beginning of the service, it may be used on occasion in place of a hymn elsewhere in the liturgy.

📖 Anytime other than Lent or Advent

🎤 I wrote this setting for the congregation of St. James's Piccadilly in the West End of London, a church known for its lively, radical ministry and its connection to the Episcopal Church in America. St. James's welcomes a large number of visitors to its worship so this setting was designed to be easily taught by a CANTOR and learned quickly by everyone. The regular congregation has also found it very satisfying. This setting can be sung as CALL AND RESPONSE, as almost every phrase of music is repeated. As the congregation becomes more confident, they will readily begin to sing the full setting.

At the words "Lord Jesus Christ" the melody is transposed into the TONIC minor, moving from C major to C minor and back to C major at "For you alone." Use this piece to teach the contrast in sound and mood between the major and minor tonalities.

🎼 For an accompaniment variation use a violin, viola, flute, or other melody instrument on the top line of the accompaniment and a cello, bass trombone, or bass euphonium on the bass line. These instruments will not have to transpose. If others instruments are desired, be sure to check for their need to transpose.

? *Can you draw a picture of all the things we praise God for in this song?*

6

Words: from The Book of Common Prayer (1979) of the Episcopal Church USA.
Music: Fiona Vidal-White, from *St. James Piccadilly* © 1988 Fiona Vidal-White.
All rights reserved. Used by permission.

All

♪ A CAPPELLA

✠ If the Gloria is not used as the hymn of praise at the beginning of the service, it may be used on occasion in place of a hymn elsewhere in the liturgy.

📖 Anytime other than Advent and Lent

This Glory to God was written to be sung unaccompanied. The Gloria is based on the PENTATONIC SCALE, which allows accompaniment by any combination of the five notes used in the melody. The vocal sound needs to be vigorous and grounded. The pentatonic melody consists of a few repetitive phrases that are easily learned, but that may confuse the singer in their similarity during the learning phase. A CANTOR outlining the movement of the melody with the hand will help keep people on track.

Accompany the melody with violin, add a drum beat

to the first section up to the words "Lord Jesus Christ..." at the end of the third system. Bring the drum back in at the words "For you alone are the Holy One...."

? *Imagine being "seated at the right hand of the Father." What would it be like?*

Words: from The Book of Common Prayer (1979) of the Episcopal Church USA.
Music: Jonathan Dimmock (b. 1957), from *Missa Appalachia* © 2002 Jonathan Dimmock.
All rights reserved. Used by permission.

Give thanks to the Lord our God
Rendei graças ao Senhor

B

A CAPPELLA, guitar

Prayer or healing service; anytime when thanksgiving and sorrow are combined; anniversaries of national or local disaster; Burial

Advent

This Brazilian setting of part of Psalm 106 combines a beautiful soaring melody and words of rejoicing with a minor key. The octave jump at the beginning needs attention when teaching. The image of a diving springboard is helpful — the middle C on "give" should be a preparation for the C an octave higher on "thanks." Make sure the D♭ is accurately pitched in the following phrases: "good, very good" (measure three) "and forever" (measures seven–eight). The high C at "and forever" (measure twelve) also needs attention to pitch.

Pronunciation

Ren – dei   gra – ças   ao   Se – nhor   por – que   e-le é   bom
rrehn-DEHee   grrah-sahs   AHoo   Seh-nyor   porr-keh   eh-lee   bohm

por que   su – a   mi - se – ri – cór – di - a
*porr keh   soo-ah   mee-seh-ree-**cawrr**-dee-ah*

du – ra   pa – ra   sem – pre   pa – ra   sem – pre.
doo-rah   pah-rah   sehm-prreh   pah-rah   sehm-prreh.

Ben – di – to   se – ja   o   Se – nhor,
Behn-dee-toh   seh-zhah   oo Seh-nyor,*

De – us de   Is – ra – el   de   e – ter – ni – da – de
deh-oosDEH   ees-rrah-ehl   deh   eh-tehrr-nee-dah-dee

e   to – do o   po – vo   di – ga A – men.
eh toh-doo   poh-voo   dee- gah - mehn.

rr = rolled r
*the "j" is pronounced as the "s" in measure

? *What does it mean when we say or sing "Amen"?*

Give thanks to the Lord our God
Rendei graças ao Senhor

Give thanks to the Lord our God for our God is good, ver - y good,
Ren - dei gra-ças ao Se - nhor, por-que e - le é bom, e - le é bom;

for God's lov - ing kind-ness lasts for - ev - er and for - ev - er. Oh
por que su-a mise-ri - cór - dia, du-ra pa-ra sem-pre pa - ra sem-pre. Ben-

bless-ed, bless-ed be our God; God of Is-ra - el, now and for - ev - er.
di - to se - ja o Se - nhor, De-us de Is-ra - el de e - ter - ni - da - de

Let all the peo-ple say A - men, al - le - lu - ia!___
e to - do o po - vo di - qa A - men,

al - le - lu - ia,___ al - le - lu - ia,___ al - le - lu - ia!___

Gloria, gloria

B

Guitar, A CAPPELLA

Liturgy of the Word, especially during the Christmas season

Anytime other than Lent or Advent

The refrain may be sung alone as a round. The complete Gloria text for CAN-TOR may be sung simultaneously with the round or as verses with the refrain interspersed at the points marked. In this style of music, layering the parts available, adding and taking away, creates the beauty of the whole. Don't be tempted to do everything all the time!

The following procedure works well:

- Cantor sings the refrain unaccompanied.

- Congregation sings refrain doubled by melody instrument.

- Congregation sings the refrain several times as a round until it is secure. Choir members or instrumentalists may support the congregational parts.

- Cantor sings verses with the refrain sung at the end of each. Congregation sings *softly* or hums the round while cantor is singing, increasing the volume when cantor stops singing. Various instrumental parts could be added during this part. Instrumental accompaniments for Music from Taizé are available from GIA Publications, Inc. www.giamusic.com.

- The refrain is sung once more after the final verse. As each part of the round ends, singers should join the others still singing so that all finish with "alleluia" together.

? *How could you help bring "peace to his people on earth"?*

Gloria, gloria

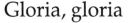

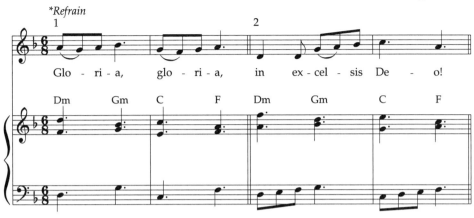

Refrain

Glo - ri - a, glo - ri - a, in ex - cel - sis De - o!

Dm Gm C F Dm Gm C F

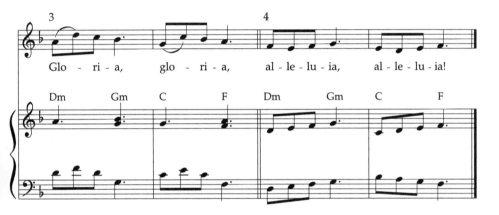

Glo - ri - a, glo - ri - a, al - le - lu - ia, al - le - lu - ia!

Dm Gm C F Dm Gm C F

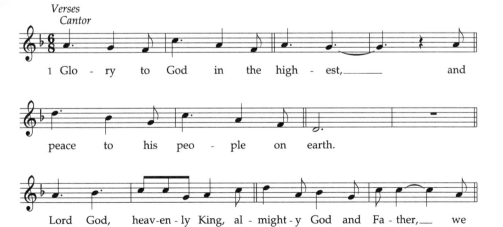

Verses
Cantor

1 Glo - ry to God in the high - est,_____ and

peace to his peo - ple on earth.

Lord God, heav - en - ly King, al - might - y God and Fa - ther,___ we

Refrain ad lib.

wor - ship you, we give you thanks, we praise you__ for your glo - ry.__

2 Lord Je - sus Christ, on - ly Son of the Fa - ther,__

Lord God, Lamb of God, you take a - way the sin of the world:

have mer - cy on us; you are seat - ed__ at the right hand

Refrain ad lib.

__ of the Fa - ther:__ re - ceive our prayer.__ 3 (For)

you a - lone are the Ho - ly One, you a - lone are the Lord,

you a - lone are the Most High, Je - sus Christ,

with the Ho - ly Spir - it, in the glo - ry of God the Fa - ther.

To refrain

A - men, a - men, a - men, a - men!

* The refrain may be sung as an ostinato throughout all or part of the text, or it
may be sung as a response at the beginning and after each section of the text.

Words: from The Book of Common Prayer (1979) of the Episcopal Church USA.
Music: Jacques Berthier (1923–1994) © GIA Publications, Inc., 7404 S. Mason Ave.,
Chicago, IL 60638 [www.giamusic.com]. All rights reserved. Used by permission.
You must contact GIA Publications, Inc. to reproduce this music.

I thank you, Jesus

B

♪ A CAPPELLA or piano

✠ Special times of thanksgiving; ordinary time

📖 The season after the Epiphany with its themes about Jesus and his ministry

⚷ This African American song of praise states simple and essential beliefs about Jesus. Jesus is our Savior, our family, and our companion or guide in life. You may teach this song in the method of gospel groups that learn by ROTE:

- bass part up to the word "God"
- tenor part up to the word "God"; bass and tenor together
- alto part up to the word "God"; add to the bass and tenor
- add the melody with the lower three parts responding
- continue in this way, phrase by phrase until the music is learned

𝄞 The written rhythm pattern is performed in a relaxed style more as triplets than the printed dotted eighths and sixteenths. The word-painting in the third line, with its repeated note melody, suggests the steadfast journey on which Jesus has accompanied us. As you sing, build in intensity through the line to the word "way," where the pitch changes.

? *How would Jesus be like your mother, father, sister, or brother?*

way.   Thank you, Je-sus,
way.   Been my fa-ther,

thank you, Je-sus, thank you, Je-sus,_____ my Sav-ior
been my moth-er, been my sis-ter,_____ my broth-er,

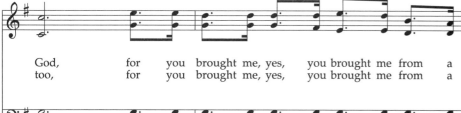

God, for you brought me, yes, you brought me from a
too, for you brought me, yes, you brought me from a

might-y, a might-y long way,____ a might-y long way.
might-y, a might-y long way,____ a might-y long way.

Glory to God

👫 All

🎵 A CAPPELLA

✠ Hymn of praise

📖 During any season except Lent

⛓ This Glory to God does not contain the full text of the Gloria, but it contains the essence of praise in worship. It is a good introduction to the Gloria for children, both because of its simplicity and the opportunity for children to lead it. Teach the congregation to sing this by ROTE, which means that they learn it by listening, not by looking at the music. Begin with the first two phrases, each of which require the congregation to echo what the leader sings. Next, explain how the Alleluias are built up into chords. Experiment with different groups singing each note of the building chord. Begin the "Alleluia" section quietly, increasing the volume as each chord note is added, slowing the TEMPO on the last "Alleluia! Amen."

🎼 This is a simple two-section song of praise that appeals to all ages in worship. Either a CANTOR or a group of singers (ideally a children's choir or a church school class) can sing the part marked "Cantor," setting a strong declamatory style for the piece. When the congregation has learned it well, variations on who sings which part may be made. After the cantor sings the first measure, one side of the congregation could continue that part with the other side of the congregation singing the echoing part. The three groups in the "alleluia" section could be divided between men, women, and children or between groups within the congregation. Use hand gestures to cue the congregation.

❓ *How does it feel to hear people singing notes different from yours?*

Lord, have mercy
(Kyrie eleison)

This ancient text comes from the fourth century and was originally secular. "Lord, have mercy" was an acclamation of the people when the emperor approached, much as "God save the Queen" is used today. After its appropriation as a sacred acclamation, the Kyrie made its way from East to West, retaining its Greek language. The "Christe eleison" verse was added.

Although many consider the text to be penitential, it can also be an acclamation of joy (see #30). One of the four settings available in this section is more penitential sounding (#14) because it is in a minor key. "Lord, have mercy" without its "Christ, have mercy" verse is also used as an acclamation in the Prayers of the People. In Advent and Lent, the Kyrie (or Trisagion) is used liturgically in place of the Gloria or other song of praise.

Lord, have mercy

All

♪ A CAPPELLA

✠ Retreats; prayer service

📖 Anytime, especially Lent

🗝 The composer of this Kyrie grew up in Appalachia. It captures the haunting sound of the folk music of that geographic area.

🎵 Add two percussion instruments: a low-pitched, reverberant drum, rain stick, or finger cymbals on the first beat of each measure, and another drum playing

throughout. Begin with two measures of percussion introduction. The tune could be doubled by a melody instrument (flute, violin, recorder). An interesting sonic effect may be created in a reverberant space by having two widely spaced groups sing this as a round at one measure. (The second group begins when the first group reaches the word "mercy.") In this arrangement it is essential that singers count accurately.

? *Does this music remind you of other pieces?*

May be sung throughout by congregation.

Words: from The Book of Common Prayer (1979) of the Episcopal Church USA.
Music: Jonathan Dimmock (b. 1957), from *Missa Appalachia* © 1989 Jonathan Dimmock.
All rights reserved. Used by permission.

Kyrie eleison

B

♪ A CAPPELLA, guitar

✠ Parish or youth retreat; prayer response

📖 Anytime

This infectious rolling melody comes from the central South American country of Paraguay. To help young children learn the meaning of Kyrie eleison, the men of the congregation could sing the words "Lord, have mer-cy" as follows:

Lord   have   mer - cy.   Lord   have   mer - cy.___

Teach this part first and then add the melody.

Kyrie eleison is not always a slow, penitential song or response. This one should be felt in two pulses per measure that move at a leisurely walking TEMPO. The guitars could add this rhythm on each measure:

strum:

? *What do you imagine you have in common with someone from Paraguay?*

Ky - ri - e   e - le - i - son.___   Ky - ri - e   e - le - i - son.___   Ky - ri -
Chri - ste   e - le - i - son.___   Chri - ste   e - le - i - son.___   Chri -

e   e - le - i - son.___   Ky - ri - e   e - le - i - son!___
ste   e - le - i - son.___   Chri-ste   e - le - i - son!___

repeat Kyrie

Words: from The Book of Common Prayer (1979) of the Episcopal Church USA.
Music: Paraguayan © 1995 World Council of Churches, 475 Riverside Dr., New York, NY 10027.
All rights reserved. Used by permission.

Kyrie eleison

B

♪ A CAPPELLA

✠ Times of penitence; meditation; contemplation; anniversaries of national or local disaster

📖 Lent

🔑 This song is essentially eight measures long with a repeat that incorporates small variations, the most challenging being in the bass part. It may be best attempted by congregations who have learned to sing some simpler songs in four-part harmony or by those that have readers scattered throughout.

🎼 This Kyrie setting has a lovely slow swing to it. Each harmony part should bring out the Kyrie motif (rhythmically like the first two measures of the soprano part) as they sing it. If you wish to sing this as a threefold Kyrie, repeat at the end of the second line, with the basses holding the low C on "-son" instead of singing the descending scale. "Christe" may be substituted for "Kyrie" on this repeat of the first section, holding the first syllable "Chri-" for the first measure and putting "ste" on the second measure.

? *What would you like to ask God's mercy for today?*

Words: from The Book of Common Prayer (1979) of the Episcopal Church USA.
Music: John L. Bell (b. 1949) © WGRG The Iona Community (Scotland) (admin. GIA Publications, Inc., 7404 S. Mason Ave., Chicago, IL 60638 [www.giamusic.com].) All rights reserved. Used by permission.
You must contact GIA Publications, Inc. to reproduce this music.

All

A CAPPELLA

At the beginning of the Eucharist; prayer response

Anytime, especially Lent

The close harmonies of this Kyrie are characteristic of the music of the Russian Orthodox Church, from which it comes. Russian liturgical music is often sung very slowly. Also characteristic is the doubling of the bass voice an octave lower. If the four-part version is sung in the key of G major (the same as the three-part version) the bass part could be doubled at the octave by a few men who can sing notes in that range. Because the top two parts are parallel harmonically, they could be taught simultaneously, adding the lower part(s) next. If a nine-fold Kyrie is desired, sing each phrase three times.

Sing very slowly, but at a TEMPO that allows the phrase "Kyrie eleison" to be sung in one breath. If your church owns hand bells, play the lowest G that you have on the downbeat of measures one and three and on the very last note. Play the lowest D that you have on the downbeat of measure two. Let the sound reverberate (do not damp). In the four-part version written in the key of E major use the bell pitches E and B.

? *Why do we sing this song, which means "Lord, have mercy," in a different language?*

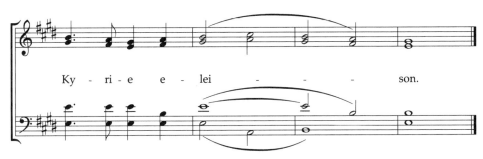

Words: from The Book of Common Prayer (1979) of the Episcopal Church USA.
Music: Russian Orthodox © World Council of Churches, 475 Riverside Dr., New York, NY 10027 [www.wcc-coe.org]. All rights reserved. Used by permission.

Holy God (Trisagion)

"Trisagion" is a Greek word derived from *tris* and *hagios* meaning "thrice holy." It is part of our liturgical heritage from the Eastern churches and has been sung since the fifth century. The trifold petition "Holy God, Holy and Mighty, Holy Immortal One, have mercy upon us" is easy for children to recall because the hymn as a whole is often repeated three times. The two settings printed here are different; #16 is in a minor key with close harmonies and sung A CAPPELLA, as is much Eastern church music. The Holy God at #17 is a more elaborate setting with optional hand bells, flute or oboe, and organ.

B, C, D

♫ A CAPPELLA

✠ In place of the Kyrie during Lent

📖 Lent

The Trisagion may be sung as an alternative to the Kyrie in Lent. The name means "thrice holy," and this ancient hymn is sung in Eastern churches when the clergy enter with the scriptures and at other points in the service. This Russian-sounding setting with its characteristic close harmonies conveys a sense of awe and mystery.

This version is for three female voices or two female and one fairly high tenor. The congregation may sing only the top part with organ accompanying with chords. The top two parts move in parallel thirds, making them easy to learn. The third part is more CHROMATIC and will need more practice and attention to the tuning of the changing D♮, D♯, and the F♯ in the penultimate measure. If you would like to sing this in four parts, transpose down to C minor (starting notes C and E♭) with the bass doubling the tenors. The piece should be sung three times.

Holy, holy, holy God

Holy God

Ho - ly, ho - ly, ho - ly God, Ho - ly and Might - y,

Ho - ly and Im - mor - tal, have mer - cy on us.

Words: Traditional.

All

Organ, piano, flute or oboe, hand bells

In place of the Kyrie during Lent

Lent, Advent

This melody is built on a rising and falling minor scale, from D to A. Its simplicity is contrasted with the more complex organ accompaniment, which may distract singers unless it is soft enough to allow the melody to be heard clearly. The piece should be performed three times.

This setting from *Music for the Holy Eucharist II* by Peter Crisafulli is a work in layers written intentionally to build in complexity. Begin the singing accompanied only by the organ. On the first repeat add the solo instrument, and on the final repeat add the hand bells.

Ho - ly God,   Ho - ly and Might - y,

Ho - ly Im - mor - tal One, have mer - cy on us.   mer - cy on us.

Bells needed

Words: from The Book of Common Prayer (1979) of the Episcopal Church USA.
Music: Peter Crisafulli, from *Music for the Holy Eucharist Rite II* © 2002 Peter Crisafulli.
All rights reserved. Used by permission.

Alleluia

The word "Alleluia" is very ancient and comes from the Hebrew *Hallelu Yah,* meaning "Praise God!" It may be spelled "alleluia" or "hallelujah" and is an acclamation or word of spontaneous thanks and praise to God. There are many opportunities for singing "Alleluia": as a response to readings, at the beginning or end of a service, at a time of celebration such as prayers for those with birthdays and anniversaries, at baptism, for confirmation or marriage, and as a spontaneous response to the good news. Each of the pieces in this section comes from a different country and has different characteristics. Alleluias may also be sung as a congregational or choral prelude and during Gospel processions.

All

A CAPPELLA, percussion

See section introduction

Any season except Lent

This lively, energetic song could be an easy accompaniment for movement: the Gospel procession, the procession to the baptismal font, the offertory procession, or the encircling of the altar for communion.

The basses have responsibility for subsequent repeats of the piece. In the last measure they should sing the printed G as an eighth note followed by three more eighth notes on D, E, and then F♯. A beaded gourd or maracas may play

for each measure except for measure eight when

should be used. End the piece with a long shake. A steel drum or band, if available, would add authenticity to this Caribbean song.

Halle, halle, hallelujah!

Hal - le, hal - le, hal - le - lu - jah!

Hal - le, hal - le, hal - le - lu - jah!   Hal - le - lu - jah!

Hal - le, hal - le, hal - le - lu - jah!

Hal - le - lu - jah!   Hal - le - lu - jah!

ᛏ᛫᛫ All

♪ A CAPPELLA

✠ See section introduction

📖 Any season except Lent

Western music is characterized by melodic movement and structure, whereas the driving force in African music is strong rhythm that evokes physical movement.

The harmony parts in this infectious acclamation are easy to learn. Those singing the alto part must learn to be independent from the others because they begin one measure later. They should also note the abbreviated word at the end of the first line. The first syllable of "Hallelujah" should be stressed, which will emphasize the interweaving of the parts. Repetition increases the enthusiasm for this song.

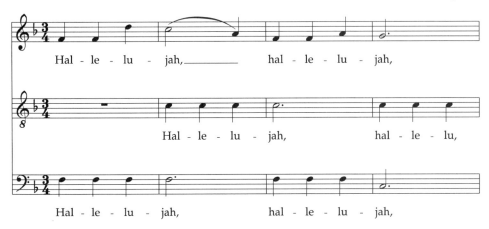

Hal - le - lu - jah,_____ hal - le - lu - jah,

Hal - le - lu - jah, hal - le - lu,

Hal - le - lu - jah, hal - le - lu - jah,

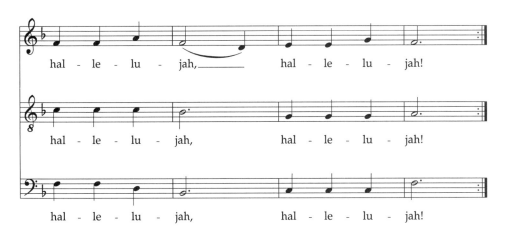

hal - le - lu - jah,_____ hal - le - lu - jah!

hal - le - lu - jah, hal - le - lu - jah!

hal - le - lu - jah, hal - le - lu - jah!

All

A CAPPELLA, piano, organ, melody instrument, and percussion

See section introduction

Any season except Lent

This alleluia is taken from a Gospel acclamation by Fintan O'Carroll and Christopher Walker. The original includes verses for a variety of Sundays throughout the Christian year. It is available in octavo form from OCP Publications, www.ocp.org.

Sing this with a lilting, lifting sound. A melody instrument such as a flute or violin could play the tune, and percussion, such as a BODHRAN or Irish drum, could play

The piano accompaniment could be sung in four parts by A CAPPELLA voices.

Al - le - lu - ia, al - le -

A   E   D   E   A

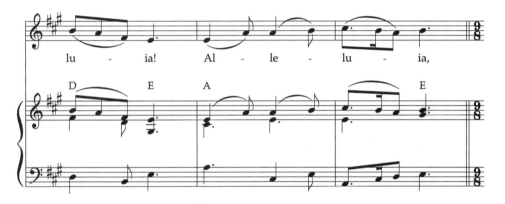

lu - ia!   Al - le - lu - ia,

D   E   A   E

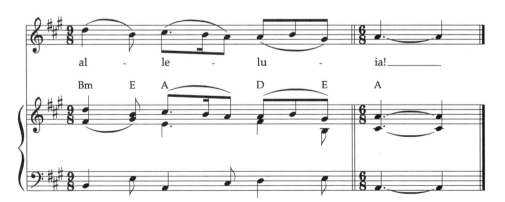

al - le - lu - ia!_____

Bm   E   A   D   E   A

👥 All

🎵 A CAPPELLA with hand clapping

✠ See section introduction

📖 Any season except Lent

☞ This piece is such fun to sing! The two "voices," cantor and congregation, have similar rhythmic patterns in an overlapping form making a never-ending circle of sound. This effect is heightened because even though the key of the piece is C major, the harmonic make-up consists of only two chords: F A C (IV) and G B D (V). There is a sense that the praise never ceases, so do not try to "resolve" the final chord.

🎼 South African music, such as this alleluia, is often accompanied by hand clapping. The pattern to use here is best understood as based on two large beats in each 6/8 measure. The hand clapping should be four even claps per measure. What results is a two-against-three rhythmic accompaniment. Other phrases could be substituted for "Alleluia" as long as they fit the rhythm, for example: "Praise to God in the highest," "Thank the Lord for his goodness," " Sing a new song to praise God," etc.

Allelu, alleluia

Cantor

Al - le - lu, al - le - lu - ia. Al - le - lu, al - le -

Al - le - lu, al - le - lu - ia.

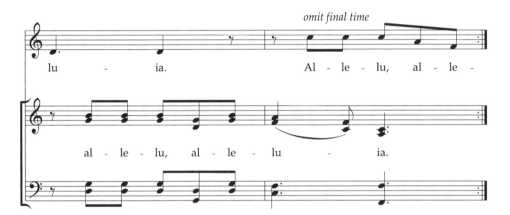

omit final time

lu - ia. Al - le - lu, al - le -

al - le - lu, al - le - lu - ia.

Heleluyan *Alleluia*

👥 All

♫ A CAPPELLA, percussion

✠ See section introduction

📖 Any season except Lent

🗝 Coming from the Native American tradition, this alleluia needs to reflect that culture's deep reverence for the earth. It may be interpreted, musically, by a strong first beat in each measure and a sense of weight on each note. The TEMPO should be slow rather than fast.

♪ If available, use a Native American drum that is large and low to the ground, allowing for several players to surround it. All should play

with an emphasis on the first beat in each measure. In singing, make sure the dotted rhythm is well marked. When singing this as a round, each part could be reinforced by a wooden flute or penny whistle. Trying moving each group of singers to a different area in a reverberant room for a dynamic effect.

Heleluyan *Alleluia*

He - le - lu - yan, he - le - lu - yan: he - le, he - le - lu - yan;
Al - le - lu - ia, al - le - lu - ia: al - le, al - le - lu - ia;

he - le - lu - yan, he - le - lu - yan: he - le, he - le - lu - yan.
al - le - lu - ia, al - le - lu - ia: al - le, al - le - lu - ia.

* May be sung as a round.

Words: Traditional.
Music: *Heleluyan,* Muscogee (Creek) Indian, transcr. Charles H. Webb © 1989 The United Methodist
Publishing House (admin. T.C.C. – The Copyright Co., 1026 16th Ave. S, Nashville, TN 37212
[www.thecopyrightco.com].) All rights reserved. International copyright secured. Used by permission.
You must contact T.C.C. to reproduce this music.

Prayers and Responses

In this section you will find simple musical refrains that may be used as prayer responses or sung prayers in which everyone can participate.

The Prayers of the People

The various forms of the Prayers of the People were included in The Book of Common Prayer to encourage a freer kind of prayer that could be written by the community, using these forms as guidelines. Indeed, the simplest form is an outline of general headings or framework for the concerns of the gathered community found on page 383 of The Book of Common Prayer. It is appropriate for the people's responses to be sung. The following printed forms could utilize some phrases or refrains from this book:

Forms I, IV, and V use the response "Lord, have mercy" or "Lord, in your mercy, hear our prayer." The first two measures of #12 or the entire #30 could be the sung response for Form I. The response in Forms IV and V could be #23 with the intercessor singing the first phrase and the people joining in the remainder.

Form II allows for a silent or extemporaneous spoken petition by the people. Consider carefully whether you want a sung response at all. One alternative is a sung response at the beginning and end of prayers. Teach the response before the service if possible. At the beginning of the prayers, sing the response and then indicate that everyone should repeat it. After each petition cue the congregation, giving at least two preparatory beats. In an informal prayer service, people may offer their own petitions. To accommodate these, the cantor should determine the length of a short period of silence before beginning the sung response.

Sung prayer

It is important that people occasionally move away from the fixed structure of liturgy, and even the freer forms of Prayers of the People, to experience meditative prayer. Many of the short songs found in this collection may be used as sung prayer or community devotion. The music and text are prayer, and the consecutive repetitions of these simple songs free the rational mind to be able to pray while singing. Do not be tempted to limit the number of repetitions for this kind of prayer. Some will want to continue singing while others continue praying the words silently or just humming the melody. It is particularly beautiful when the song naturally fades away, followed by the profound silence that comes when a song has been "fully sung," leaving us open to a moment of deep prayer. CANTORS should remember to observe these times of silence as fully as the times of singing! Remember that these pieces are an expression of the Holy Spirit moving within us, perfectly described in the this hymn from the Iona Community (#110 "She sits like a bird").

> She dances in fire, startling her spectators,
> waking tongues of ecstasy where dumbness reigned;
> she weans and inspires all whose hearts are open,
> nor can she be captured, silenced or restrained.

All

♪ A CAPPELLA

✠ Response for Prayers of the People; any time of intercessory prayer

📖 General

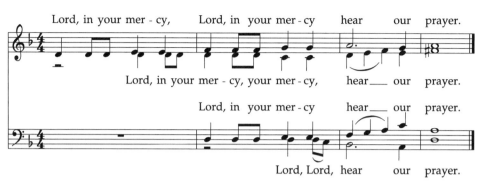

Words: from The Book of Common Prayer (1979) of the Episcopal Church USA.
Music: John L. Bell (b. 1949) © 1995 WGRG The Iona Community (Scotland) (admin. GIA Publications, Inc., 7404 S. Mason Ave., Chicago, IL 60638 [www.giamusic.com].) All rights reserved. Used by permission. *You must contact GIA Publications, Inc. to reproduce this music.*

A feature of this piece is its use of dissonance resolving to consonance. There are rules and conventions in music that intervals like the second and seventh are not so pleasant to hear, but if these lead to a more satisfying chord, the tension and resolution created is pleasing. Listen to the entrance of the alto part against the soprano, which resolves when the tenor enters. The same occurs as the bass enters against the tenor, resolving when all arrive at the word "hear."

As a final "bonus" the piece ends with a major chord, although the piece is in a minor key. This tension and resolution could illustrate our request to God for mercy. We come knowing our failings yet believing in God's forgiveness.

🎼 This music is written very simply but sounds far more complex. Ask the congregation to sing each vocal part in their own register, beginning with the sopranos and ending with the basses. Then ask everyone to recite the SEQUENCE of voice-part entries: "Lord in your, Lord in your, Lord in your, Lord, Lord" pointing to each vocal group as their part would enter. To give the parts support, choir members may be placed among the congregation.

? *How do you know that God has heard your prayer?*

All

Piano, organ

Liturgy of the Word; after communion; retreats; following Bible study; thanksgiving for parish or ministry accomplishments

Anytime, especially Lent

This piece, and #25 "I will praise your name" are refrains by Leon Roberts, excerpted from psalm settings in *Lift Every Voice and Sing* II published by Church Publishing. They both have the distinctive gospel feel of a strong backbeat, in this case on the second and fourth beat in each measure.

This refrain has an irresistible energy, movement, and glorious CHROMATIC harmonies that are so typical of African American music. Do not elide the first two words as "Hislove," but make sure the word "his" is clear and a bit short each time it is sung because it immediately sets the rhythmic energy. CRESCENDO from the beginning to end of the piece, keeping the sound well-sustained. Repeat the refrain without pause at the end, leaving just enough time to catch a breath and begin again. The piano accompaniment should be accented on the second and fourth dotted quarter notes.

? *What helps you know that God's love is everlasting?*

All

Piano, Hammond organ

Liturgy of the Word; after communion; retreats; following Bible study; thanksgiving for parish or ministry accomplishments

Anytime

This piece and #24 "His love is everlasting" are refrains by Leon Roberts, excerpted from psalm settings in *Lift Every Voice and Sing* II published by Church Publishing. They both have the distinctive gospel feel of a strong backbeat. The refrain should be felt in a slow or "big" two beats per measure with the second beat being the strongest. We are used to praise being a noisy, unrestrained affair, but this expression of praise is rooted in fervent prayer and confidence in God and should be sung with deep conviction.

Piano and Hammond organ (or a jazz organ sound on an electronic keyboard) may be played together to accompany this refrain. Both accompanists should be encouraged to add rhythmic and harmonic "fills" between the printed chords, especially in the final measure when the song is repeated. Using a drum kit with this music would help keep it moving and emphasize the strong pulse.

Words and Music: Leon C. Roberts (1950–1999) © 1987 Leon C. Roberts.

All

Guitar, accordion, bongo drums, GUIRO

Prayer response; hymn of praise; general

Trinity Sunday, Year C

The name of this music, given by the composer, is merengue, the national dance of the Dominican Republic. It is a dance song form in two beats per measure and is often accompanied by accordion and a number of various hand percussion instruments, including a GUIRO, or ridged hollow gourd, that is played with a wooden stick scraping across the ridges and double hand drums called tambouras. Bongo drums would work equally well.

The joy and liveliness of this dance-hymn could be captured if the music is used for the congregation to move from one place to another, perhaps from seats to standing around the altar or from the church into the parish hall or vice versa. Teach the youngest children to sing "Holy, holy, holy" at the beginning of lines 1, 2, and 3, and if possible from "your glory . . . " to the end. They could play shakers on the pattern

and finger cymbals on the first beat of the measure, letting them ring.

Pronunciation

San - to   can - tan se - ra - fi - nes.
Sahn – toh   cahn - tahn seh - rah - fee - nehs.

Dios   es   el   Se - ñor.
Dyohs ehs ehl Seh - nyohr.

es   fuer - te   nue - stro   Dios.
ehs fwehr - teh   nweh – stroh   Dyohs.

Tu   glo - ria   lle - na los   cie - los,
Too gloh - reeAH   yeh - nah-lohs seeEH - lohs,

la   tie - rra   lle - na es - tá.
*lah teeEH – rrah   yeh – nice - **tah**.*

Ho - san - na en   las   al - tu - ras,
Oh - sahn - nine   lahs   ahl - too - rahs,

ho - san - na   la   can - ción.
*oh - sahn - nah lah cahn - **seeOHN**.*

? *What do you think the angels look like?*

Holy, holy, holy *Santo, santo, santo*

"Ho - ly, ho - ly, ho - ly," an - gel hosts are sing - ing.
"San - to, san - to, san - to," can - tan se - ra - fi - nes.

"Ho - ly, ho - ly, ho - ly is the Lord our God.
"San - to, san - to, san - to, Dios es el Se - ñor.

Ho - ly, ho - ly, ho - ly is God, the Lord of might. Your
San - to, san - to, san - to es fuer - te nue - stro Dios. Tu

glo - ry fills the heav - ens, your glo - ry fills the earth." Ho -
glo - ria lle - na_los cie - los, la tie - rra lle - na_es - tá." Ho -

san - na in the high - est, ho - san - na is our song.
sa - na_en las al - tu - ras, ho - sa - na la can - ción.

Words: based on Isaiah 6:3, English paraphrase Bert Polman, 1985.
Music: *Merengue*, Spanish; harm. AnnaMae Meyer Bush, 1985 © 1987 CRC Publications,
2850 Kalamazoo Ave. SE, Grand Rapids, MI 49560 [www.crcpublications.org].
All rights reserved. Used by permission.

Your kingdom come, O Lord

All

🎵 A CAPPELLA

✠ Prayer response; Liturgy of the Word

📖 Propers 12, 20, 27, and 28, Year A; Advent; Lent

Each Sunday we pray this phrase as part of the Lord's Prayer. Using this repeatable phrase as a response is most effective when other readings focus on the coming of the kingdom in the books of the prophets and the kingdom of heaven in the Gospels.

The first phrase should be quiet with all voices sounding as one. The next two phases should build in strength, leading to the musical high point with the soprano rising D octave. The final phrase should become softer, observing the FERMATAS by giving each beat weight and taking a lifting breath at the comma.

? *What would you imagine the kingdom of heaven to be like?*

Your kingdom come, O Lord

Your king-dom come, O Lord. Your king-dom come, O Lord. _ Your

king-dom come, O Lord. _ Your king-dom come, O Lord.

Words: from The Book of Common Prayer (1979) of the Episcopal Church USA.
Music © WGRG The Iona Community (Scotland) (admin. GIA Publications, Inc., 7404 S. Mason Ave.,
Chicago, IL 60638 [www.giamusic.com].) All rights reserved. Used by permission.
You must contact GIA Publications, Inc. to reproduce this music.

O bless the Lord

All

A CAPPELLA

Prayer response; Liturgy of the Word; grace before or after food; congregational or choral prelude

Psalm 103 is appointed for Ash Wednesday, but the jubilant mood of this piece suggests a different occasion may be more appropriate, such as Proper 19, Year A; Eighth Sunday after Epiphany, Year B; Proper 3, Year B; Third Sunday in Lent, Year C. Because "O bless the Lord" is only a small portion of the psalm text appointed on these days, it should not replace the psalm.

This lively song of praise, based on Psalm 103:2, is easy and very satisfying to sing in harmony. If you have no basses, one or more sopranos could sing the bass melody an octave higher. The two phrases should sound like one with a smooth handover from the bass lead "O bless the Lord" to the response "O my soul."

Be sure that the upper three parts sustain their notes to overlap with the bass leading line just as the basses sustain "Lord."

How might you remind yourself of God's love?

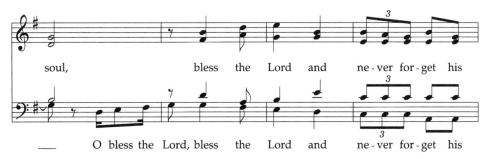

Words: based on Psalm 103:2.
Music: John L. Bell (b. 1949) © WGRG The Iona Community (Scotland) (admin. GIA Publications, Inc., 7404 S. Mason Ave., Chicago, IL 60638 [www.giamusic.com].) All rights reserved. Used by permission.
You must contact GIA Publications, Inc. to reproduce this music.

C, C*

Piano or organ

Prayers of the People; intercessions in daily prayer

Advent

The Prayers of the People may be sung. This form, by Roman Catholic composer Michael Joncas, gives a response to the people and petitions to a cantor much in the same way that S107–S109 does in The Hymnal 1982. When deciding whether to use all the petitions or to create others, consult The Book of Common Prayer, page 359, for a listing of intercession categories.

When playing the refrain accompaniment on the piano, bring out the two inner voices (alto and tenor), which support the sung melody. Those with small hands may need to rearrange the accompaniment so that the harmonic structure may be fully represented.

? *Who do you think would be "those who seek and serve the common good"?*

God ever-faithful

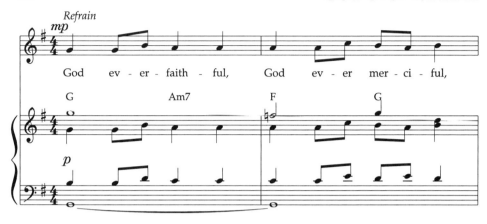

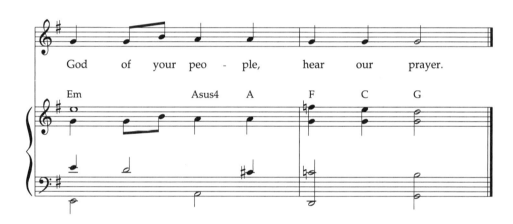

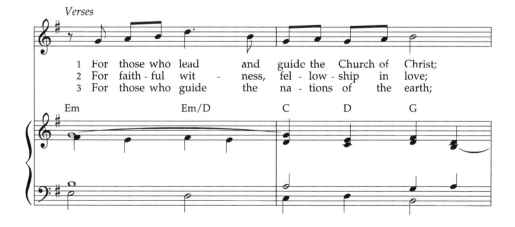

Additional verses

4 For those who seek and serve the common good;
that justice reign, we pray to you, O Lord:

5 For neighbors' needs, for shelter from the storm;
for homes of peace, we pray to you, O Lord:

6 For those in sorrow, anguish, and despair;
that they find hope, we pray to you, O Lord:

7 For those oppressed, for those who live in fear;
that they be freed, we pray to you, O Lord:

8 For all the sick, the dying, and the dead,
be life and grace, we pray to you, O Lord:

9 That we might live in peace from day to day;
that wars will cease, we pray to you, O Lord:

10 That we may stay faithful, open to your Word;
your Kingdom come! We pray to you, O Lord:

11 For all the dreams held deep within our hearts;
for all our needs, we pray to you, O Lord:

12 Entrusting all we are into you hands,
we call your name, and pray to you, O Lord:

Kyrie eleison

Kyrie eleison

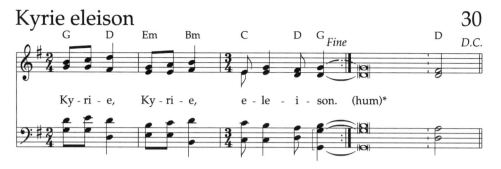

Ky - ri - e, Ky - ri - e, e - le - i - son. (hum)*

* Petitions may be sung or spoken here.

All

♪ A CAPPELLA or with instruments. (Instrumental accompaniments for Music from Taizé are available from GIA Publications, Inc., www.giamusic.com.)

✠ Prayers of the People; any time of intercessory prayer

📖 Lent

Prayer responses are not always slow and quiet. This one from TAIZÉ is bright and quick. The musical rhythm matches the word stresses perfectly. Make sure you observe them, stressing the "K" of Kyrie, and leaning on the SYNCOPATION of "e-LE-i-son."

Following the Kyrie eleison phrase, singers should immediately begin to hum as the petitions are sung or spoken, moving to the chord change at the end of the line on indication by the cantor. Since humming is not an easy way to sing, try an "Nnnnnnn" sound, with tongue behind the top teeth, or "Ooo," with lips slight parted. Take breaths quietly wherever needed during the sustained sound.

? *What or who would you like to include in the prayers?*

Words: from The Book of Common Prayer (1979) of the Episcopal Church USA.
Music: Jacques Berthier (1923–94) © Les Presses de Taizé (France) (admin. GIA Publications, Inc., 7404 S. Mason Ave., Chicago, IL 60638 [www.giamusic.com].) All rights reserved. Used by permission. *You must contact GIA Publications, Inc. to reproduce this music.*

All

♪ A CAPPELLA or with drum, rattles, or hand clapping

✠ Liturgy of the Word; grace before meals

📖 General

This brief acclamation in Swahili from Central Africa is best sung in its native language with the Hallelujah verse.

The harmony parts are quite easily taught. Begin with the melody and add the alto. Then teach the bass part and add it to the soprano and alto. Finally, teach the tenor part and add it to the bass part before combining with the soprano and alto. Repeat this song several times. Throughout Africa hand clapping often accompanies singing. One group could clap

with another group clapping

Pronunciation

Mu – ngu   ni   mwe – ma
Moo – ngoo*   nee   mweh – mah

* ng as at end of "song"

? *What are some things that make you know that God is good?*

Mu - ngu   ni mwe - ma.   Mu - ngu   ni mwe - ma.
Know that   God is   good.   Know that   God is   good.
Ha - le,   ha - le - lu - ya.   Ha - le,   Ha - le - lu - ya.

Mu - ngu   ni mwe - ma,   ni mwe - ma,   ni mwe - ma.
Know that   God is   good,   God is   good,   God is   good.
Ha - le,   ha - le - lu - ya,   Ha - le - lu - ya,   ha - le - lu - ya.

Words: Traditional.
Music: Democratic Republic of Congo. Source unknown © copyright control. Arr. Edo Bumba © 1997 WGRG The Iona Community (Scotland) (admin. GIA Publications, Inc., 7404 S. Mason Ave., Chicago, IL 60638 [www.giamusic.com].) All rights reserved. Used by permission.
You must contact GIA Publications, Inc. to reproduce this music.

Lord, I pray

B*

♫ A CAPPELLA, piano, organ

✠ Prayers of the People in church school; morning prayer at home; Rites of Passage

📖 Lent; Advent; Epiphany

This prayer for primary-school children serves as an internal reminder of God's help and presence throughout the day. The text encourages decision making, even in the heat of the moment, to be grounded in Christian love, and it encourages us to seek God's guidance in everything we do. Each verse has a different focus: (1) forgiving those who sin against us, (2) giving thanks for blessings, (3) asking for God's presence in temptation or fear.

The length of this song suggests that it would need to be learned over a period of time. It could be printed out on a large classroom banner and learned throughout a season or the year and coordinated with study of the Lord's Prayer or Psalm 23.

Point out the simple shape of the tune, ABAC; it would be easy to learn using SOLFEGGIO.

A: sol sol do — mi mi sol —

B: do re-mi fa fa mi mi re —

A: sol sol do — mi mi sol —

C: do ti-la sol fa mi re do —

? *What can you do when someone wrongs or troubles you?*

Lord, I pray

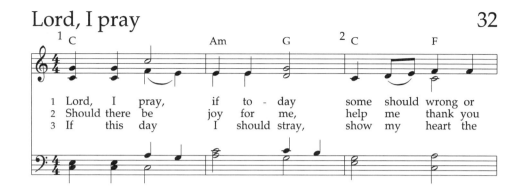

1 Lord, I pray, if to-day some should wrong or
2 Should there be joy for me, help me thank you
3 If this day I should stray, show my heart the

trou-ble me, make me kind; bring to mind
as I should. Let me through all I do
road to take. Should I fear, please be near;

your for-give-ness makes me free.
praise you, Lord, for all things good.
hear my prayer for Je-sus' sake.

This may be sung as a round or canon in two parts.

Words: Jean C. Keegstra-DeBoer, 1949, alt.
Music: Dutch melody, arr. Grace Schwanda © 1983 CRC Publications, 2850 Kalamazoo Ave. SE, Grand Rapids, MI 49560 [www.crcpublications.org]. All rights reserved. Used by permission.

A*

♪ A CAPPELLA

✠ Bedtime or upon arising in the morning; Morning Prayer; church school

📖 Third Sunday of Advent, Year B

🔑 Young children will readily learn this song and remember it as their first formal prayer. The melody contains two useful patterns for children to learn: "do-mi-sol-do" at the beginning, and at the end the descending scale from high "do" in the last line. Remember to explain that "thee" is an old fashioned way of saying "you."

🎶 Very small children will learn "the three things" more easily if gestures are used: indicate the eyes for "to see," the heart for "to love," pointing outward for "to follow." During this, older children may count off each of these three by holding up the appropriate number of fingers.

? *How could your family pray together every day?*

Day by day, dear Lord three things of thee I pray:___ to

see thee more clear - ly, to love thee more dear - ly, and

fol - low thee more near - ly, day by day.

Words: att. Richard of Chichester (1197–1253).
Music: Fiona Vidal-White © 2004 Fiona Vidal-White.

Amen, siyakudumisa
Amen, we praise your name

♟ All

♪ A CAPPELLA

✠ Great Amen; prayer response; moving from one place to another

📖 Anytime

⟟ South African music commonly uses a caller (cantor), who starts the song encouraging the singers to join in. A confident cantor with a strong voice is the best leader. The harmonies are very easy because they are parallel throughout between the soprano, alto, and tenor. These parts may be taught together, calling attention to the last phrase in which the tenor stays on one note. Then teach the bass part, which is harmonically predictable.

𝄞 Repeat the song several times, keeping the TEMPO moving.

Pronunciation

Ma – si – thi:	A – men,	si – ya – ku – du – mi – sa	Ba – wo
Mah – see - tee:	*Ah - mehn,*	*see – yah – koo – doo – mee – sah*	*Bah - woh*

? *This song uses a cantor, who calls us to sing. How does that feel?*

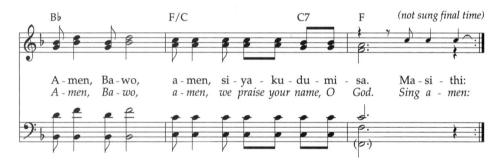

All

A CAPPELLA

Prayers; healing services; retreats

Advent; Epiphany; Lent

This open-ended song of prayer is particularly good at an informal service where it may be sung repeatedly. Focused on the theme of mission, it may be either joyous and moderately loud or slow and quiet.

The initial phrase could be sung by the cantor alone or by everyone. Other verses such as the following may be added: bless me; heal me; hear me; teach me. Invite singers to suggest other-one syllable words for additional verses.

Pronunciation

Thu - ma   mi - na,   So - man - dla.
Too - mah   mee - nah   Soh - mahnd - lah.

? *What do you think Jesus could fill you with?*

Additional verses

3 *Call:* Lead me, Lord, *Response:* Lead me, Jesus.
4 *Call:* Fill me, Lord, *Response:* Fill me, Jesus.

Holy, holy, holy Lord (Sanctus and Benedictus)

The Sanctus (Holy, holy, holy Lord) comes from Isaiah 6:1–3 and can be compared to Revelation 4:8. The Jewish synagogue used this text, and it has been an acclamation of the people from as early as the fourth century. The Benedictus (Hosanna. . . . Blessed is the one) is the text associated with Jesus' entry into Jerusalem in Matthew 21:9. Historically the Sanctus (with the Benedictus) has been an acclamation for the people. Even though Rite One in The Book of Common Prayer introduces the Sanctus with " . . . evermore praising thee, and saying . . . " the instructions on page 14 of The Book of Common Prayer indicate that the use of "said" should be understood to include "sung" and vice versa. Since children may be in church school or children's chapel during the Gloria, the Sanctus is the most important music of the ORDINARY for them to learn. In this book you will find that the moods of various Sanctus settings are greatly different. Is it a song of praise? Yes, absolutely. Is it a song of awe-filled mystery? Yes. A song of comfort in hard times? Yes. A song of worship? Yes.

B

♫ A CAPPELLA, melody instrument and percussion

✠ Retreats; parish meetings; any eucharistic celebration

The beauty of this Appalachian folk melody is its simplicity heightened by the PENTATONIC structure.

This piece has an earthy honesty about it and should be sung unaccompanied. A melody instrument, ideally a fiddle, may be added with a drum playing one beat per measure or this pattern.

Ho - ly,   ho - ly,   ho - ly,   Lord,   God   of   pow-er   and

might,_____   hea-ven   and   earth   are   full   of   your   glo - ry.

Ho - san - na   in   the   high - est._____   Bless-ed   is   the

one   who   comes   in   the   name   of   the   Lord. Ho - san - na,   ho - san - na,

ho - san - na   in   the   high - est,   the   high - est._____

B

♪ A CAPPELLA, instrument accompaniment, bells

✠ Any eucharistic celebration

📖 Advent; Lent; season of Pentecost

⚷ This Sanctus is a song of mystery (see the Sanctus introduction). The words that cue us to sing say that we join the "...Angels and Archangels...." Imagine two groups of angels or creatures that cover their faces with their wings and glow with unimaginable beauty on either side of God's throne, singing ANTIPHONALLY.

    This Sanctus is written in two parts. The second is an echo of the first. It is helpful to establish a strong four-beat pattern to secure the coordination of the two parts. The second part enters two beats after the first. Singers, especially those singing the second part, need to feel the three beats at the end of each echoed phrase (Holy...Heaven...Blessed).

𝄞 This piece may be sung in unison on the melody alone or doubled by any melodic instrument (flute, violin, or recorder). The second part, which is an echo of the melody, may be played by a cello. Divide the congregation into two groups with the cantor or leader cueing the entrances of each part. (This takes a little practice!) A large bell, such as a Tibetan bowl bell, organ chimes, or a large hand bell may be rung on the first beat of each measure and allowed to sound until it dies away.

Holy, holy, holy Lord

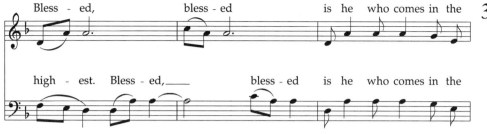

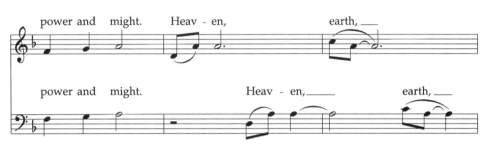

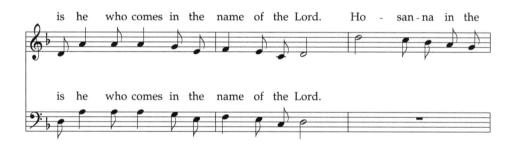

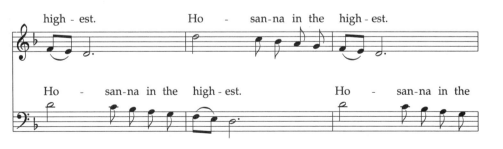

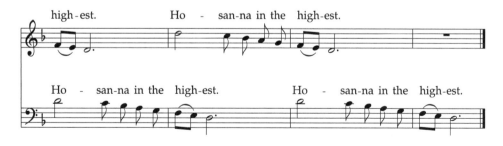

Words: Traditional.
Music © 1988 WGRG The Iona Community (Scotland) (admin. GIA Publications, Inc., 7404 S. Mason Ave., Chicago, IL 60638 [www.giamusic.com].) All rights reserved. Used by permission. *You must contact GIA Publications, Inc. to reproduce this music.*

Holy, holy, holy

B

♪ A CAPPELLA, piano or organ

✠ Rites of Passage; festivals; any eucharistic celebration

📖 Christmas; Easter

This setting is lively and should be sung with the conviction that we represent the best of God's kingdom on earth. This setting would work well at a festival service with visitors or newcomers who may not be familiar with the music. Each musical phrase repeats in an AABB form.

This may be sung in unison or in harmony with the voice parts singing the piano or organ accompaniment. The melody line should be sung LEGATO. Singers should be encouraged to breathe deeply at the end of each phrase. Voice parts are not complicated — begin with sopranos, add bass, then add altos, then tenors. Since this text of the Sanctus is from England, it is slightly different from The Book of Common Prayer because it does not contain the words from the Benedictus (blessed is the one).

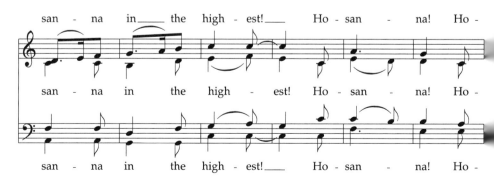

san - na! Ho - sa - na in___ the high - est!___

san - na! Ho - san - na in the high - est!

san - na! Ho - san - na in the high - est!___

Words: Traditional.
Music: John L. Bell (b. 1949) © WGRG The Iona Community (Scotland) (admin. GIA Publications, Inc.,
7404 S. Mason Ave., Chicago, IL 60638 [www.giamusic.com].) All rights reserved. Used by permission.
You must contact GIA Publications, Inc. to reproduce this music.

C

Keyboard, guitar, bass guitar, drum kit

Any eucharistic celebration

This gospel style setting should be felt in a slow duple pulse with accents on beats three and six in the 6/8 METER so that there is a strong duple/triple feel.

The gospel style may be accompanied by a piano alone. For a contemporary feel use a drum kit and a bass guitar playing the printed bass line. The most authentic keyboard sound to add to guitar and drums would be an electronic Hammond organ. This is sometimes labeled "jazz organ" on electronic keyboards.

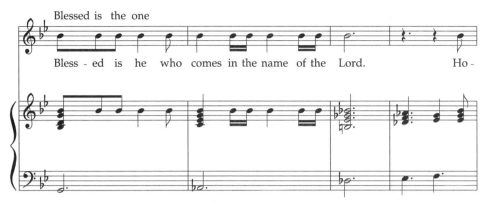

Blessed is the one

Bless - ed is he who comes in the name of the Lord. Ho -

san - na in the high-est.

Words: from The Book of Common Prayer (1979) of the Episcopal Church USA.
Music: Carl MaultsBy, from *The Saint Mary Mass* © 1989 Malted Milk Music,
575 Riverside Drive #51, New York, NY 10031-8545. All rights reserved. Used by permission.
You must contact Malted Milk Music to reproduce this music.

Holy, holy, holy Lord

C

♪ Keyboard, guitar, drum

✠ Any eucharistic celebration

🗝 This gospel setting of the Sanctus provides an opportunity to teach SYNCOPA-TION. The composer has added detailed markings to heighten the syncopation: marked accents (>) on numerous words and syllables and the STACCATO mark (·), which shortens the note before some accents, making them sound even more accented.

♪ The gospel style may be accompanied by a piano alone. For a contemporary feel use a drum kit and a bass guitar playing the printed bass line. The most authentic keyboard sound to add to guitar and drums would be an electronic Hammond organ. This is sometimes labeled "jazz organ" on electronic keyboards.

Lord's Prayer

The Lord's Prayer appears in two forms in the Gospels. In Luke 11:2–4 it appears as the response to the disciples' request, "Lord, teach us to pray, as John taught his disciples" (11:1 NEB). In Matthew 6:9–13 the Lord's Prayer is included in the Sermon on the Mount.

The Lord's Prayer became a regular part of the eucharistic liturgy in A.D. 400, when it was used as personal preparation for receiving the sacrament. It is believed that it may have been used earlier than that by people in their homes during the week when they consumed bread and wine brought from the Sunday service (see Marion Hatchett, *Commentary on the American Prayer Book* [HarperSanFrancisco, 1995], 378).

The traditional Lord's Prayer English-language version in The Book of Common Prayer has not changed since the English prayer book of 1559. The "new" version (printed beside the traditional version in The Book of Common Prayer, p. 364) is the work of the ecumenical International Consultation on English Texts in the 1970s. This common translation for use in most mainline denominations was undertaken to provide a more understandable text in contemporary language forms. For example, the use of the archaic "thy" and "thou," which were the familiar form of address in the Elizabethan era, are no longer well understood in the twenty-first century, especially by children. Only settings of this contemporary Lord's Prayer have been included in this collection for their benefit.

- B

- A CAPPELLA

- Anytime

- Proper 12, Year C

- This melody, which seems very much like plainsong, is adapted from traditional Native American music collected by Frances Densmore in Minnesota. The Ojibway word "Nossinan," which means "Our Father," may be substituted or sung simultaneously with the English.

- Today the Ojibway people sing Christian music slowly, but historically it was probably sung more quickly.

Nossinan* / Our Father in heaven, hal - low'd be your Name,   your kingdom come,

your will be done, on   earth as in hea - ven.   Give us today our dai - ly bread.

Forgive us our sins as we forgive those who sin   a - gainst us.

Save us from the time of tri - al,   and deliver us from e - vil.

For the kingdom, the power, and the glory are yours, now and for ever.

A - - men. _____

* *Ojibway word. Option for "Our Father" pronounced noh-sih-nahn.*

Words: from The Book of Common Prayer (1979) of the Episcopal Church USA.
Music: Monte Mason, from *Red Lake Mass* © Monte Mason. All rights reserved. Used by permission.

B

Piano, organ

Anytime

Proper 12, Year C

This setting of the Lord's Prayer could be used in the same service as the Sanctus setting by the same composer found at #39 in this book.

The gospel style may be accompanied by a piano alone. For a contemporary feel use a drum kit and a bass guitar playing the printed bass line. The most authentic keyboard sound to add to guitar and drums would be an electronic Hammond organ. This is sometimes labeled "jazz organ" on electronic keyboards.

Our Father in heaven

Lamb of God (Agnus Dei)

The Lamb of God is one of several texts that are collectively referred to as fraction anthems because they are to be sung following the fraction (breaking of the bread). It is an optional part of the liturgy, but when children are present, this brief song can vocally illustrate the action at the Table. "Lamb of God" signifies Jesus or the eucharistic bread.

B

♪ A CAPPELLA, melody instrument, hand bells or chimes, hand drum

✠ Any eucharistic celebration

📖 Second Sunday after Epiphany, Year A

⚷ The simplicity of this Appalachian melody is embellished by the sustained vocal sound in the alto and tenor. The melody could be sung alone throughout.

𝄞 This fraction anthem could be accompanied by a melody instrument with chimes or hand bells doubling the alto and tenor vocal parts. For a more sustained sound use violin, viola, and cello. A hand drum playing

throughout could be added.

O Lamb of God

Cantor or Congregation

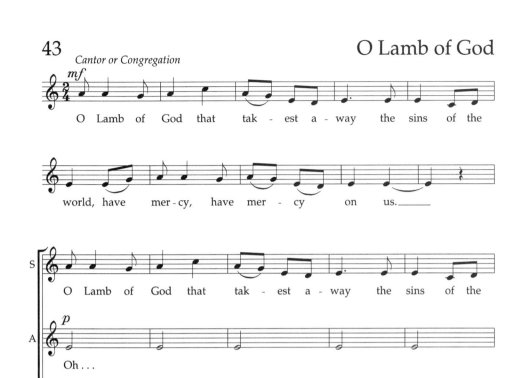

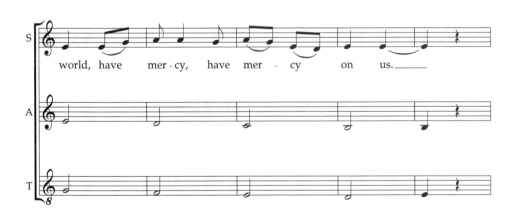

The choral parts may be played by the organ. However, the organ should not play the melody.

Words: from The Book of Common Prayer (1979) of the Episcopal Church USA.
Music: Jonathan Dimmock (b. 1957), from *Missa Appalachia* © 1989 Jonathan Dimmock.
All rights reserved. Used by permission.

O Lamb of God

All

A CAPPELLA

Any eucharistic celebration

This wonderfully simple setting is easy for all congregations. The congregation echoes each phrase sung by the cantor and holds the last note to overlap and harmonize with each cantor phrase.

The variety of invocation suggestions offered may be used as the middle verse replacing the words "Lamb of God." These phrases could be coordinated with the season or with specific references to Jesus from the PROPERS of the day. Multiple invocations should be used only if extra time is needed for preparing the bread and wine for communion.

**O Lamb of God, you take a - way

the sins of the world: have mer - cy on us.

Grant us your peace, grant us your peace.

* *The congregation echoes each phrase of the cantor at the interval of one measure.*

** *Additional Invocations*

Advent	**Lent**	**General**
O Morning Star	O Tree of Life	O Bread of Life
O Word of God		O Cup of Joy
Emmanuel	**Easter**	O Prince of Peace
	O Risen Lord	
Christmas	O Cornerstone	
O Word made flesh	O Spring of Life	
Emmanuel		

Words: from The Book of Common Prayer (1979) of the Episcopal Church USA.
Music: Ralph R. Stewart © 2000 G.I.A. Publications, Inc., 7404 S. Mason Ave., Chicago, IL 60638 [www.giamusic.com]. All rights reserved. Used by permission.
You must contact G.I.A. Publications, Inc. to reproduce this music.

Lamb of God

B

Organ, flute

Any eucharistic celebration

This simple setting of the Lamb of God may be easily taught using SOLFEGGIO syllables or numbers that correspond to the degrees of the scale in the key of D minor. The first petition uses do through sol (or 1 through 5) and is then repeated. The last petition begins on high do and descends to sol and fa (or 5 and 4), ending on sol (5).

The flute part printed here adds an interesting countermelody.

Communion

The singing of communion hymns is an important way to involve children. A child looks forward to that moment of walking to the altar to receive communion. While others receive, children will join in singing.

There are two kinds of hymns in this section: the traditional STROPHIC and the cyclical. The strophic hymn has multiple verses, each sung to the same tune. This amount of text may be challenging for non-readers; however, care has been taken to include hymns with refrains or enough repetitive phrases to engage young children. The cyclical hymn is one that has a single verse that can be repeated several times. These are useful as people move to communion, because frequent use allows memorization, thus eliminating the need to carry music.

All

Piano or organ

Communion; commissioning services; healing services

Third Sunday after Epiphany, Years A and B; Propers 5, 8, 17, Year A; Second Sunday in Lent, Year B; Proper 23, Year B; Baptism; Rites of Passage; Ordination

This short prayer sums up what we need from God. God accepts us as we are and makes of us far more than what we can be on our own. We are "sealed" at our baptism. See The Book of Common Prayer, page 308. The baptizand is marked on the forehead with a cross and the words "... you are sealed by the Holy Spirit in baptism and marked as Christ's own for ever."

This song may be sung unaccompanied with voices singing the harmony of the accompaniment. It may also be repeated several times.

Gestures

First phrase: *hold hands out wide in open gesture of prayer.*
Second phrase: *scoop open hands to meet each another at chest level.*
Third phrase: *place both hands over heart.*

? *What would you like a "seal upon my heart" to look like?*

Take, O take me as I am

Take, O take me as I am; sum-mon out what I shall

be; set your seal up-on my heart and live in me.

Behold, I make all things new

All

Piano or guitar

Prayer response; song for healing; congregational prelude

Fifth Sunday of Easter, Year A; Advent; Holy Innocents (December 28)

This song reminds us that in the Eucharist we are made new through Christ. The word "behold" is translated in newer versions of scripture as "see" or "look."

Each repetition of the word "behold" may be echoed. Divide the congregation into two groups having one sing first and the other echo. Switch the groups on subsequent repetitions of the song

What have you seen today that God has made new?

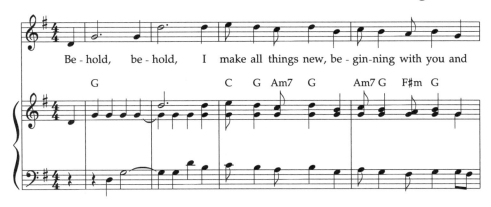

Be - hold, be - hold, I make all things new, be - gin-ning with you and

G   C   G   Am7   G   Am7 G   F#m G

Orff instrument accompaniment

Alto Metallophone

Bass Metallophone

start-ing from to - day.   Be - hold,   be - hold,   I

C/E   G/D   Am7/C   G/D   Dsus4   D   G

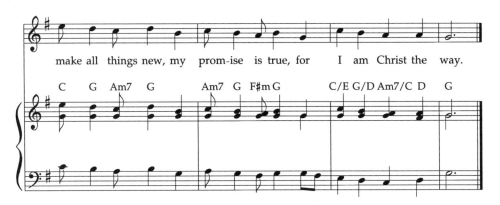

make all things new, my prom-ise is true, for I am Christ the way.

C   G   Am7   G   Am7   G   F#m G   C/E   G/D   Am7/C   D   G

C, C*

Piano, guitar

During communion; Liturgy of the Word

Anytime; Proper 13 and 14, Year B; Fifth Sunday in Lent, Year B; alternate verses for Advent, Christmas, or Lent

This hymn is rich in eucharistic imagery. In the Gospel of John, Jesus refers to himself as the "Bread of Life" and speaks of his forthcoming death as grain falling to the earth and dying. Help children understand how this is related to Jesus' words concerning the bread that we hear each week (The Book of Common Prayer, pp. 362, 368, 371, and 374). Scripture also refers to God's people being scattered but brought together by Christ, whose body was broken for us.

This song works well either for the congregation or as a choir anthem. Text may be more clearly revealed when some listen while others sing. Contrasting groups may divide the verse and refrain: cantor and congregation, adults and children, or high voices and low voices.

Because this song begins with a series of short textual phrases, it is in danger of losing its forward movement. In the refrain, the tied quarter notes on "Christ" in the second line and "us" in the third are places where attention must be given to carry the phrase forward. The eighth rests ( ) in the verses shape the line for clarity and should not be used for taking a breath. The quarter rests ( ) allow time for taking deep breaths. Hold fully the tied notes at the end of the middle and final phrases of the verses.

? *Who is the Bread of Life?*

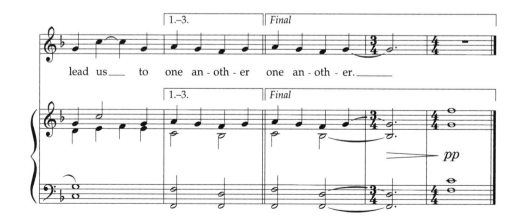

Verses

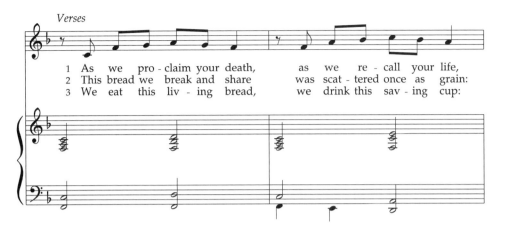

1 As we pro - claim your death, as we re - call your life,
2 This bread we break and share was scat - tered once as grain:
3 We eat this liv - ing bread, we drink this sav - ing cup:

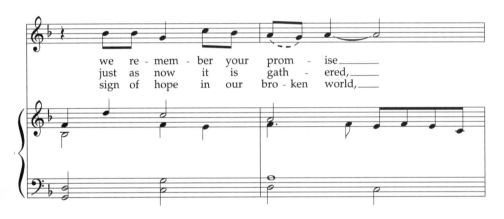

we re - mem - ber your prom - ise_____
just as now it is gath - ered,_____
sign of hope in our bro - ken world,_____

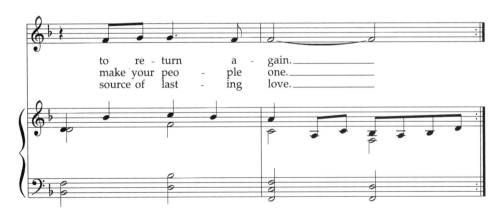

to re - turn a - gain._____
make your peo - ple one._____
source of last - ing love._____

Additional alternate verses on the next page.

Alternate Verses

VERSES for Advent:

1 Be with your people, Lord, send us your saving Word:
  Jesus Christ, light of gladness, come among us now. *Refrain*

2 Bring to our world of fear the truth we long to hear:
  Jesus Christ, hope of ages, come to save us now. *Refrain*

VERSES for Christmas:

1 A child is born for us, a son is given to us,
  in our midst, Christ, our Lord and God comes as one who serves. *Refrain*

2 With our own eyes we see, with our own ears we hear
  the salvation of all the world, God's incarnate Word. *Refrain*

3 You are the hope of all, our promise and our call,
  radiant light in our darkness, truth to set us free. *Refrain*

VERSES for Lent:

1 Our hunger for your Word, our thirsting for your truth,
  are the sign of your life in us till we rest in you. *Refrain*

2 To those whose eyes are blind you give a light to see;
  dawn of hope in the midst of pain, love which sets us free. *Refrain*

Alternate Verses for Ordinary Time:

1 Hold us in unity, in love for all to see;
  that the world may believe in you, God of all who live. *Refrain*

2 You are the bread of peace, you are the wine of joy,
  broken now for your people, poured in endless love. *Refrain*

Guitar lead sheet

Capo 3:

REFRAIN:

Bread of life, hope of the world,

Je-sus Christ, our broth - er:___ feed us now, give us life,

lead us___ to one an - oth - er one an - oth - er.___

Fine

VERSES:

1. As we pro - claim your death, as we re - call your life,
2. The bread we break and share was scat - tered once as grain:
3. We eat this liv - ing bread, we drink this sav - ing cup:

we re-mem-ber your prom - ise___ to re - turn a - gain.___
just as now it is gath - ered, make your peo - ple one.___
sign of hope in our bro-ken world, source of last - ing love.___

All, A*

A CAPPELLA, guitar or piano, hand chimes

Appropriate when children administer communion to each other

Anytime

Very young children will easily learn this song as their own. It is intended for use when few adults are present, such as in church school or children-only chapel. When small children offer communion to each other, they may say a simple phrase such as: "the bread of Jesus" and "the wine of Jesus," or phrases related to this song, "the Bread of Life" and "the cup of Love." Help children understand that we say this to emphasize the importance of the action just as we have a special way of presenting the birthday cake at a party.

Older children may want to add the Optional Descant, which is sung twice during each verse of the song. Hand chimes, which are lighter in sound than hand bells, may double the descant.

? *What do you like best about receiving communion?*

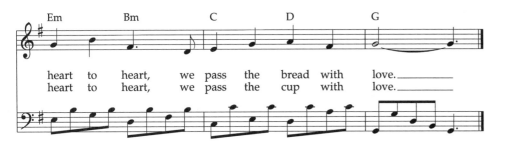

Optional Descant

Ha - le - lu - jah,   thank   you,   Lord.

All

♪ Piano, steel drums, conga drums, percussion instruments

✠ After communion; sending hymn at end of a retreat

📖 Proper 9, Year C; Fourth Sunday in Lent, Year B; Proper 13, Year A; Proper 11, Year B

Calypso, the style of music and dance from Trinidad, developed in the nineteenth and twentieth centuries. This "communion calypso" has been popular since the 1970s. Originally calypso functioned as oral newspapers, a cultural relationship highlighted by Fred Kaan's text "pass the word around."

This song is lively and should be sung with exuberant abandon. Dance should be encouraged. Jamaican folk instruments that could be added to a steel band and conga drums are cowbell, tambourine, and a ridged wooden or metal cylinder that is scratched with a metal comb. Some electronic keyboards may have a sound such as "vibraphone," which can be played to approximate the sound of a steel drum.

? *Can you draw a picture of verse 3 of this hymn?*

Let us talents and tongues employ

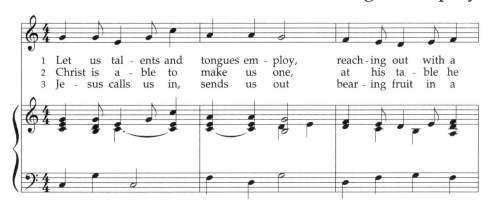

1 Let us tal-ents and tongues em-ploy, reach-ing out with a
2 Christ is a-ble to make us one, at his ta-ble he
3 Je-sus calls us in, sends us out bear-ing fruit in a

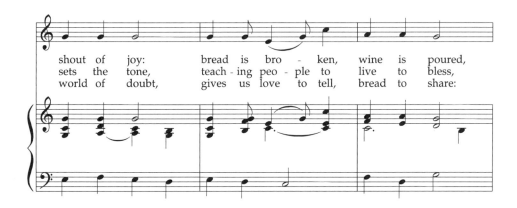

shout of joy: bread is bro-ken, wine is poured,
sets the tone, teach-ing peo-ple to live to bless,
world of doubt, gives us love to tell, bread to share:

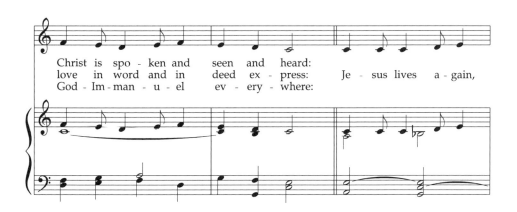

Christ is spo-ken and seen and heard:
love in word and in deed ex-press: Je-sus lives a-gain,
God-Im-man-u-el ev-ery-where:

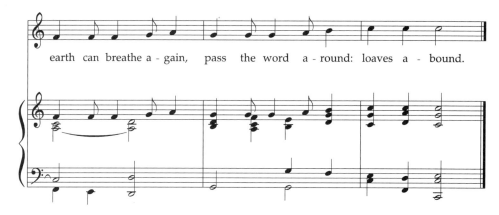

earth can breathe a-gain, pass the word a-round: loaves a-bound.

Words: Fred Kaan (b. 1929).
Music: *Linstead*, Traditional Jamaican Melody, arr. Doreen Potter (1925–1980).
Words and Music © Oxford University Press/Church of Scotland, 198 Madison Ave., New York, NY 10016-4314 [www.oup.org]. All rights reserved. Used by permission.

Gentle Jesus, risen Lord

B, B*

Piano and guitar

During communion; offertory

Anytime

The congregational response "...we come to your table" and its expanded form in the refrain are simple enough for immediate memorization by even the youngest children.

The cantor part could be sung by a children's choir as the congregation receives communion while singing the memorized responses and refrain.

? *Who calls you to the table when your family has a meal together?*

Gentle Jesus, risen Lord

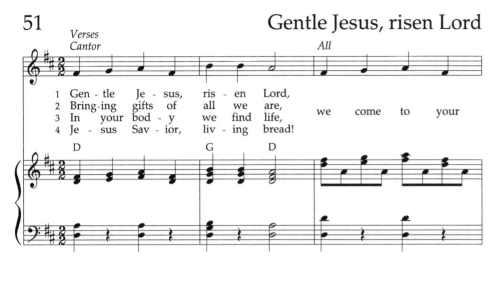

1 Gen - tle Je - sus, ris - en Lord,
2 Bring-ing gifts of all we are,
3 In your bod - y we find life,
4 Je - sus Sav - ior, liv - ing bread!

we come to your

ta - ble;

with our hearts so full of joy,
gifts of life and love and joy,
life you give for us to share,
bread of heav - en, bread of hope,

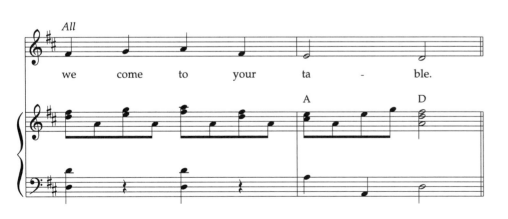

we come to your ta - ble.

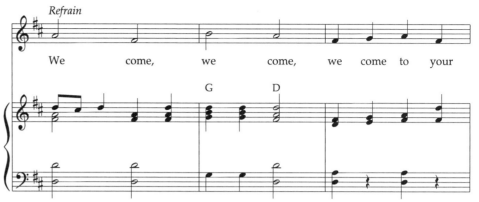

We come, we come, we come to your

ta - ble. We come, we come,

we come to your ta - ble.

C, C*

A CAPPELLA or melody instrument and hand drum

Congregational procession from the place of the Word to the Table

Easter season

This American folk tune is from a nineteenth-century shape-note collection called *The Southern Harmony,* 1835. It is PENTATONIC, has an insistent beat, is simple in form, and truly satisfying to sing. The evangelistic contemporary text names our hunger for God. Ask the children questions about the images in this hymn: What is holy manna? Who ate manna in the wilderness? What does the writer mean when she uses the word "wilderness"? Who are the people wandering in the wilderness right now? What is grace? Discuss with them the action of gathering scattered people around the communion table. Very young children can learn the last two lines as a refrain.

This hymn is in the same musical style as the "Holy, holy, holy Lord" and "O Lamb of God" from the *Missa Appalachia* (see #36 and #43).

A melody instrument such as a fiddle or recorder may accompany the singing. A hand drum may be added playing

throughout, or

A simple movement pattern may be used with this music. All should begin on the same foot, taking three steps forward and one back. The step back is more like leaning back on the right foot:

All who hun-ger gath-er glad - ly; ho-ly man-na is our bread. etc.
L   R   L   Rback   L   R   L   Rback etc.

?   *What do you like the taste of most?*

All who hunger gather gladly

1 All who hun-ger gath-er glad-ly; ho-ly man-na
2 All who hun-ger, nev-er stran-gers, seek-er, be a
3 All who hun-ger, sing to-geth-er, Je-sus Christ is

is our bread. Come from wil-der-ness and wan-d'ring.
wel-come guest. Come from rest-less-ness and roam-ing.
liv-ing bread. Come from lone-li-ness and long-ing.

Here in truth we will be fed. You that yearn for
Here, in joy we keep the feast. We that once were
Here, in peace, we have been fed. Blest are those who

days of full-ness, all a-round us is our food.
lost and scat-tered in com-mun-ion's love have stood.
from this ta-ble live their days in grat-i-tude.

Taste and see the grace e-ter-nal.
Taste and see the grace e-ter-nal.
Taste and see the grace e-ter-nal.

Taste and see that God is good.
Taste and see that God is good.
Taste and see that God is good.

Leaving

These two songs capture the spirit of the post-communion prayers: "Send us now into the world..." and "Send us out to do the work..." (The Book of Common Prayer, pp. 365, 366). It is sometimes difficult to know how we can help create community and purpose outside our church life except by remembering that Christ is always with us. We need to acknowledge the struggles presented by our role as Christ's own in the world, but we also need to acknowledge that our work is strengthened by the weekly worship with other Christians. This is particularly true following retreats or religious conferences. We go home feeling as if we have lived a little slice of heaven, and relocating is hard. The same is true for children at the end of vacation Bible school. It is important to acknowledge this and take time to address the feelings.

B

Piano or guitar

Closing of a prayer service; end of a retreat or conference

Because the prayer after communion is not optional in the principal Sunday Eucharist, this "sending hymn" would be redundant following it. However, it would be very useful at the end of a retreat or conference when it is sometimes challenging to negotiate "re-entry" after a Spirit-filled time away.

Depending on the size of the group and the dismissal time and mood of the closing events, this song could be sung repeatedly with people invited to leave the space at will, continuing to hum the tune as they depart. Piano and guitar should not sound together.

? *Can you name two people you know who have God's love in their hearts?*

Let us now depart in your peace, blessed Jesus.

Capo 3 (D) (G) (D) (A7) (D) (G) (D) (A7)
play D   F   B♭   F   C7   F   B♭   F   C7

Send us to our homes with God's love in our hearts.

(D) (G) (D) (G) (Fm) (G) (D) (A7)
F   B♭   F   B♭   Am   B♭   F   C7

Let not the bus-y world claim all our loy-al-ties.

(D) (Bm) (Em) (A7) (D) (G) (Em) (A7)
F   Dm   Gm   C7   F   B♭   Gm   C7

optional

Keep us ev-er mind-ful, dear Lord, of thee. A-men.

(D) (Bm) (G) (Em) (D) (A7) (D) (G) (D)
F   Dm   B♭   Gm   F   C7   F   B♭   F

C, C*, D*

♫ Guitar, piano, percussion instruments

✠ After communion; closing song for any gathering

⚷ South American folk tunes such as this are energetic, simple, and repetitive melodies that encourage quick learning. Divided into four-measure phrases, the melodic repetitions follow this pattern: verse ABAB; refrain CDCD.

𝄞 A GUIRO (oblong, hollow gourd instrument with ridges that are scraped with a wooden stick) may play this rhythm:

The quarter note and the tied notes should be emphasized. If no instruments are available, clap the rhythm.

If your congregation cannot manage the entire text in Spanish, work only on the refrain.

Pronunciation

O – re – mos por la paz, can – te – mos de tu_a – mor.
Oh – reh – mohs poor lah pahs cahn – teh – mohs deh twah – mohr.

Lu – che – mos por la paz, fie – les a ti, Se – ñor.
Loo – cheh – mohs poor lah pahs, feeEH – lehs ah tee, Seh – nyor.

? *How would you finish the sentence, "I hope . . . "?*

54 May the God of hope *Dios de la esperanza*

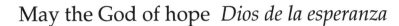

1 May the God of hope go with us ev-ery day,___
2 God will be our shep-herd as we go our way___

1 ¡Dios de la es-pe-ran-za, da-nos go-zo y paz!___
2 Dios se-rá nues-tro pas-tor en el ca-mi-no

bring-ing light and hope to ev-ery land and race.___
we must not for-get that God is al-ways there.___

luz y es-pe-ran-za en la os-cu-ri-dad.___
Pe-ro Dios siem-pre nos a-yu-da-rá.___

fill-ing all our lives with love and joy and peace.___
and will not for-sake us when we go a-stray.___

Al mun-do en cri-sis, ha-bla tu ver-dad.___
no nos a-ban-do-na-rá cuan-do nos per-di-mos.

Refrain

Pray-ing,___ let us work for peace; sing-ing,___ share our
O-re-mos___ por la paz, can-te-mos___

May the God of jus-tice speed us on our way,___
E-ven though the load of life is hard to bear,___

Dios de la jus-ti-cia, mán-da-nos tu luz,___
La___ vi-da es u-na car-ga pe-sa-da,

joy with all;___ work-ing___ for a world that's new,
de tu a-mor.___ Lu-che-mos por la paz,

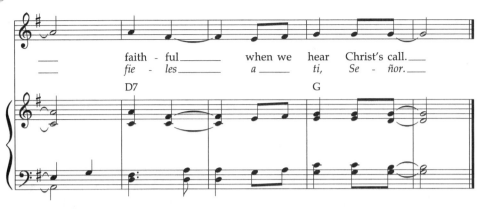

faith - ful_____ when we hear Christ's call.____
fie - les_____ a _____ ti, Se - ñor.____

D7   G

Words: Verse 1: Traditional Spanish, tr. Alvin Schutmaat © Alvin Schutmaat. All rights reserved.
Used by permission of Mrs. Pauline Schutmaat.
Verse 2: Tom Mitchell, tr. Frank W. Roman © Choristers Guild, 2834 W. Kingsley Rd., Garland, TX
75041-2498 [www.choristersguild.org]. All rights reserved. Used by permission.
Music: Argentine Folk Melody.

Blessings

The blessing at the end of the Sunday liturgy is optional because we have already received the blessing of the Eucharist. There is nothing left to do after the post-communion prayer except be dismissed to do the mission of the church. Communal sung blessings may be used at various times, such as the closing of a prayer service, retreat, or vestry meeting. Children could also sing the blessing together at the end of a church school session. Parents could join their children in singing each night at bedtime, or when a parent departs on a trip, or as a grandparent bids farewell after a visit. Holding hands while singing helps communicate the special nature of what is being shared.

B

Xylophones, wind chimes, ORFF INSTRUMENTS

Children's choir anthem; in place of the priest's blessing

Western collections of hymns are slowly beginning to include music from Asian Christians. This melody comes from China and has been adapted by noted church music professor and ethnomusicologist, Dr. I-to Loh. There are many ethnic styles and scales in Eastern music. This melody uses the PENTATONIC SCALE, which our Western ears find familiar. Use the word "God's" as an alternative substitute for the masculine pronoun "his." The most important feature of Asian music is the melody.

Several sets of wind chimes and finger cymbals playing throughout the church is a simple accompaniment for this hymn. Xylophones or ORFF INSTRUMENTS may play repeated patterns using any of the pitches in the hymn melody. Because the PENTATONIC SCALE is used, all the pitches sound equally well together.

May the Lord,— might-y God, bless and

keep us for-ev - er; grant us peace,—

per - fect peace, cour-age in ev-ery en-deav - our.

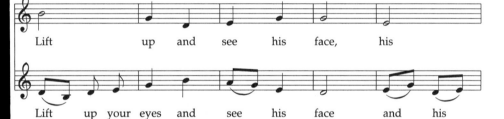

Lift up and see his face, his

Lift up your eyes and see his face and his

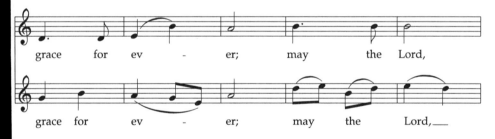

grace for ev - er; may the Lord,

grace for ev - er; may the Lord,—

might-y God, bless and keep us for-ev - er.

might-y God, bless and keep us for-ev - er.

Words: Traditional Liturgical Text.
Music: *Wen Ti*, Chinese Origin, adapt. I-to Loh (b. 1936) © 1983 Abingdon Press (admin.

All

Piano, guitar, percussion

At the end of children's chapel; prayer service

Originally written as a gentle lullaby for my young children, this song could be sung at bedtime by parent and child. The text, known as the Aaronic bene-diction or blessing, is found in the Old Testament book of Numbers, 6:24–26, and was probably used in the temple at Jerusalem. The pronoun "you" has been changed to "us" so that this may be a communal prayer.

Add a triangle or small bell on the first beat of every measure. A guitar may begin on an E major chord and alternate it with an A major chord until the measure before the ending, which requires a B7 chord.

May the Lord bless us

May the Lord bless us and keep us,

and make his face to shine u-pon us

and be mer - ci - ful, mer - ci -

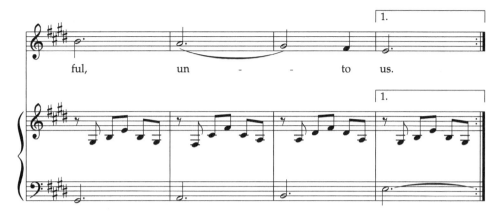

ful, un - to us.

us.

May also be sung unaccompanied.

Words: Aaronic Blessing, adapt.
Music: Fiona Vidal-White © 2004 Fiona Vidal-White.

C, C*

♫ Guitar, A CAPPELLA

✠ At the close of the liturgy; at the exchange of the peace

📖 Sixth Sunday of Easter, Year C

☛ A simple strum pattern for the guitarist will add to the folk sound of this South American melody:

downward strum ↓   upward strum ↑   Beats: 1   2   3

                                        Strum: ↓   ↓   ↑   ↓   ↑

🎼 A cantor could sing the verses of this song with the congregation singing the refrain in Spanish.

Pronunciation

La paz del Se - ñor, (repeat)   la paz del Re - su - ci - ta - do
Lah pahs del Seh - nyor,   *lah pahs del Reh – soo – see – tah – doh*

1–3 La paz del Se - ñor, la paz del Se - ñor,
1–3 *The peace of the Lord, the peace of the Lord,*

la paz del Re - su - ci - ta - do,_____
the peace of the One who is ris - en,_____

la paz del Se - ñor a ti y_a mi,
(2) se ha - ce pre - sen - te a_hora y_a - quí
(3) no pue - de vi - vir encer - ra̱da en si,
the peace of the Lord to you and me,
(2) *peace makes it - self pre - sent here and now.*
(3) *should not be en - closed in you or me,*

D.C. after (E7) each repeat

a to - dos al can - za - rá.
a - pré - sta - te re - ci - bir - la.
a - pré - sta - te com - par - tir - la.
to ev - ery - one reach - es out._____
Be rea - dy God's peace to re - ceive._____
but shared a - mong all who be - lieve._____

Advent

Advent is a time of dilemmas for Christian educators. Do we teach our children about the religious meaning of Christmas to counteract their focus on Santa Claus and gifts, or about Advent, knowing that Christmas will be over in a flash? How can we teach them Christmas carols, which most of them don't know, while at the same time singing songs about Advent? I believe the answer is to focus on Advent in our regular services and education time, and to have special times for Christmas preparations like singing carols and making gifts for others. The message of Advent is much too important to miss: we wait not only for Jesus' birth, but for the coming of God's kingdom in this world. Important themes for the season are how we have not built our world as God would wish; how we can find ways to help others; and how we can make a real effort to detach ourselves, even briefly, from the madness of a commercial Christmas.

All

Organ, piano, or A CAPPELLA

Congregational prelude

Advent

The beauty of this piece is its urgency and excitement about Christ's coming. Call attention to how the music highlights the text: the word "prepare" is sung ahead of the beat and illustrates our excited anticipation to get ready. This occurs again in the last line at the word "is," which sounds rushed — it's hard to wait!

To sing this in the CALL AND RESPONSE way, think of line one as "A," line two as "B," and line three as "C." Then follow this scheme:

CANTOR sings A and B

Congregation repeats A and B

Cantor sings C

Congregation repeats C

Cantor sings A

Congregation sings B

The cantor should help the congregation by clearly indicating with hand signals who is to sing each phrase.

? *What does it feel like when you are so excited you can't wait for something? What might that something be?*

Christ_____ is com - ing:___ pre - pare the way.___

Christ_____ is com - ing:___ pre - pare the way.___

Fine

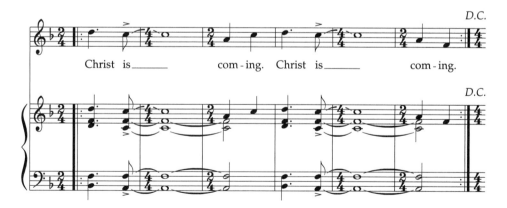

Christ is_____ com - ing. Christ is_____ com - ing.

D.C.

D

Piano, organ, guitar

Liturgy of the Word

Advent; Epiphany

An important message of Advent is comparing what God wishes us to do with what we have done. The first two lines of verses 1 through 4 show contrasting pairs (light/darkness, peace/troubled, food/hungry, shelter/homeless) and then asks God for the help we need to change. The text is confessional but does not dwell on penitence; rather, it moves from the problems to the solutions. Talk to older children about the ideas in each verse: Who do we think of as longing for light, but waiting in darkness? Who is looking for peace although our world is troubled?

This is one of the more complex hymns in this collection, so begin by teaching the refrain. The first line repeats (Christ, be our light), so learning that is the entry level for this piece. Also consider having the choir sing verses 2 and 4 with the congregation always singing the refrain and the remaining verses.

? *What do you long to see changed in this world? What can you do this Advent to resolve your longing for change?*

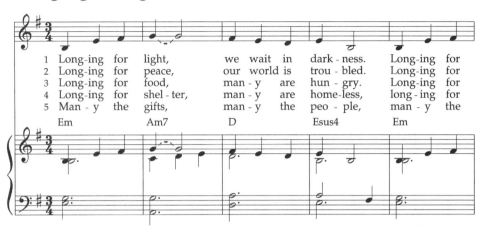

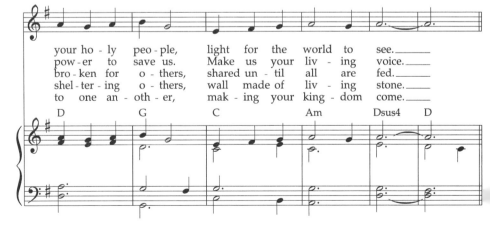

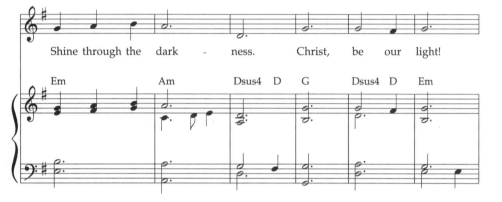

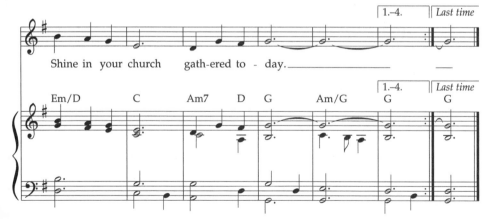

B, C

Organ, piano, melody instrument and hand drum, or guitar

Alternative to the Magnificat, especially in Evening Prayer

Third Sunday of Advent, Year B; For Social Justice; Marian feasts

The text of this hymn is a PARAPHRASE of the Magnificat, the song Mary sang when she visited Elizabeth, the mother of John the Baptist. Mary speaks of God's power that raises up the lowly and brings down the powerful. Jesus is the fulfillment of the promise made to our ancestors.

Mary is often seen as a passive participant in the story of Jesus' life, but these words portray Mary as brave and faithful to God — a woman of spirit! The lively folk tune captures the spirit of her words and reveals the active force of her witness today.

The challenge of learning this hymn with small children is the long text. The very youngest children could learn to sing their own version using this portion of the text:

> My heart sings out with joyful praise,
> My heart sings out with joy. (repeat)
> Fa, la, la, la;
> Fa, la, la, la;
> Fa, la, la, la, la, la.
> My heart sings out with joyful praise,
> My heart sings out with joy.

The verses could be taught one each week in Advent in church school. The Swedish folk tune is an AABA form with a constant skipping rhythm. A melody instrument such as a violin, flute, or recorder could accompany the tune. A small hand drum would add interest with a pattern

on each phrase.

What do you learn about Mary as a person from this song?

60 My heart sings out with joyful praise

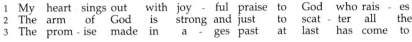

1 My heart sings out with joy - ful praise to God who rais - es
2 The arm of God is strong and just to scat - ter all the
3 The prom - ise made in a - ges past at last has come to

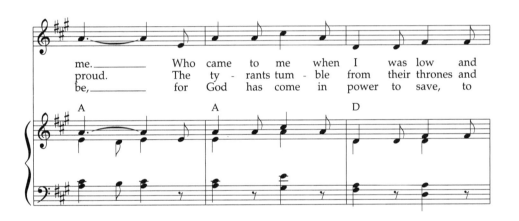

me._____ Who came to me when I was low and
proud. The ty - rants tum - ble from their thrones and
be,_____ for God has come in power to save, to

changed my des - ti - ny._____ The Ho - ly One, the
van - ish like a cloud. The hun - gry all are
set all peo - ple free._____ Re - mem - bering those who

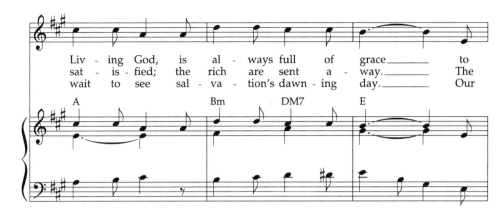

Liv - ing God, is al - ways full of grace_____ to
sat - is - fied; the rich are sent a - way._____ The
wait to see sal - va - tion's dawn - ing day._____ Our

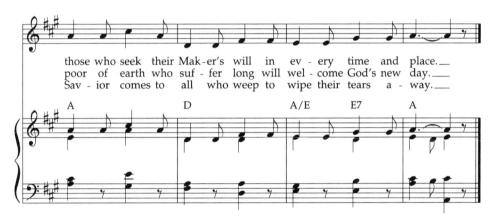

those who seek their Mak - er's will in ev - ery time and place.
poor of earth who suf - fer long will wel - come God's new day._____
Sav - ior comes to all who weep to wipe their tears a - way._____

Words: Ruth Duck.
Music: *Marias Lovsäng*, Swedish Folk Melody, arr. John L. Hooker (b. 1944) © GIA Publications, Inc.
7404 S. Mason Ave., Chicago, IL 60638 [www.giamusic.com]. Used by permission. All rights reserved.
You must contact GIA Publications, Inc. to reproduce this music.

B, D

♪ A CAPPELLA or instrumental accompaniment (see below)

✠ Communion or healing; prayer response

📖 Second Sunday of Advent, Years ABC; Nativity of St. John the Baptist (June 24); Feast of St. Mark (April 25); For Social Justice

🔑 Advent is the time when we prepare for the coming of Christ — not only the historical Jesus in scripture, but also Christ coming today through us as we help bring about God's kingdom here on earth. Examples of how we can do that are in the way we care for the earth and in making sure we share the world's resources so no one is poor or hungry.

A major theme in the season of Advent is that Jesus fulfills the prophesy of the coming of the Messiah. All four Gospels quote the prophet Isaiah, which is the text of this song. The Gospel of Mark, the earliest Gospel, opens with the Isaiah quote. John the Baptist plays a key role in this prophecy.

🎼 This brief refrain may be sung repeatedly alone or as a CANON in two, three, or four parts as marked. The secondary canon may be added to the first, or it could also be played on a flute. For a simple harmonic part, sing the words to the accompaniment pattern or use a neutral vowel such as "oo." The instrumental part included here may be played on flute, hand bells, chimes, or the bell sound on an electronic keyboard.

? *What would you do if you knew that Jesus was coming to your town, your school, or your home today?*

Prepare the way of the Lord

Canon

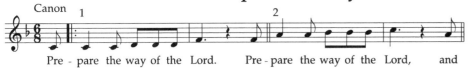

Pre - pare the way of the Lord. Pre - pare the way of the Lord, and

all peo-ple will see the sal - va - tion of our God.___ Pre -

Secondary Canon

Al - le - lu - ia. Al - le - lu - ia. Al - le -

lu - ia. Al - le - lu - ia.

Accompaniment

Capo I: (E)   (A)   (E)
F   B♭   F

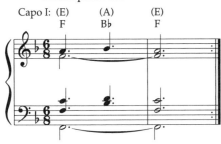

Instrumental part

Words: based on Luke 3:4, 6, adapt. The Taizé Community.
Music: Jacques Berthier (1923–1994) © 1984 by Les Presses de Taizé (France). (Words and Music admin.
GIA Publications, Inc., 7404 S. Mason Ave., Chicago, IL 60638 [www.giamusic.com].)
All rights reserved. Used by permission.
You must contact GIA Publications, Inc. to reproduce this selection.

A*, B*

♫ Piano, A CAPPELLA, small percussion instruments

✠ Congregational prelude; Liturgy of the Word

📖 Advent, particularly Year A

Because it contains numerous scriptural references for the season, this song could be sung throughout Advent. To manage the wordiness for very young singers, teach one verse each week. There is a simple pattern in both text and tune repeated in each verse:

Pattern	Verse 1 words
A	Stay awake, be ready.
B	You do not know the hour when the Lord is coming.
A	Stay awake, be ready.
C	The Lord is coming soon.
D	Alleluia, Alleluia!
C	The Lord is coming soon.

This song falls into the "children's song" category, but it can still be fun for adults. The claps are intended to be an aural highlight for the words. Small percussion instruments such as bells, CLAVES, or GUIRO could be added to the claps. Think of the noise as a wake-up call rather than an artistic enhancement! The short sung phrases before the claps should be cut off as indicated in the rhythm so the claps stand alone.

    The long phrase in the second line should not break before the second "Stay awake." Use the time of the claps to take a deep breath.

    Verses 3 and 4 do not have a word on the pick-up note to measure three. When learning *not* to sing a particular note, children can touch their fingers on their lips on the absent beat. Another possibility is to clap three times at that spot instead of the usual two. If adults are reticent about clapping, ask the accompanist to play two strong chords on the clapping beats.

? *How might you change your life this Advent?*

Words and Music: Christopher Walker (b. 1947) © 1988, 1989, 1990 OCP Publications, 5536 NE Hassalo, Portland, OR 97213 [www.ocp.org]. All rights reserved. Used by permission. *You must contact OCP Publications to reproduce this selection.*

All

Keyboard, drum kit, piano

Liturgy of the Word

Advent, especially Second Sunday of Advent, Year B; Nativity of St. John the Baptist (June 24)

This setting of Isaiah 40:3–4, 9 combines a gospel style refrain of "Prepare ye the way of the Lord" with a chant for the subsequent verses.

The printed accompaniment for the refrain is simple and could be played by young musicians on keyboard and drums. Alternatively it could be played by instruments less associated with gospel music: cellos playing the bass and tenor parts, with hand chimes for the three upper voices, and a flute doubling the melody an octave higher.

The simple refrain offers the opportunity to teach some basic musical concepts: counting an introduction of four measures and singing a triplet pattern against two beats. To count the introduction, use the first beat in the measure to count off the measures: <u>1</u>-2-3-4, <u>2</u>-2-3-4, <u>3</u>-2-3-4, <u>4</u>-2-3-4. Singing a triplet against two quarter notes is largely a matter of feeling the triplet as a relaxed pattern.

Each verse has a different rhythm to match the words. To learn them speak each one in rhythm before singing. Also, the verses could be sung by a cantor or by a choir.

? *What do you think God wants us to do to "prepare the way of the Lord"?*

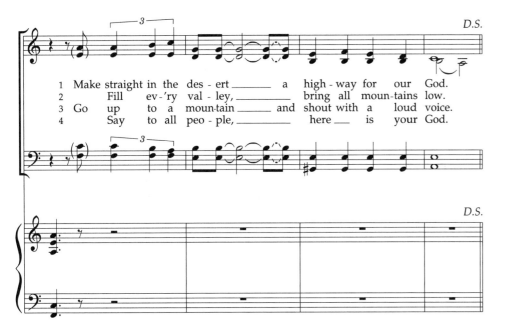

D.S.

1 Make straight in the des-ert _____ a high-way for our God.
2 Fill ev-'ry val-ley, _____ bring all moun-tains low.
3 Go up to a moun-tain _____ and shout with a loud voice.
4 Say to all peo-ple, _____ here _____ is your God.

D.S.

Words: Isaiah 40:3–4, 9.
Music: James E. Moore Jr. (b. 1951) © 1992 GIA Publications, Inc., 7404 S. Mason Ave., Chicago, IL 60638 [www.giamusic.com]. All rights reserved. Used by permission.
You must contact GIA Publications to reproduce this music.

Christmas

The *Godly Play* story of the church calendar discusses how the mystery of the principal feasts in the church year can be missed, and why time is needed "for getting ready to come close to the mystery." Advent is the "getting ready" time to come close to the mystery of Christmas. Helping prepare children to see the mystery of "God with us" during Advent is a worthy goal of educators and will ultimately bring them closer to understanding Christmas as formative to their faith.

Help your parish resist the temptation of abandoning all intentions of child-friendly worship on this important festival in deference to the "Christmas and Easter folk." Some churches schedule an early children's Christmas Eve service that appeals to families as well as adults or the elderly who do not wish to attend a late service.

Our Christmas carol repertoire has become dominated by European carols of the nineteenth century, and while Charles Dickens and Prince Albert shaped many of our secular Christmas rituals, most of us would not turn to this historic period for advice on education or the role of children in society. Some of these carols depict Jesus as an unreal baby, " . . . no crying he makes . . . ," and Mary as an unreal birthing mother "how silently, how silently the wondrous gift is given." (See chapter 7 in *The Singing Thing* by John Bell, GIA Publications, Inc., www.giamusic.com.)

A goal of the Christmas music in this collection is to expand our repertoire to include songs with a theological integrity and a contemporary honesty. Celebrate the Christmas season for its entire twelve days up to Epiphany, which continues the story with the manifestation, or "epiphany," of Christ. Consider ending a Christmas pageant with the birth and celebrating the arrival of the kings on Epiphany. While it is a challenge to help children understand the real meaning of Christmas, thoughtful worship during the Christmas season after Christmas day itself can bring a clearer understanding of the full mystery and unique integrity of Advent, Christmas, and Epiphany in the church year.

All

♪ A CAPPELLA, guitar and drums, piano, violins

✠ Congregational prelude; Gospel procession; hymn of praise

📖 Christmas season

⚷ The composer based this song on a lively Chilean dance form called the *cueca*, which is also popular in Argentina. The piano accompaniment provided here uses the *cueca* rhythm, which alternates between 6/8 and 3/4.

𝄞 Singing this simple song in two parts is quite easy because the harmony part matches the rise and fall of the melody line. Two violins could assist by playing the vocal lines. Make sure the rhythms are crisp and lively. If possible, alternate the English and Spanish texts.

Pronunciation

Glo - ria   en las al - tu - ras a Dios! y en la tie - rra
Glo - reeAH ehn lahs ahl - too – rahs ah Dyohs! yehn lah teeEH - rrah

paz   pa - ra a - que - llos   que a - ma el Se - ñor.
pahz pah - rah – keh - yohs kehAH - mehl Seh – nyor.

❓ *What do you think it would feel like to be an angel singing to welcome Jesus?*

Words: Traditional.
Music: Pablo Sosa (b. 1933) © Pablo Sosa.

A*, B*

Piano, guitar

Liturgy of the Word; offertory

Christmas pageant; Epiphany

This well-known song originated from a twelfth-century Latin carol, *Orientis Partibus,* the first line of which is "from the east the donkey came." The tune may have been sung in thirteenth-century France at the "Donkey's Festival," which celebrated the flight of the Holy Family into Egypt. It became popular in British hymnals at the turn of the twentieth century.

A beloved carol known by the name "The Friendly Beasts," this memorable text and tune will be easy for children. The rhythm of each verse is unique, so attention should be given to rehearsing it accurately. Should fewer verses be desired for the congregation, select two of the four animal verses and either repeat the first verse at the end or sing the printed final verse. The omitted verses could be sung by a solo voice.

? *What other creatures do you think helped look after Baby Jesus?*

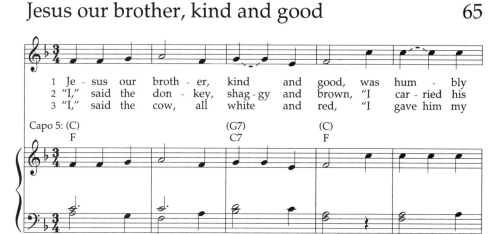

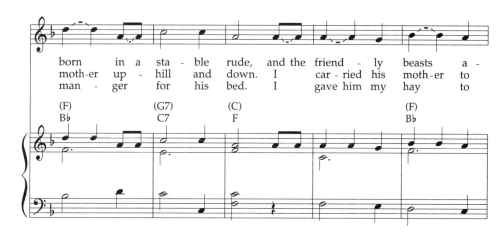

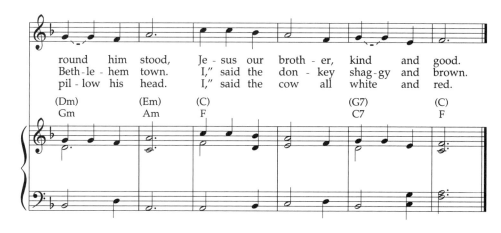

4 "I," said the sheep with curly horn,
"I gave him my wool for his blanket warm.
He wore my coat on Christmas morn.
I," said the sheep with curly horn.

5 "I," said the dove from rafters high,
"I cooed him to sleep, so he should not cry.
We cooed him to sleep, my mate and I.
I," said the dove from rafters high.

6 Thus every beast by some good spell,
in the stable dark was glad to tell
of the gift he gave Emmanuel,
the gift he gave Emmanuel.

Words: att. Robert Davis (1881–1950).
Music: Pierre de Corbiel, arr. Margaret W. Mealy (b. 1922) © 1961 General Convention of the Episcopal Church. All rights reserved. Used by permission.

A*, B

A CAPPELLA, piano, rain stick, hand chimes, METALLOPHONE, or flute

To accompany movement such as a procession of crèche figures; at communion; during pageant

Christmas Eve; Christmas season

Small children readily identify with the baby Jesus either personally or because they have younger siblings. They understand being looked after and loved by a mother and father. Consider alternating "arms of Mary" with "arms of Joseph." Because of its simplicity, this song can be taught immediately before the liturgy or during a children's homily.

The four-part setting is included here so that adults may enjoy this lullaby as well. Let the children sing the unison melody alone first. This setting should be accompanied by hand chimes or METALLOPHONE or sung A CAPPELLA. The four-part setting is incompatible with the printed piano accompaniment.

To help with remembering the words, add the following gestures:

"Sleep, sleep, gently sleep, close your eyes, you're..."	*hands folded as pillow*
"...cradled in the arms of Mary,"	*rocking gesture*
"...sleep, sleep, gently sleep,"	*hands folded as pillow*
"...in the arms of Mary."	*rocking gesture*

Call attention to the descending scale on "sleep, sleep, gently sleep" which helps the baby fall asleep. In the next line imagine that the baby fusses a bit, so rock him with the dotted notes. The last phrase calms him again until he's asleep.

Add a rain stick, turning slowly, on the first beat of every two measures. Remember, when using many forces, do not use everything all at once!

? *I wonder what you would do for the baby Jesus if you were there?*

Sleep, sleep, gently sleep

Choral arrangement with metallophone by Fiona Vidal-White © 2006

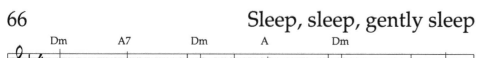

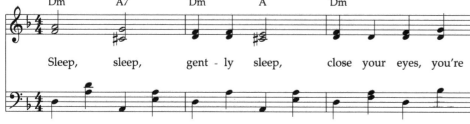

Sleep, sleep, gent-ly sleep, close your eyes, you're

cra-dled in the arms of Ma-ry, sleep, sleep,

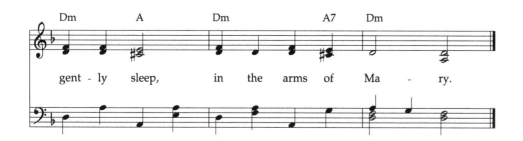

gent-ly sleep, in the arms of Ma - ry.

Sleep, sleep, gen-tly sleep, close your eyes, you're cra-dled in the arms of Ma-ry,

Sleep, sleep, gen-tly sleep, close your eyes, and sleep,_____

Sleep, sleep, gen-tly sleep, close your eyes, and sleep,_____

Sleep, sleep, gen-tly sleep, sleep sleep,_____

Metallophone

sleep, sleep, gen-tly sleep, in the arms of Ma - ry. Ma - ry.

sleep, sleep, gen-tly sleep, in the arms of Ma - ry. Ma - ry.

sleep, sleep, gen-tly sleep, in the arms of Ma - ry. Ma - ry.

sleep, sleep, gen-tly sleep, in the arms of Ma - ry. Ma - ry.

👪 All, B*, C, C*

🎵 Piano, conga drums, small percussion instruments

✠ Liturgy of the Word; offertory; procession from one place to another

📖 Christmas season; Feast of Epiphany

🔑 The large group of islands that extends from the tip of Florida almost to the coast of Venezuela and divides the Atlantic Ocean from the Caribbean Sea is known as the West Indies, or the Caribbean. The music from this widespread area has similar characteristics of repetitive patterns and infectious rhythm.

🎼 The driving force of this music is the rhythm. Resist the temptation to simplify the SYNCOPATION in church, highlighting it with large conga drums and various rattles, shakers, or maracas. A strong pianist is helpful if the percussion instruments are not available.

? *What do you think the "glorious kingdom" that Jesus came from is like?*

The Virgin Mary had a baby boy

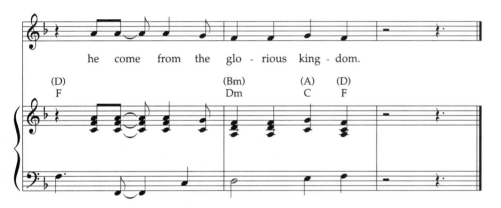

B, C

A CAPPELLA, finger cymbals, viola or cello

Liturgy of the Word; offertory

General or Christmas season

An important feature of Chinese music is the melody, in contrast to African or Caribbean music, which features strong rhythmic patterns. Chinese is a tonal language and sung sounds often slide between pitches. The dotted eighth note followed by the sixteenth note pattern in the first measure, for example, should be sung LEGATO, or smoothly, rather than MARCATO, or marked crisply.

An *erh-hu,* a small two-stringed Chinese instrument that is played like a cello, might accompany this piece, with the melody played in the tenor range. A cello might be substituted, but should be as bright a sound as possible and should slide between pitches, especially on single words that are sung to two SLURRED notes.

? *Can you write a short poem or song of the good news?*

Lis-ten, my friends and hear the good news: Je - sus now has

come to save you, one with God, he came from heav'n,

came to save all peo - ple on earth.

Lis-ten, my friends and hear the good news: Je - sus Christ has

come to bring hope, one with God, he came to save me;

came to save me, came to save you!

* *finger cymbals*

Words: Anon. Chinese, tr. Lucy Ding, para. C. Michael Hawn © 1999 Choristers Guild, 2834 W. Kingsley Rd., Garland, TX 75041-2498 [www.choristersguild.org]. All rights reserved. Used by permission.
Music: Traditional Chinese.

B, C

Guitar, percussion, A CAPPELLA

Christmas pageant; at the Station at the Christmas Crèche (see *Book of Occasional Services 2003,* Church Publishing Inc.)

Christmas Eve; Christmas season; Feast of Epiphany

The descending thirds pattern punctuated with the dotted quarter and eighth in the bass clef create a rocking motion for this lovely lullaby. The accompanist should be careful to clearly distinguish between the triplets and duplets in the third measure of each phrase.

The three harmony parts of this song may be sung A CAPPELLA with men's voices singing the bass part in short percussion-like syllables with an explosive consonant such as "buh" or "puh." The accompaniment could also be played by two melody instruments (violins or flutes) and a cello or bass guitar. If you would like a longer musical set for a scene in a pageant, combine this song with #66 "Sleep, sleep, gently sleep." A light percussive pattern

for children using fingertips on the palm of the hand is a gentle accompaniment.

Pronunciation

Ni - ño lin - do, an - te ti me rin - do,
Nee – nyoh leen - doh, ahn – teh tee meh reen - doh,

Ni - ño lin - do, e - res tú mi Dios.
Nee – nyoh leen – doh, eh – rehs too mee Dyohs.

? *Do you think the singer of this carol is a grown-up or a child? Why?*

Child so love-ly,   here I kneel be-fore you,
Ni - ño lin - do,   an - te ti me rin - do,

child so love - ly,   you are Christ, my God.
ni - ño lin - do,   e - res tú mi Dios.

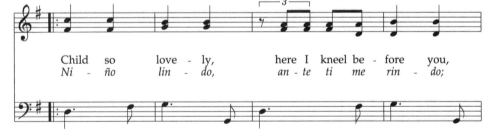

Child so love - ly,   here I kneel be - fore you,
Ni - ño lin - do,   an - te ti me rin - do;

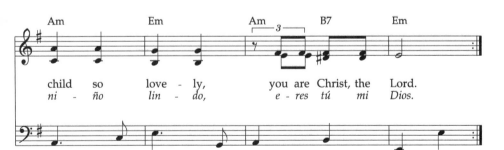

child so love - ly,   you are Christ, the Lord.
ni - ño lin - do,   e - res tú mi Dios.

B*, C, C*

Drum, shakers, rattles, mambilira (similar to the Western xylophone)

Offertory; during communion or a pageant

Christmas Day; Christmas season

Known as the "warm heart of Africa" because of the friendliness of the people, Malawi is a small landlocked country in the southeastern part of that continent. Blantyre, the name of this melody, is the largest city in southern Malawi; it was founded as a mission station by the Church of Scotland and named for the birthplace of David Livingston, the famous Scottish missionary and explorer.

The musical QUESTION AND ANSWER phrases of this song make it an excellent means for teaching a basic compositional technique. The tune of the first phrase that accompanies the text, "That boy-child of Mary was born in a stable," ends without sounding complete — as if a question has been asked. The next musical phrase on the words "…a manger his cradle in Bethlehem" quotes the first part of the initial musical question, but brings the music to a close (cadence) with a satisfying "answer." The same technique is used in the two phrases of the verses.

Keep the TEMPO of this song moving. To add interest to the verses, divide the QUESTION AND ANSWER musical phrases between two groups with everyone joining in on the refrain. If the song feels too long, sing the refrain only after each pair of verses.

A xylophone with wooden bars, such as an ORFF INSTRUMENT, could play the two treble parts. Add various rattles and shakers made from gourds on

emphasizing the first of each triplet. A tik-tak drum, also known as a whirling drum, would help create an authentic sound. This is a small two-sided drum on a stick from which are suspended small nuggets of wood on strings. Whirling the stick back and forth between the palms of the hands cause the nuggets to strike the heads.

?   *What question do you want to ask about the story of Jesus' birth?*

That boy-child of Mary

That boy-child of Ma-ry was born in a sta-ble, a man-ger his

cra-dle in Beth-le-hem.

Fine

1 What shall we
2 His name is
3 How can he
4 Gift of the
5 One with the
6 Glad-ly we

call him, child of the man - ger? What name is
Je - sus, God ev - er with us, God giv - en
save us, how can he help us, born here a -
Fa - ther, to hu - man moth - er, makes him our
Fa - ther, he is our Sav - ior, heav - en - sent
praise him, love and a - dore him, give our-selves

D.C.

giv - en in Beth - le - hem?
for us in Beth - le - hem.
mong us in Beth - le - hem?
broth - er in Beth - le - hem.
help - er in Beth - le - hem.
to him in Beth - le - hem.

Words: based on Luke 2:7, adapt. Tom Colvin (b. 1925). Music: *Blantyre*, Traditional Malawi melody, adapt. Tom Colvin (b. 1925). Words and Music © 1969 Hope Publishing Co., 380 S. Main Pl., Carol Stream, IL 60188 [www.hopepublishing.com]. All rights reserved. Used by permission.
You must contact Hope Publishing to reproduce this selection.

Epiphany

The word "epiphany" means *to show* or *reveal*. The Feast of the Epiphany, on January 6, marks the arrival of the kings, or magi, to see Jesus. So far the witnesses to Jesus' birth have been his family, God's representatives the angels, and representatives of Joseph and Mary's own race and religion, the shepherds. What we learn from the visit of the kings is that Jesus came not just to his own family, community, country, and religion, but to the whole world — to those far away and those of different faiths and nations, as represented by the magi, who were astrologers from other lands. The Festival of the Three Kings celebrated on the Epiphany is very important to people in Hispanic or Latin cultures, particularly Puerto Ricans. The night before Epiphany children put food and water out for the kings' camels and are rewarded with a gift.

The Epiphany, one of the principal feasts of the church, comes at the end of the Christmas season, bringing closure to those twelve days and helping us turn from the birth of Jesus to the manifestation of his work in the world. What we celebrate on the Sundays after the Epiphany are those events and actions in Jesus' ministry that revealed him to the world. The Epiphany could be celebrated by a short pageant dramatizing the arrival of the kings. Include a potluck dinner with foods from many countries to emphasize that Christ's message reaches out to all.

Los magos que llegaron a Belén
The magi who to Bethlehem did go

👥 D

🎵 Guitars, double hand drums (bongos), maracas, piano

✠ Offertory; Epiphany pageant

📖 The Epiphany; Three Kings Festival

🔑 This carol is included in this collection to honor the Hispanic or Latin importance of the Three Kings Festival and to offer Anglo congregations a rhythmic and joyful alternative to "We three kings." Like that familiar carol, this one sets the context of the story in an introduction calling the kings the "heralds of the coming of Messiah." The kings sing a verse together about their mission, and then each sings a solo of homage to the baby Jesus, interpreting the meaning of his gifts to him. In the *estribillo*, or refrain, the singers hail the guiding star which revealed God and continues to assure us of God's presence.

🎼 The entire congregation may sing this carol, or it may be dramatized by assigning parts to different groups and soloists. The challenge to non-Spanish speakers is fitting the rhythm of the words to the melody. The infectious energy of the tune will nearly teach itself. The congregation could sing only the introduction and the refrain with soloists with the kings singing the four verses. If this song is used dramatically with non-Spanish speakers, teach the children the introduction in advance, so the congregation may sing only the refrain.

As you teach the children, appeal to their desire to sing the words correctly. Ask them to memorize sections as homework between services or rehearsals. Recite the words in rhythm, and clap the rhythm alone before putting words and music together.

An outline of the shape of this song is as follows:

Introduction	All, or choir/children
Verse 1	All kings
Refrain A labeled (1–3)	All
Verse 2	King I
Refrain A	All
Verse 3	King II
Refrain A	All
Verse 4	King III
Refrain B labeled (4)	All

Pronunciation

Introduction

Los ma - gos que lle - ga - ron a Be - lén
*Lohs mah - gohs keh yeh - gah – rohn ah Beh - **lehn***

a - nun - cia - ron la lle - ga - da del Me - sí - as
*ah – noon - seeAH- rohn lah yeh - gah - dah del Meh - **see** - ahs*

y no - so - tros, con a - le - grí - a,
*ee noh - soh - trohs, cohn ah - leh - **gree** - ah,*

la a - nun - cia - mos hoy tam - bién.
*lah – noon – seeAH- mohs oy   tahm - **beeEHN.***

Refrain A

Oh bri - llan - te es - tre - lla que a - nun - cias   la au - ro - ra
Oh bree - yahn - tehs – treh - yah kehAH – noon - seeAHS lau - roh - rah

no nos fal - te nun - ca tu luz bien - he - cho - ra.
noh nohs fahl – teh noon - kah too loos beeEHN – eh - choh - rah.

Refrain B

Glo - ria en   las al - tu - ras al Hi - jo de Dios,
Gloh – reeAHehn lahs ahl – too - rahs ahl ee - hoh deh Dyohs,

Glo - ria en   las al - tu - ras y en la tie - rra a - mor.
Gloh – reeAHehn lahs ahl – too - rahs yehn lah teeEH – rrah – mohr.

❓ *What do you think the kings were thinking and talking about on their long journey?*

Los magos que llegaron a Belén
The magi who to Bethlehem did go

71

3 Co-mo_es Dios el ni-ño
le re-ga-lo in-cien-so,
con a-ro-ma dul-ce
que su-be_has-ta_el cie-lo.
Estribillo

3 To the Child of God
rich incense I am bringing,
with aroma sweet
that heavenward is winging.
Refrain

4 Al ni-ño del cie-lo
que ba-jó a la tie-rra,
le re-ga-lo mi-rra
que ins-pi-ra tris-te-za.
Estribillo

4 To the Child who came
to bring us heaven's gladness,
I have come with myrrh,
a sign of coming sadness.
Refrain

Words: Manuel Fernández Juncas, tr. Carolyn Jennings © 1995 The Pilgrim Press, 700 Prospect Ave., Cleveland, OH 44115-1100 [www.thepilgrimpress.com]. All rights reserved. Used by permission.
Music: *Los Magos*, Traditional Puerto Rican Carol

C, D

Piano, guitar, flute, percussion

Liturgy of the Word; offertory; Epiphany pageant

Feast of the Epiphany

The delightful text is written from the point of view of onlookers who are trying to make sense of the unfolding events of the Epiphany — much like us. In the curious way of children, many questions are asked. Answers are not given; instead, the singers look, follow, and wonder. Though the text is quite busy, the music is very simple. The first musical phrase (who are these eastern strangers?) is the material for the entire verse, since the second half uses the same melodic shape beginning on a different pitch. The refrain (second page) is a simple ABAB form.

As one of the few songs in this collection more effectively sung as a performance, this powerful text could be easily incorporated into a dramatic presentation. Separate verses could be interspersed between episodes of pageant dialogue to give the audience a child's-eye view of the action. The congregation could be incorporated by singing the last half of each verse, beginning at the top of the second page. An oboe or perhaps a flute could introduce the melody with a hand drum playing a repeating pattern

To be most effective, finger cymbals should play infrequently, such as on the downbeat of the last measure of each phrase (measures four, eight, twelve, sixteen, etc.).

? *Imagine you are with the people in this hymn. What do you see? What do you think about what you see?*

72 **Who are these eastern strangers?**

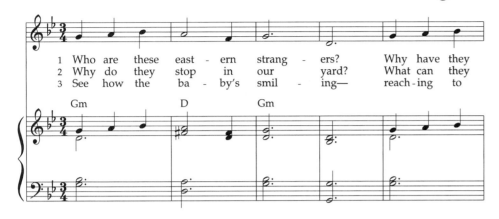

1 Who are these east-ern strang-ers? Why have they
2 Why do they stop in our yard? What can they
3 See how the ba-by's smil-ing— reach-ing to

come so far? Why do they gaze in-
hope to see? Why do they come with
hold the myrrh! Why is his mo-ther

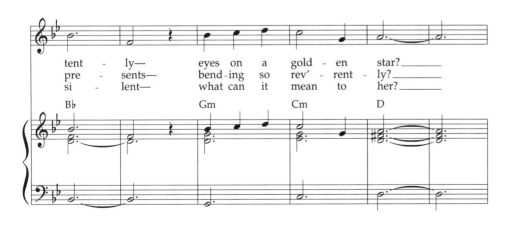

tent-ly— eyes on a gold-en star?
pre-sents— bend-ing so rev-'rent-ly?
si-lent— what can it mean to her?

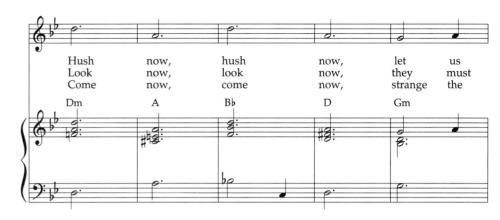

Hush now, hush now, let us
Look now, look now, they must
Come now, come now, strange the

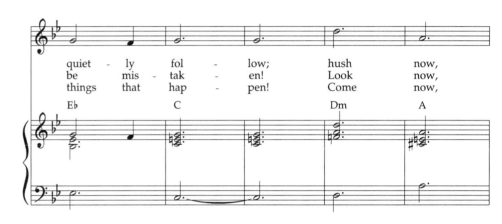

quiet-ly fol-low; hush now,
be mis-tak-en! Look now,
things that hap-pen! Come now,

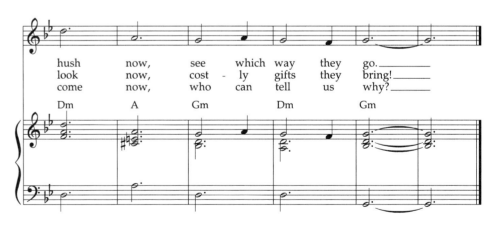

hush now, see which way they go.
look now, cost-ly gifts they bring!
come now, who can tell us why?

Words: Cecily Taylor.
Music: *Eastern Strangers,* Mike Daymond.
Words and Music © 1999 Stainer & Bell Ltd. (admin. Hope Publishing Co., 380 S. Main Pl., Carol Stream, IL 60188 [www.hopepublishing.com].) All rights reserved. Used by permission.
You must contact Hope Publishing to reproduce this selection.

A*, B*

Guitar, A CAPPELLA, piano

Congregational prelude; Liturgy of the Word; Gospel procession; offertory

Season of Epiphany, especially the Last Sunday after the Epiphany, Year B; the Transfiguration

The Christian image of light is an important and very powerful one for children, who are often afraid of the dark and the unknown. There is plenty of material for discussion here: Who are the prophets? How is the word of the Lord a light? (see Ps. 119:105). Who or what is the Morning Star? (see Rev. 22:16). And, of course, there is the star in the Epiphany story. Take this opportunity to discuss our old friends, metaphor and simile. An example might be how we refer to the persons of the Trinity, who are difficult to describe. We give them names and liken them to something else to help us understand something that is beyond our complete understanding. Note that you can change the word in each verse at "See the light of the _____ ." To learn the logic of the word changes, ask the children, "What can we see the light of? What makes a light in our stories?" Then show them how that word fits into the music.

Especially suited to very young pre-readers, this song is a good one to learn in church school or children's chapel through the season of Epiphany. Because the verse is repetitive and rhythmically engaging, younger children will easily learn this part, while readers will be able to sing the more complicated refrain. (For this reason think of "Look up!" as the refrain, rather than what is printed.) Add two claps or percussion beats after the third "Look up!" — to punctuate the text and help measure the two-beat rest. This would be an excellent song for children to sing as an anthem. Alternatively, the congregation could join the readers singing the refrain. Simple ORFF INSTRUMENT parts are included.

? *What does the dark make you think of or feel? And the light?*

Look up!

1 Look up! Look up! Look up! See the light of the

pro - phets.* Look up! Look up! Look up! See the

light of the pro - phets.* For the word of the Lord is a

light, shin - ing in the dark - ness___ un - til the

day dawns, and the Morn - ing Star a - ris - es in your hearts.

Orff instrument accompaniment

* *Alto metallophone*

Stanzas (play 4x) ... *Refrain*

* *or use any bell sound on keyboard; handbells, tone chimes*

* *2 angels, 3 star, 4 Jesus*

Words: based on 2 Peter 1:19.
Music: June Fischer Armstrong © 1991 CRC Publications, 2850 Kalamazoo Ave. SE,
Grand Rapids, MI 49560 [www.crcpublications.org]. All rights reserved. Used by permission.

Blest are the poor in spirit

B, C, D

A CAPPELLA, strings, organ

Prayer; healing; offertory; communion

All Saints; Fourth Sunday after the Epiphany, Year A; Sixth Sunday after the Epiphany, Year C; Proper 1, Year C

The structural elements of this song make it ideal for bringing together singers of differing abilities. The close harmonies and nearly parallel movement between parts of the Amen antiphon allow it to be easily learned. The richness of the antiphon contrasts with the plaintive clarity of the verses. The antiphon moves in single steps up or down with two exceptions: from "it" to "shall" in the first line and from the first to the second syllable of "Amen" in moving from line one to line two. Singers should be alerted to these variants. The tenor G♯ is an important pitch in the final major chord. Allow adequate rehearsal time for the cantor or choir to learn the changing text rhythms for the various verses.

The sustained sound of a string quartet or the organ could support the harmonies of the antiphon, which may be used alone as a prayer or a response to reading. When using the verses, sing the antiphon as printed and then hum the harmonies as an accompaniment while a cantor or choir sings the verses. To extend the mood of this TAIZÉ-like chant, the organist could improvise quietly on this song once the singing has ended. A choir and cantor could be used together by singing the verses responsively, i.e., the cantor sings, "Blest are the poor in spirit...," and the choir responds, "...the kingdom of heaven is theirs."

? *Can you think of other people, or groups of people, whom God will bless?*

Blest are the poor in spirit

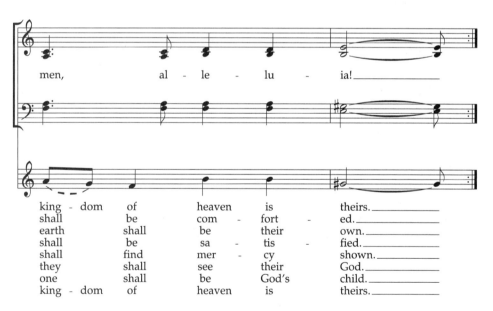

Yo soy la luz del mundo
I am the world's true light

A, D*

A CAPPELLA, guitar or vihuela, violin, trumpets, bass or guitarrón (see below)

Liturgy of the Word; offertory; processions; retreats; youth meetings; congregational prelude

Season of Epiphany; Fourth Sunday in Lent, Year A; Baptism

Light is a major theme from Advent through Epiphany. We hear about it in scripture, collects, and psalms. Jesus said not only that he was the light of the world, but also that we are the light of the world (see Matt. 5:14). This lively song gives us an opportunity to reflect Christ's light in our lives by singing and rejoicing! The profound proclamation "God is our light, God is our peace, God is our love" is our witness to the world. Note that the word "our" is an addition to the English translation in Part 3 so that the text rhythm will easily match the musical rhythm.

When teaching this song use three cantors or groups of singers, each to lead a group in the congregation. Teach Part 1 to everyone. When it is secure, teach Part 2 to everyone. Put the two parts together noting that Part 1 begins with a pick-up one beat before Part 2. Now stop the singing (this is the hard part!) and teach everyone Part 3. Combine all three parts by adding them consecutively: Part 1 sings, Part 2 joins on the repeat of 1, Part 3 joins 1 and 2 after they have sung together.

Once this song is well known, it may be sung by all as a round with everyone moving on to the next part when they have finished the first. To keep all parts together, remind singers to listen as well as to enjoy themselves! An interesting contrast would be created by singing or humming one part quietly once or twice before the full exuberant singing is let loose. To bring the singing to a close, the cantor should signal the last round and conduct a RALLENTANDO, or all could repeat one of the three parts in unison as an ending.

A mariachi-style accompaniment would bring out the Mexican flavor of this song. The guitar or vihuela, a guitar with a rounded back, should play a rhythmic down and up strum, and the violin and trumpet should play the melody together. If there is a second trumpet available, it should play a third lower than the melody where possible, especially on Part 3. The low-pitched guitarrón, a large guitar with a convex back, could provide the bass by playing

on the pitches of the chords indicated.

Pronunciation

Part 1

Yo soy la luz del mun - do. El que me si - ga ten - drá
Yoh soy lah loos dehl moon - doh. Ehl keh meh see - gah tehn - **drah**

la luz que le da la vi - da.
lah loos keh leh dah lah vee - dah.

Y nun - ca an - da - rá en la os - cu - ri - dad.
Ee noon - cahn — dah - **RAHehn** *laus - koo - ree - dahd.*

Part 3

Dios es la luz, Dios es la paz, Dios es a - mor.
Dyohs ehs lah loos Dyohs ehs lah pahs, Dyohs ehs ah — mohr.

? *How can we be the light that Christ wants us to be?*

Yo soy la luz del mundo
I am the world's true light

Part 1

Yo soy la luz del mun - do. _ El que me si - ga ten - drá la
I am the world's true light. _____ If you will fol - low me, your

luz que le da la vi - da. Y nun - ca an - da - rá en la os - cu - ri - dad.
life will re - flect my bright - ness and you'll nev - er walk in the night.

Part 2

A - le - lu - ya, a - le - lu - ya,

a - le - lu - ya, a - le - lu! La, la, la, la, la, la.

Part 3

Dios es la luz, Dios es la paz, Dios es _ a - mor. _____
God is our light, God is our peace, God is _ our love. _____

Dios es la luz, Dios es la paz, Dios es _ a - mor.
God is our light, God is our peace, God is _ our love.

Words and Music: based on John 8:1, att. Rodolfo Ascencio, tr. C. Michael Hawn © 1999 Choristers Guild, 2834 W. Kingsley Rd., Garland, TX 75041-2498 [www.choristersguild.org]. All rights reserved. Used by permission.

When Jesus saw the fishermen

B, B*, C

A CAPPELLA, guitar

Liturgy of the Word; children's chapel; vacation Bible school; themes of mission

Epiphany season, especially the Third Sunday after the Epiphany, Years A and B; Proper 5, Year A; St. Andrew (November 30)

This song is a ballad, or a storytelling text, and surrounds the calling of the disciples with a simple tune that can be sung as a round. Learning this song could inspire an illustrative art project for children. Print the words in the center of a large page with wide margins, leaving room for the children to illustrate the text. Or create a wall poster illustrating each verse.

Teach only the first verse to pre-readers. Readers can easily learn all the verses during a few weeks. When singing as a round, do not hold the last note more than the indicated length, so that the round continues without a break. The song could be sung by all with a repeat of the first verse sung as a round at the end. ORFF INSTRUMENT parts are provided.

What would you do if Jesus said, "Come and follow me"? Is there anything that would hold you back?

When Jesus saw the fishermen

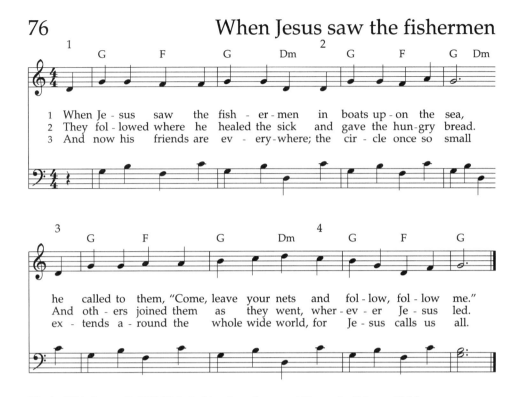

1 When Je - sus saw the fish - er - men in boats up - on the sea,
2 They fol - lowed where he healed the sick and gave the hun - gry bread.
3 And now his friends are ev - ery - where; the cir - cle once so small

he called to them, "Come, leave your nets and fol - low, fol - low me."
And oth - ers joined them as they went, wher - ev - er Je - sus led.
ex - tends a - round the whole wide world, for Je - sus calls us all.

Orff instrument accompaniment

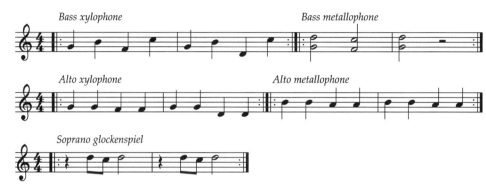

Bass xylophone

Bass metallophone

Alto xylophone

Alto metallophone

Soprano glockenspiel

B, C, C*, D*

♪ Piano or electronic keyboard, guitar, bass, and drum kit, organ

✠ Liturgy of the Word; offertory; after communion

📖 Trinity Sunday, Year C; Second Sunday in Epiphany, Year B; Lent; For the Mission of the Church; Commissioning for Lay Ministries (see *Book of Occasional Services 2003,* Church Publishing Inc., p. 179); Ordination; Rites of Passage

⚿ Growing out of the liturgical reforms in the late 1960s and early 1970s, this hymn first gained popularity in the Roman Catholic Church. The verses portray the "voice of God" and the refrain is a more personal statement that quotes from the calling of Isaiah (see Isa. 6:1–8), the calling of the boy Samuel (see 1 Sam. 3:1–18), and the questioning of the disciples at the Last Supper (see Matt. 26:22 RSV). The result is a refrain that is a personal commitment to mission with a subtle nod to our human capacity for betrayal.

𝄞 The original performance intent of this song was that verses should be sung by a soloist with the congregation joining in at the refrain. This honors the two different "voices" between the verses and the refrain (see above). This provides a clue about first teaching the refrain only to the congregation. The choir or a cantor should sing the verses with guitar accompaniment. The full support of a praise band would cue the congregation to sing at the refrain. An unamplified guitar alone is generally inadequate to lead singing unless the congregation is very small.

When the congregation is ready to sing the verses, note the entry on the second beat of the measure for the verses and the "empty" measure in the middle of the verse at the top of the second page of music. Encourage LEGATO singing that highlights the flowing musical line.

? *This song names God "the Lord of sea and sky," "the Lord of snow and rain" and "the Lord of wind and flame." What name would you give God?*

I, the Lord of sea and sky

Here I am, Lord.___ Is it I, Lord?___ I have

heard you call-ing in the night._____ I will go, Lord,___

___ if you lead me,___ I will hold your peo-ple in my

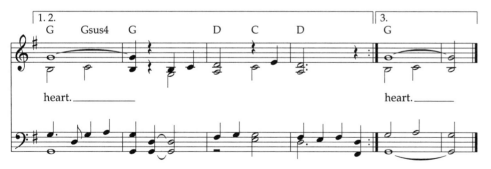

heart._____ heart._____

B, C, D

♪ Piano, A CAPPELLA

✠ After communion; Liturgy of the Word

📖 Epiphany season; Proper 9, Year A; For Social Justice

One kind of Christian action or mission is to envision what we will do as members of Christ's body. This is an action song in that sense. The activity of Christian mission is embodied by the rhythms of this song especially if it is enhanced by a choir singing the accompaniment A CAPPELLA. Besides, it is hard to stay still while singing this song! Physical movements for children are added below to help interpret the words.

The printed accompaniment could be played on the piano as all sing the melody in unison; however, if there is a choir or part of the congregation that could sing the accompaniment without the piano, the song then becomes an energetic and powerful dialogue between the two groups. The accompaniment part should be light and bouncy so as not to overpower the melody line. Light hand claps on the off-beat could also be added for rhythmic interest.

Gestures

Verse 1

We will lay	*With both hands, hold the neck of a sack over right shoulder*
our burden down	*Lower it over to the left*
In the hands of	*Show the palm of the left hand*
the risen	*Show the right palm*
Lord	*Raise both hands in* ORANS *position*

Verse 2

We will light	*Fold hands as if in prayer, tuck thumbs inside forming a "flame"*
the flame of love	*Raise hands, then part them moving out in two circles*
	coming together to make the "flame"
…hands of…	*repeat actions above*

Verse 3

We will show	*Touch chest with both hands then lower them, palms out*
both hurt	*Cross wrists, clench fists*
and hope	*Open hands out*
…hands of…	*repeat actions above*

Verse 4

We will walk	*Move arms back and forth to suggest walking*
the path of peace	*Make peace sign*
Hand in hand with	*Take the hands of the people next to you*
the risen Lord	*Raise linked hands*

? *Which verse of this song do you like best? Why?*

* *The accompaniment may be sung by a choir using the words above.*

Words and Music: John L. Bell (b. 1949), The Iona Community © 1989 WGRG The Iona Community (Scotland) (admin. GIA Publications, Inc., 7404 S. Mason Ave., Chicago, IL 60638 [www.giamusic.com].)

B, C, D

A CAPPELLA, guitar, maracas, marimba

After communion

Anytime; Rites of Passage; Commissioning for Lay Ministries; Commissioning for a Church Planter, Missioner, Mission Team

The church in Nicaragua is working to fight poverty, war, and suffering. Its songs reflect an understanding of God's mission that is straightforward and practical. It interprets our baptismal covenant in plain language. This song is about what each of us can do with our hands, if we ask God to help us. The music itself has a strong first and third beat that adds a sense of strength and decisiveness.

The traditional music of Nicaragua is often accompanied by a rhythmic guitar strum emphasizing the strong first and third beats, maracas (they were there when Columbus arrived!), and a marimba, which is like a xylophone with wooden bars. Play the soprano and tenor line on the marimba, which has the warm sound of tuned wooden bars struck by a moderately soft mallet. Make a contrast vocally between rhythmic percussive singing in the first half and a more sustained LEGATO style, although not too sentimental, in the second half. Return to the rhythmic singing for the last phrase. Make sure to observe the rest at the end of each phrase and feel the drive of the line that carries through to the last word "I," "now," "place," and "comes." Once is never enough with this song; sing it over.

Gestures

Sent by the Lord am I	*Arms lifted, palms up: clap, clap*
my hands are ready now	*Arms lifted, palms facing out: clap, clap*
to make the earth a place	*Arms lifted, palms out: clap, clap*
in which the kingdom comes.	*Arms lifted, palms up: clap, clap*
(repeat)	
The angels cannot change	*Touch fingertips to shoulders, then thumbs, rotate fingers out like wings and flap (this is American Sign Language)*
a world of hurt and pain	*Cross wrists, clench fists*
into a world of love,	*Arms crossed hands open*
of justice and of peace.	*Lower arms to be parallel to each other at waist level*
The task is mine to do,	*Left hand beats chest*
to set it really free.	*Cross wrists, clench fist, break open and lift arms on "free"*
Oh, help me to obey;	*Fold hands on chest, bow slightly*
help me to do your will.	*Stand up and lift arms*

? *What could you do with your hands to make the earth the place in which the kingdom comes? Choose a task and arrange to do it.*

Sent by the Lord

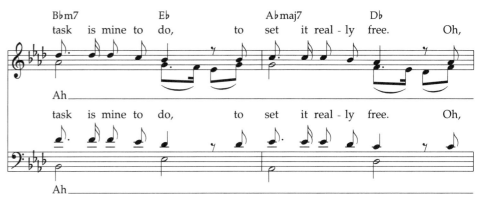

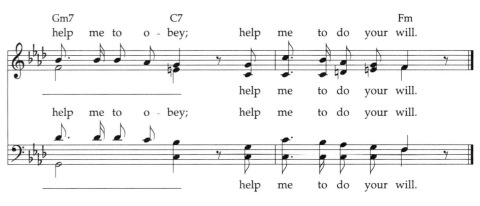

All

♪ A CAPPELLA, piano, guitar

✠ Liturgy of the Word; prayer response; communion; anthem at the candle lighting in evening worship

📖 Christmas; Epiphany; Baptism

Originally part of a longer song, this CANON-like refrain creates a mesmerizing halo of sound especially when used at an evening service. The singers on the second voice part will need to know that the exact imitation of the canon ends on their last two words.

Teach the top voice part first, singing it alone a few times. As the melody becomes more familiar divide into the two parts with the cantor leading the congregation on the top part and the choir or another cantor leading the second part.

? *Why is Christ a "light"?*

The light of Christ

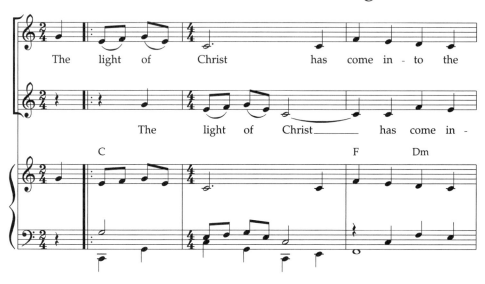

Words and Music: Donald Fishel (b. 1950) © 1974 Word of God Music (admin. T.C.C. – The Copyright Company, 1026 16th Ave. S, Nashville, TN 37212 [www.thecopyrightco.com].) All rights reserved. International copyright secured. Used by permission.
You must contact T.C.C. to reproduce this selection.

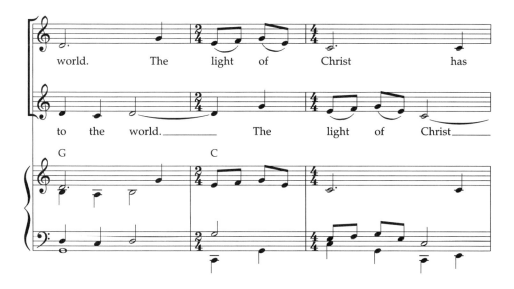

All

Piano, guitar

Liturgy of the Word; communion

Epiphany; Proper 10, Year A (Revised Common Lectionary); Rites of Passage

The text of this song from Psalm 119:105 is not appointed for use in the Episcopal lectionary, but does appear in the Revised Common Lectionary used by many Episcopalians and other denominations. These words are congruent with texts, especially from the psalms and collects, on a variety of other occasions.

Children are fascinated by echoes. In this simple AABA song each time the text is "Your word" there is an echo indicated by smaller type. It is almost as if the word is rolling across the countryside. In the middle of the song an entire phrase is echoed.

Teach this piece first without the echoes. Divide the congregation into two groups, with the echo group being smaller or just instructed to sing more softly. This group could be physically separate from the main group, perhaps seated in a gallery or balcony. The cantor should clearly cue each group, making sure that the parts hold their last note so that it overlaps with the other. All should sing " . . . is a lamp to my feet." The TREBLE CLEF of the piano accompaniment is the picking pattern for the guitar, which could also be played an octave higher by two flutes. A bass guitar playing the bass clef of the piano part would be a good anchor for the sound. The guitars should be lightly amplified to be an effective accompaniment if the singing group is more than about a dozen.

? *Why do we use the metaphors of light and dark for good and evil?*

Your word

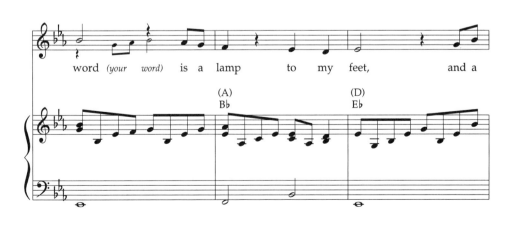

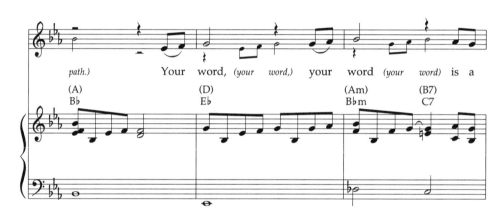

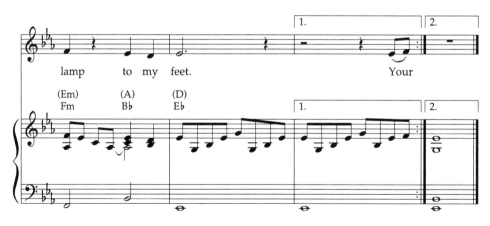

Words: Psalm 119:105.
Music: Frank Hernandez © 1990, Birdwing Music (ASCAP) (admin. EMI Christian Music Publishing, PO Box 5085, Brentwood, TN 37024-5085). All rights reserved. Used by permission.

Lent

From earliest Christian times, Lent has been the time for the preparation of catechumens, unbaptized adults who wish to become Christians. During this season they hear the stories (scripture), worship, pray, and discover their gifts for ministry. At the end of Lent during the Great Vigil of Easter, they are baptized. They receive communion for the first time as Christians and from then on are full members of the Christian community. (Historically, catechumens could attend only the Service of the Word, leaving before communion to study together.) A central theme of Lent, therefore, is this catechumenal process of preparation for the Sacrament of Baptism and, for baptized Christians, the reexamination of their baptismal commitments.

The theme of discipleship, from the season of Epiphany, continues, but as we reflect on Jesus' journey and the events leading to the crucifixion, we also think about the hard questions: How can I make my life more like Jesus' life? How do I learn to say "I'm sorry" to those I have hurt? Is there something I cling to that stops me from doing what I say I will do when I renew my baptismal vows? How can I help those who have less than I do, and work toward making the world a fairer place? All children, however young, think about these issues in their own way. They hope to do good and make a difference in the world just as adults do. Jesus does not measure the size of any task we do, but the sincerity with which we do it.

👥 B, C, D

♪ A CAPPELLA, piano

✠ After a reading; offertory; prayer response

📖 Sixth Sunday after Epiphany, Year A; Ash Wednesday; Fourth Sunday in Lent, Year C; Proper 1, Year A; Proper 7, Year B

⌐ There are so many different ways in which we need reconciliation — from personally to nationally. This contemporary song from Korea, a country quite literally divided by conflict, is a plea to God to "make us one body." The apostle Paul speaks about the body of Christ in the context of the sacrament of the Holy Eucharist: "Because there is the one bread, all of us, though many, are one body, for we all share in the one bread" (1 Cor. 10:17, RSV). And yet we forget, becoming territorial and openly hostile to others to keep what we have — position, possessions, or wealth.

The melody of the first phrase of this song is the musical idea of the entire composition. Each subsequent phrase varies the first slightly; consequently, it is easy to learn.

♭ Equally effective sung either in unison or in harmony, this plaintive music matches the longing in the text. Singers should strive for a flowing LEGATO sound which would be enhanced by a cello playing the bass line in dotted half notes for each changing pitch in the easy stepwise movement. The scale may be completed by adding a passing tone in the next-to-last measure by inserting an F between E and the G in the final measure.

? *If we know that we are all one in the body of Christ, why do we keep falling out and need to be reconciled, or joined together, again?*

Come now, O Prince of Peace

1 Come now O Prince of Peace, make us one bo - dy,
2 Come now, O God of love, make us one bo - dy,
3 Come now and set us free, O God, our Sa - viour,
4 Come, Hope of u - ni - ty, make us one bo - dy,

come, O Lord Je - sus, re - con - cile your peo - ple.
come, O Lord Je - sus, re - con - cile your peo - ple.
come, O Lord Je - sus, re - con - cile all na - tions.
come, O Lord Je - sus, re - con - cile all na - tions.

If you love me

B*, B, C

Piano, guitar, ORFF INSTRUMENTS, organ

After a reading; offertory; after communion

Pentecost; Fifth Sunday of Easter, Year B; Lent

The first verse of this text quotes Jesus speaking to his disciples as recorded in the Gospel of John (John 14:15). The text answers the question, "What should I do to be a good Christian?" If we love God, we must follow God's rules (commandments), follow God's path, and care for all people as an expression of that love. Use this song when the Ten Commandments are taught or with lessons on caring for others. Several weeks may be required to teach all four verses to young children.

The melody is a combination of repeated notes, scale steps, and skips of a third and a fourth. Older children will enjoy learning how these intervals sound and matching them. Verse 3 contrasts with the other verses both melodically and harmonically. Such contrasts make the song more interesting. Verses 1, 2, and 4 are in F major. Verse 3 is written in its relative minor, D minor. Both keys share the same KEY SIGNATURE — one flat. Play the two different melodies, asking the children to listen to the difference and then describe what they hear.

Verses 1, 2, and 4 may be sung as a three-part CANON at a distance of one measure. The canon should be allowed to end before continuing to verse 3. ORFF INSTRUMENTS using the patterns below add a gentle accompaniment to this song. The pedal point, or sustained pitch in the bass line, could be effectively played on the organ.

? *Can you write a summary of what this song tells us to do, in five or six bullet points? If so, you could write it on an index card and carry it in your backpack or wallet.*

Orff instrument accompaniment

1 If you love me, tru-ly love me, keep my com-mand-ments
2 If you love me, tru-ly love me, come now and my dis-
4 If you love me, tru-ly love me, in-to the world a-

day by day. If you love me, tru-ly love me,
ci- ple be. If you love me, tru-ly love me,
rise and go. If you love me, tru-ly love me,

Fine

fol- low for-ev- er in my way.____
fol- low and so re- mem- ber me.____ *to verse three*
there ev- 'ry-where my wit- ness show.____

3 Through the land my peo-ple feed, al- le- lu- ia,

C D.C.

in their sor- row, in their need, al- le- lu- ia.

Words and Music: Natalie Sleeth (1930–1992) © 1980 Hinshaw Music, Inc., PO Box 470,
Chapel Hill, NC 27514 [www.hinshawmusic.com]. All rights reserved. Used by permission.

C, D

piano, A CAPPELLA, flute or violin, hand drum

Liturgy of the Word; offertory

Lent; Good Friday

Each verse of this contemporary Lenten hymn recounts Jesus' experiences of temptation, suffering, and betrayal and then offers a prayer for strength and guidance when one is faced with similar situations. As we sing it, we ask to be reminded of Jesus' example when we are tempted, when we want to give up, and when we deny him.

The METER of this hymn is one of the most popular: 87.87 D. The "D" means "double." To substitute a different tune for this text, look in the hymnal Metrical Index and try other 87.87 D tunes to this text (The Hymnal 1982 Accompaniment Edition, Hymns Volume, p. 1039).

I wrote this *Southern Harmony*–style tune to make this wordy hymn easier to learn. It may be accompanied by a flute or violin playing the melody and a hand drum playing a

pattern for measures in 4/4 and a

pattern measures in 6/4. Each verse of this hymn could be divided between two groups of singers, highlighting the change in the text between the story from scripture and the prayer response.

? *What do you think it feels like being in the desert? How do we remember that Jesus is with us when we are distracted by these feelings?*

Forty days and forty nights

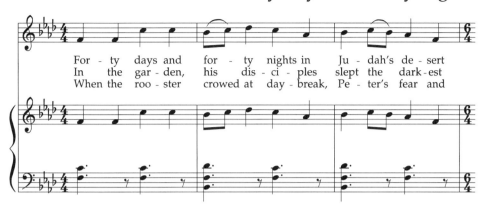

Forty days and forty nights in Judah's desert
In the garden, his disciples slept the darkest
When the rooster crowed at daybreak, Peter's fear and

Jesus stayed. All alone he fought temptation,
hours away. but our Lord did not condemn them
panic grew. He denied three times the charge that

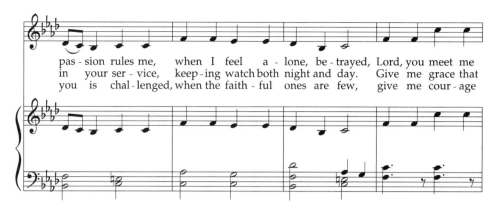

passion rules me, when I feel alone, betrayed, Lord, you meet me
in your service, keeping watch both night and day. Give me grace that
you is challenged, when the faithful ones are few, give me courage

in the desert, strong in faith and unafraid.
I may never such a love as yours betray.
and conviction to proclaim my Lord anew.

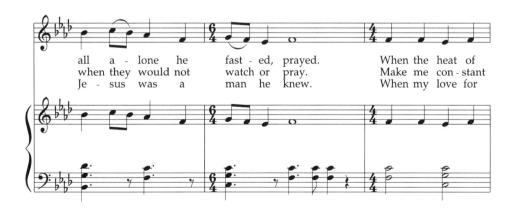

all alone he fasted, prayed. When the heat of
when they would not watch or pray. Make me constant
Jesus was a man he knew. When my love for

✝ C, D

♫ Organ, piano, guitar

✠ Liturgy of the Word; offertory

📖 Advent; Lent; Easter Vigil; All Saints (see specifics below)

⚷ Few hymns about only one particular story from scripture have been included in this collection. This one, however, is like a glorious "five-for-one" offer. The hymn is about the ancient and continuous story of our ancestors in faith — Abraham, Sarah, Moses, Miriam, Joseph, Mary, Zacchaeus, and Martha — and what we can learn from them. Select the verses you need for an occasion, ending the hymn with verse 5.

Because of its length, this isn't the easiest song for younger children to memorize, but it is a wonderful learning tool for older children. Display the text in the church school classroom or chapel so children can learn about each of the characters in the verses. Discuss the contrast of the ancient stories and the language of this contemporary hymn written for the Iona community of Scotland in 1989.

𝄞 This lilting Celtic tune has a common form of many folk tunes — AABA. The high E♭ in the second line may come as a surprise at first, but it gives an authentic flavor to the tune, and singers will come to relish it.

Occasionally changing how hymns and songs are sung by the gathered community — who sings and who listens — is an encouragement for strong congregational singing. Listening while others sing part of a text allows a closer focus on the words and gives a greater sense of the whole, especially if the structure of the hymn gives clues about how to assign parts. You may vary the singing body for this hymn in the following ways:

- Because the verses have a two-part structure, the first and second halves could be sung by two different groups.

- If singing all verses, consider assigning each verse to a different TIMBRE of voice — soprano, alto, tenor, bass.

- Assign the phrases about men (first two lines) to men's voices and the phrases about women (second two lines) to women's voices or vice versa. All should join in singing the last four phrases.

Specific lectionary references

Verse 1   *Abraham:* Second Sunday in Lent, Year A
          Sarah: Proper 11, Year C

Verse 2   *Moses:* Easter Vigil
          Moses and Miriam: Easter Day, Year A (alt. Old Testament reading)

Verse 3   *Joseph:* Fourth Sunday of Advent, Year A
          Mary: Fourth Sunday of Advent, Year B

Verse 4   *Zacchaeus:* Proper 26, Year C
          Martha: Proper 11, Year C
          Mary and Martha of Bethany: July 29

? *Which verse do you like best? Why? Can you write a verse or poem about your favorite person or persons in the Bible?*

God it was

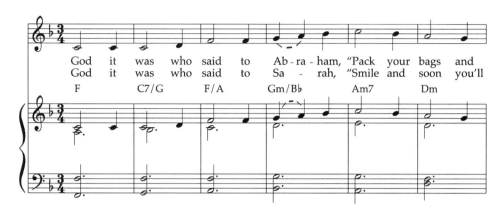

God it was who said to Ab-ra-ham, "Pack your bags and
God it was who said to Sa - rah, "Smile and soon you'll

F   C7/G   F/A   Gm/Bb   Am7   Dm

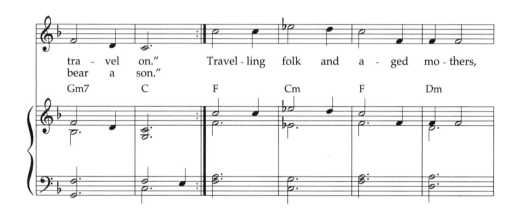

tra - vel on."   Travel - ling folk and a - ged mo - thers,
bear   a   son."

Gm7   C   F   Cm   F   Dm

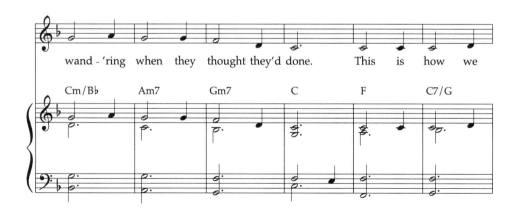

wand - 'ring when they thought they'd done.   This   is   how   we

Cm/Bb   Am7   Gm7   C   F   C7/G

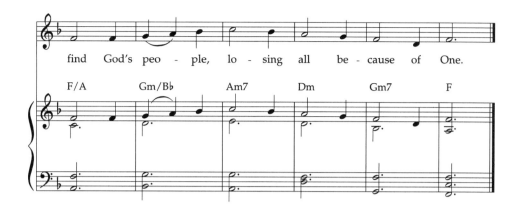

find   God's   peo - ple,   lo - sing   all   be - cause   of   One.

F/A   Gm/Bb   Am7   Dm   Gm7   F

Choose verse according to lectionary, ending with stanza five.

2 God it was who said to Moses,
   "Save my people, part the sea."
   God it was who said to Miriam,
   "Sing and dance to show you're free."
   Shepherd-saints and tambourinists
   doing what God knew they could—
   this is how we find God's people,
   liberating what they should.

3 God it was who said to Joseph,
   "Down your tools and take your wife."
   God it was who said to Mary,
   "In your womb, I'll start my life!"
   Carpenter and country maiden
   leaving town and trade and skills—
   this is how we find God's people,
   moved by what their Maker wills.

4 Christ it was who said, "Zacchaeus,
   I would like to eat with you."
   Christ it was who said to Martha,
   "Listening's what you need to do."
   Civil servants and housekeepers,
   changing places at a cost—
   this is how Christ summons people,
   calling both the loved and lost.

5 In this crowd which spans the ages,
   with these saints whom we revere,
   God wants us to share their purpose
   starting now and starting here.
   So we celebrate our calling,
   so we raise both heart and voice,
   as we pray that through our living
   more may find they are God's choice.

Words: John L. Bell (b. 1949) and Graham Maule.
Music: Traditional Scots Gaelic, arr. John L. Bell (b. 1949) and Graham Maule.

B, C, C*, D

Organ, piano

Liturgy of the Word; offertory

Lent; Easter Day; Easter season; New Year's Eve; Vocation in Daily Work

Several songs in this collection are adapted from children's choir anthems by Natalie Sleeth, who had a gift for writing both words and flowing, colorful melodies that appeal to children.

In school, children learn about flowers growing from bulbs, about butterflies emerging from cocoons, and about other life cycles referred to in this text. In the second verse the author describes more abstract ideas and ultimately leads the singer to understand the metaphorical nature of these images that reveal to us an understanding of life, death, and resurrection. There are not always simple answers. Some things "God alone can see." We need both understanding and faith.

The tune of this hymn grows out of the musical idea in the first phrase. This kind of development is a composer's way of subtly illustrating the examples from nature described in the text. Imagine the first musical phrase as a shape — a skip up, followed by scale steps up and down (1-2-3-2-1). Each new phrase in the first half of the hymn uses the same shape, changing only the width of the skip (phrase one, a fourth; phrase two, a fifth; phrase three, a third). The last half of the melody builds on the foundation of the first, leading to a satisfying musical flourish to the highest pitch in the last phrase " . . . unrevealed until its season. . . . "

? *Have you ever experienced something which seemed really bad at the time, but out of which came good?*

In the bulb there is a flower

1 In the bulb there is a flow - er; in the seed, an ap - ple
2 There's a song in ev - 'ry si - lence, seek-ing word and mel - o -
3 In our end is our be - gin - ning; in our time, in - fin - i -

F   Gm7

win - ter there's a spring that waits to be,
fu - ture; what it holds, a mys - ter - y, un - re -
rec - tion; at the last, a vic - to - ry,

F   Gm   A7   Dm

tree; in co - coons, a hid - den prom - ise: but - ter -
dy; there's a dawn in ev - 'ry dark - ness, bring-ing
ty; in our doubt there is be - liev - ing; in our

C7

vealed un - til its sea - son, some-thing God a - lone can see.

Bb   F   Dm   Gm7   C7   F

flies will soon be free! In the cold and snow of
hope to you and me. From the past will come the
life, e - ter - ni - ty; in our death, a res - ur -

F   Bb

All

♪ A CAPPELLA, piano

✠ Prayer response; Liturgy of the Word

📖 Lent; Good Friday; anytime

🔑 The moving texts of Negro spirituals, created and sung by African slaves, often reveal deep reliance on faith in Jesus throughout lives marked by pain, suffering, and hardship. Slaves were not permitted to read or write, making it necessary for them to commit their music to memory. A song leader would improvise verses or repeat well-known phrases used in many different songs, sometimes adding a refrain. In this spiritual the leader may have sung the opening phrase with others echoing "walk with me" and then singing the repeated "refrain" at the end of each verse.

The Christian life is often described as a journey. Being a Christian does not shield us from bad things; however, it does mean that we believe Jesus walks with us because he lived a human life and died a human death. In good times and bad, Jesus is there to comfort and assure us.

🎼 Choose a small group to sing "walk with me" set off by parentheses. To teach the SYNCOPATION in the last two lines insert a clap on the tied downbeat. Practice the syncopation in the third line by adding a clap to feel the downbeat before the strong syncopated word following:

When you have learned this rhythm correctly, point out that the words "journey," "Jesus," and "Walk with me" need a strong emphasis.

Help children create more new verses for this song! Ask, "Where in your life would you like Jesus to walk with you?" and work at forming your thoughts into four syllables — this is the craft of a hymn writer. The verse can be specific ("In my math test, Lord walk with me") or more general ("When I'm lonely"). Then all repeat "all along my pilgrim journey, Lord, I want Jesus to walk with me." The person with a new verse may become the song leader.

? *Have you ever asked Jesus to walk with you when you were facing something difficult? Have you ever had the conviction that Jesus is walking with you?*

1 I want Je - sus____ to walk with me (walk with me); I want
2 In my tri - als,____ Lord, walk with me (walk with me); In my
3 In my sor - rows,____ Lord, walk with me (walk with me); In my

Je - sus____ to walk with me (walk with me); All a -
tri - als,____ Lord, walk with me (walk with me); When the
sor - rows,____ Lord, walk with me (walk with me); When my

long my____ pil - grim jour - ney,____ Lord, I want
shades of____ life____ are fall - ing,____ Lord, I want
heart with - in____ is ach - ing,____ Lord, I want

Je - sus____ to walk with me (walk with me).
Je - sus____ to walk with me (walk with me).
Je - sus____ to walk with me (walk with me).

👪 B, C, D

♫ Organ, piano

✠ Liturgy of the Word; offertory; communion

📖 Easter season, especially Year A; Fourth Sunday of Lent, Year A; Proper 12, Year C; St. Philip and St. James (see below)

⛓ The Sunday reading of the verses of scripture related to this song occurs during the Easter season in Year A (Sundays 4, 5, and 6). Most of the images are from the "I am" statements by Jesus in the Gospel of John — I am the way, the truth, and the life; I am the vine, you are the branches; I am the light of the world; I am the good shepherd; I am the bread of life. These memorable phrases help us know something about who Jesus is.

♪ The relevant verse could be repeated as a Gospel acclamation. The form of the text in verses 2–5 is generally simple and matches the music. These should be taught first. Verse 1 does not have the repeated phrases and may be taught once the melody and form are learned.

Words		*Music*
A	Jesus said, I am the . . .	A
BB	Mark my footsteps — repeated	BB (measures 3 and 4)
CC	Enter in — repeated	CC (measures 5 and 6)
A	Jesus said, I am the . . .	A2 (measures 7 and 8)
B2	follow, follow, joyfully	B2 (measures 9 and 10)

Scripture References

Verse 1	Luke 11:9, Matthew 7:7
Verses 2, 3	John 14:6
Verse 4	John 15:5
Verse 5	John 8:12

❓ *Which name of Jesus do you like best? Why?*

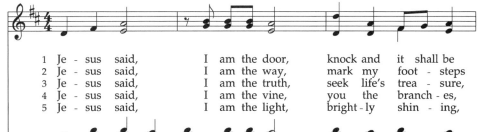

1 Je - sus said,   I am the door,   knock and it shall be
2 Je - sus said,   I am the way,   mark my foot - steps
3 Je - sus said,   I am the truth,   seek life's trea - sure,
4 Je - sus said,   I am the vine,   you the branch - es,
5 Je - sus said,   I am the light,   bright - ly shin - ing,

op - ened un - to you. En - ter in, joy - ful - ly. Je - sus said,
mark my foot - steps, fol - low me, fol - low me. Je - sus said,
seek life's trea - sure, fol - low me, fol - low me. Je - sus said,
you the branch - es, part of me, part of me. Je - sus said,
bright - ly shin - ing, come to me, come to me. Je - sus said,

I am the door,   en - ter, en - ter, joy - ful - ly.
I am the way,   fol - low, fol - low, joy - ful - ly.
I am the truth,   fol - low, fol - low, joy - ful - ly.
I am the vine,   you the branch - es, part of me.
I am the light,   shin - ing, shin - ing, come to me.

All, B, B*

Guitar, piano, A CAPPELLA

Children's chapel; church school

Lent; Baptism

This disarmingly straightforward children's song answers the question posed by the title simply and succinctly. The "I can..." phrases are understandable by pre-readers and can be taken literally, as they offer an excellent formational understanding. Remind older children of the parable of the Good Samaritan and Jesus' answer to the question "But who is my neighbor?"

This would make an excellent substitution for the Creed in church school or chapel. Pre-readers can learn the chorus, adding the verses as they get older. It would also be an excellent song for children to sing at a child's baptism or when baptismal vows are renewed.

?   *What's your favorite part of being a Christian?*

89 What does it mean to follow Jesus?

Palm Sunday

Palm Sunday is an unusual feast because there are two distinct parts. We begin by rejoicing and proclaiming Jesus a king and move to the tragic events of betrayal and the trial with Jesus' journey toward crucifixion. Here are two suggestions for active participation that engage children in this liturgy:

Procession (especially outside the church through the neighborhood)

- We Episcopalians are a timid lot when it comes to making a noise about our faith in public, and we need a little help. Do not be tempted to have children "represent" adults for the procession of palms. If adults are embarrassed to stand up and profess their faith in public, it is not right to send the children in our place.
- All attention must be on the purpose of this procession — to enact the joyful and spontaneous acknowledgment of Jesus as King that led to the events of Good Friday. A song is needed that encourages and expresses these feelings and doesn't become dull with repetition. Because people are unaccustomed to the distraction of singing while walking over unfamiliar ground or sidewalks, the song must be instantly memorable. A repeated refrain with a few words is best suited for this. Traditional hymns may be reserved for use once everyone has stopped moving.
- Whenever one group of singers wanders from another, their pitch and rhythm begins to wander too; therefore, a procession may be more successful when accompanied by melody instruments and percussion, with strong singers spread throughout the procession.
- Music leaders are needed at the beginning and end of the procession, so that as the people enter the church building they can pull the music together if the TEMPO has changed in transit!

The Passion Gospel

The reading of the Passion Gospel increases the length of the service. Some well-meaning parishes include the children in the procession and then send them off to make palm crosses. This eliminates a wonderful opportunity. This liturgy, with its appeal to the senses, its drama, and its importance for understanding Holy Week must be accessible to children, especially those who may not come to church again until Easter Sunday. Choose a Bible translation or PARAPHRASE that is immediately understandable; there is also a shorter version of the Passion Gospel in "Eucharistic Readings." Allow the children to come up close to the readers, inviting them to be part of the action even if they can't participate in the reading. The reading may be divided into shorter sections with a repeated short sung response, for example, a setting of Kyrie eleison (Lord, have mercy), omitting the Christe eleison verse, such as #13 or #14. If you use #15 sing the words "kyrie eleison" three times.

B, C, C*, D

Guitar, cymbals, bells; for procession use trumpets, hand drum, tambourine; ORFF INSTRUMENTS

Liturgy of the Palms; Liturgy of the Word

Palm Sunday; Fourth Sunday of Advent, Year A

Note that the first two verses are written from the historical view of the event itself, while the second two verses reflect our understanding of the saving event of Jesus' death and resurrection. These verses remind us that we are not just reenacting a historical event, but overlaying our post-resurrection understanding and discovering new meaning each time we participate in Palm Sunday.

The refrain and the tune use the same melody, but the refrain is in E minor, and the verse is in its relative, G major. This gives a good opportunity for teaching major and minor scales and their differing patterns of whole steps and half steps. Although the general assumption persists that minor keys indicate a somber mood and major keys a more upbeat one, some cultures, as we see in this melody, use minor scales for lively songs to great effect.

This song would make an excellent processional as long as the verses are sung by a small group and memorized. The Israeli folk tune is wonderfully infectious and a natural choice for outdoor singing. If you are using this song for procession, be sure to teach it well in advance, and remind people that they are re-creating Christ's entry into Jerusalem and being witnesses of the faith to the neighborhood — which takes courage! The accompanying instruments could be varied depending on how this song is used. Outdoor processions allow more dramatic sounds, such as brass and drums and cymbals, while singing indoors may work better with the more subtle sounds of the guitar or ORFF INSTRUMENTS.

? *What do you think it would have been like to see Jesus coming into Jerusalem?*

The King of glory comes

Refrain

Em ... B7 Em

The King of glo-ry comes, the na-tion re-joic-es.

*

B7 Em

O-pen the gates be-fore him, lift up your voic-es.

G ... C D7 G

1 Who is the King of glo-ry? What shall we call him?
2 In all of Gal-i-lee, in cit-y or vil-lage,
3 He gave his life for us, the pledge of sal-va-tion;
4 He con-quered sin and death; he tru-ly has ris-en.

Em ... D7 G *Repeat refrain*

He is Im-man-u-el, the prom-ised of a-ges.
he goes a-mong his peo-ple, cur-ing their ill-ness.
he took up-on him-self the sin of the na-tions.
And he will share with us his heav-en-ly king-dom.

* Sing small notes as a descant on the final refrain.

Orff instruments for refrain

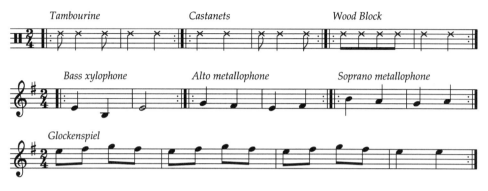

Tambourine — *Castanets* — *Wood Block*

Bass xylophone — *Alto metallophone* — *Soprano metallophone*

Glockenspiel

'Sanna

'San-na,* san-na-ni-na, san-na, san-na, san-na,____

san - na, san - na, san - na, san-na-ni-na,

All

♫ A CAPPELLA, percussion

✠ Liturgy of the Palms; Gospel acclamation on Sundays other than Palm Sunday

📖 Palm Sunday

☞ The text of this song is simply a shortened form of "Hosanna." Imagine that it is written "Zanna."

𝄞 Observation of the rests is essential for the rhythm of this exuberant song. It is effective both in unison and in harmony, so both could be alternated on the repeats. The harmonies are easy to learn with a little practice. Use a percussive accompaniment of hand clapping on the beat with a tambourine playing a pop rhythm of

Strike the tambourine against the palm of the hand or against the side of the thigh on the first sixteenth playing a tight back-and-forth motion on the remaining three sixteenths for each beat. A good teenage drummer with a kit will add a lot to this song, especially by adding fills at all the repeats.

? *What do you like or dislike about singing a song with only one word?*

san - na, san - na san - na.____ San -____

* This is a shortened form of the word 'hosanna.'

Holy Week

Some churches feel uneasy about including children in the Holy Week services. In *The Rite Light,* Michael Merriman says, "During this week we will rediscover what God has done for us, rediscover the meaning of our baptism, rediscover the meaning of our sharing in the Eucharist." In other words, Holy Week is a summation of all that it means to be Christian, and including children in this is essential. Before each section of music for the services of Holy Week are some suggestions for adapting the liturgies to be child-friendly.

Maundy Thursday

Maundy Thursday marks the beginning of the Triduum (pronounced "trih-doo-oom"), or Three Days leading to Easter. At the close of Maundy Thursday the liturgy does not end but continues on Good Friday and Easter. The joy of Maundy Thursday is that it is the day when Jesus instituted the Sacrament of the Holy Eucharist, but it is overshadowed by the imminent events of Good Friday. Learning events for children may include:

* holding a parish family event that includes elements of the Passover meal with an explanation
* making bread for the communion service
* making an Easter garden with a tomb

The optional foot-washing ritual on Maundy Thursday illustrates in a dramatic way the kind of life of love and servanthood to which Jesus calls us. Encourage children to participate. "Maundy" comes from the word *mandatum,* referring to the "commandment" that Jesus gave his disciples: "A new commandment I give to you, that you should love one another as I have loved you."

Good Friday

Joe Russell, in his excellent *New Prayer Book Guide to Christian Education* (Cowley Publications, 1996) points out that sacrifice is a key concept of Holy Week. To understand this, children need to know about the Jewish temple practice of sacrificing a lamb at Passover. The people of Israel, who were in slavery in Egypt, were given instructions to do this and to mark their doors with the blood, so that the angel of death would "pass over" them (see Exod. 12:1–14a). Pharaoh then allowed Moses to lead them out of slavery to the Promised Land.

Jesus is like this sacrificed lamb. He willingly offered himself for sacrifice because he loved the world and chose to die to save the whole world from sin. Even on the cross, Jesus forgave all those who had hurt him. This is why it is called "Good Friday." Good Friday is the time in the church year to reflect on Jesus' suffering and death for us — the holy sacrifice of the Lamb of God. However, Good Friday is always within the context of the Triduum, the three days from Maundy Thursday to Easter. Good Friday is the sad and difficult part of a story that ends with the greatest gift anyone can give another — life.

Stations of the Cross

Liturgy and activities on Good Friday might include the Stations of the Cross. This devotion grew out of a tradition according to which Christians would visit Jerusalem and walk to each of the places, or stations, on Christ's last journey to Golgotha, praying and reflecting on each of the events. Today some churches have pictures for each of the "Stations" on their walls. One of the most important ways in which children can participate is to draw their own pictures of these stations during Lent to become familiar with the story. Children's art is often a powerful aid to all for thinking about Christ's suffering. At each station, summarize the story and ask children to reflect on what they can learn from this in their own lives. Then sing a song as you move to the next station. "The Way of the Cross" (Stations) may be found in *The Book of Occasional Services 2003* from Church Publishing Inc., www.churchpublishing.org.

Music suggestions for Stations of the Cross, and other Good Friday services:

From *Lift Every Voice and Sing*
  Were you there when they crucified my Lord? #37
  He never said a mumblin' word #33
  Oh how he loves you and me #35

From *Wonder, Love, and Praise*
  Bless the Lord my soul #825
  Oh, Lord, hear my prayer #827

From The Hymnal 1982
  Were you there when they crucified my Lord? #172
  What wondrous love is this #439 (for older children)

From this collection
  Settings of "O Lamb of God" #43–45
  Settings of the Kyrie or Trisagion #12–17
  I want Jesus to walk with me #87
  What does it mean to follow Jesus? #89 (a good closing song)

When celebrating the traditional Good Friday Office and the Veneration of the Cross children could help carry a full-sized cross in procession.

If the parish holds a three-hour service on Good Friday, consider offering an ongoing menu of activities so that children can move back and forth from the service to a room of activities. Some activity ideas are:

- Color pictures of different crosses (available on C.E. Visminas Clip Art CD-ROM, Morehouse Publishing, www.morehousepublishing.com).

- Make a life-sized model of a tomb with chicken wire and paper and have quiet prayers inside.

- Make a small Easter Garden, which includes three empty crosses, a tomb with a stone that is rolled away on Easter Sunday, live mosses, and miniature flowers. It can be any size from a model on a baking tray to life-sized (search "Easter Garden" on the Web).

- Learn and sing songs from the list above.

C, D

Guitar, piano, A CAPPELLA

Communion; foot-washing; retreats

Maundy Thursday

The text of this song is a quote from John 13:34–35, a text considered to be a summary of Jesus' teaching.

This song may be performed in a number of ways, each with a very different feel. For retreats and youth meetings a guitar accompaniment would set a more informal tone. For church a choir could sing this A CAPPELLA or the congregation could sing accompanied by piano.

? *What have we learned from Jesus about loving that we can pass on to one another?*

A new commandment

Words: John 13:34–35.
Music: Anonymous, arr. N. Warren © Oxford University Press, 198 Madison Ave.,
New York, NY 10016-4314 [www.oup.org]. All rights reserved. Used by permission.

♔ C, C*, D

♪ Guitar, piano or keyboard, drum kit, organ

✠ At the footwashing; during communion

📖 Maundy Thursday; Easter; Proper 7, Year C

While it is ideal for a Latino/Anglo congregation, this bilingual text is a necessity for the parish that seeks to welcome the Spanish speaking newcomers in their neighborhoods. Identify those who are native speakers in your congregation and invite them to teach the pronunciation of this text. Some will feel called to this ministry, some won't. If needed, coach them on how to teach non-speakers so that their ministry will succeed. Don't assume that all Spanish speakers will pronounce the words the same because there are significant differences depending on one's country of origin.

If you perform this song with rock instruments, electric rhythm and bass guitars, a keyboard, and a drum kit, the strong rhythmic accompaniment will keep this song moving. If you use more traditional accompaniment, increase the TEMPO so that the song does not drag.

Pronunciation

Pan de Vi - da, cuer - po del Se - ñor,
Pahn deh Vee - dah, kwehr – poh del Seh - nyor,

po - der es ser - vir, por - que Dios es a - mor.
poh - dehr ehs sehr - veer pohr - keh Dyohs ehs ah - mohr

Us - te - des me lla - man "Se - ñor,"
Oos – teh - dehs meh yah - mahn "Seh - nyor."

me‿in - cli - no‿a la - var - les los pies:
mehEEN – klee - nohAH lah - vahr - lehs lohs peeEHS:

Ha - gan lo mis - mo, hu - mil - des,
Hah - gahn loh mees - moh, oo - meel - dehs,

sir - vién - do - se u - nos a o - tros.
seehr – veeEHN - doh - seh oo - nohs ah oh – trohs.

? *Why does God want to live in us if we are "fragile and wounded and weak," that is, not perfect?*

Pan de Vida

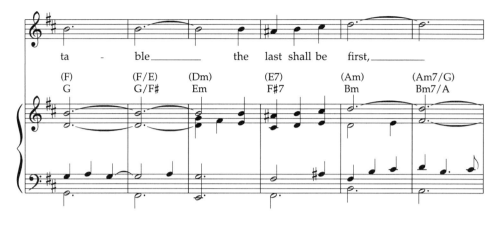

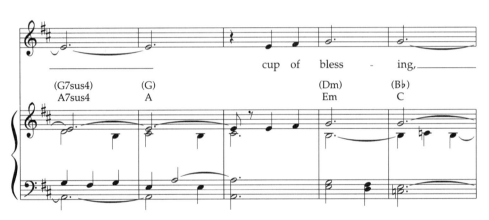

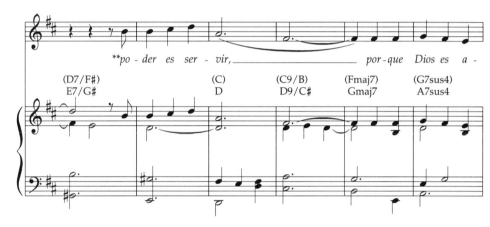

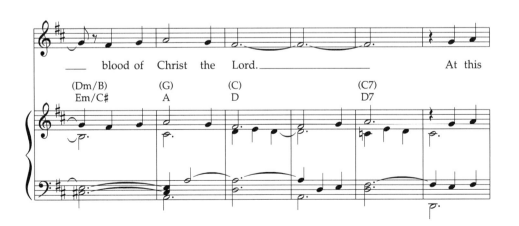

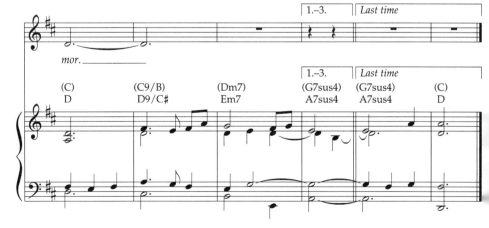

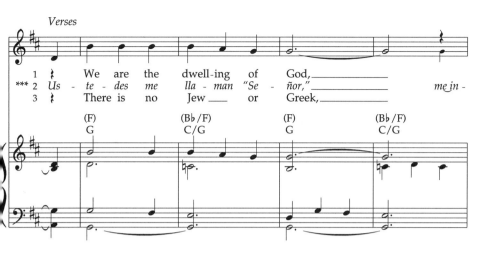

1. We are the dwell-ing of God,_____ me in-
*** 2. *Us - te - des me lla - man "Se - ñor,"_____ me_in-*
3. There is no Jew___ or Greek,_____

(F)   (Bb/F)   (F)   (Bb/F)
G   C/G   G   C/G

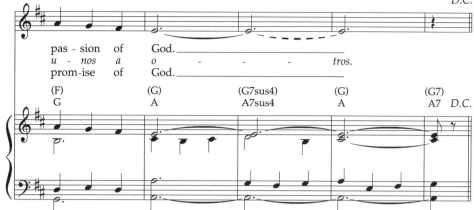

pas - sion of God._____
u - nos a o - - - tros.
prom-ise of God._____

(F)   (G)   (G7sus4)   (G)   (G7)
G   A   A7sus4   A   A7   D.C.

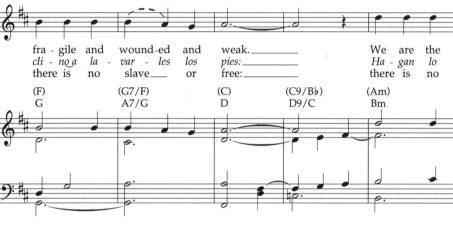

fra - gile and wound-ed and weak._____ We are the
cli - no_a la - var - les los pies:_____ Ha - gan lo
there is no slave___ or free:_____ there is no

(F)   (G7/F)   (C)   (C9/Bb)   (Am)
G   A7/G   D   D9/C   Bm

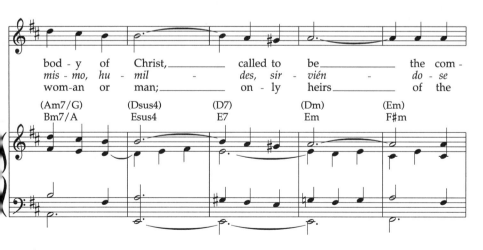

bod - y of Christ,_____ called to be_____ the com-
mis - mo, hu - mil - des, sir - vién - do - se
wom-an or man;_____ on - ly heirs_____ of the

(Am7/G)   (Dsus4)   (D7)   (Dm)   (Em)
Bm7/A   Esus4   E7   Em   F#m

* *Bread of Life, body of the Lord,*
** *power is for service because God is love.*
*** *You are the Lord, and I bow to wash your feet: you must do the same, humbly serving each other.*

Words and Music: *John 13:1–15, Galatians 3:28–29*, Bob Hurd (b. 1950) and Pia Moriarty © 1988 OCP Publications, 5336 NE Hassalo, Portland OR 92713 [www.ocp.org]. All rights reserved. Used by permission. *You must contact OCP Publications to reproduce this selection.*

Brother, sister, let me serve you

C, D

♪ Organk, piano, guitar

✠ During communion; general

📖 Lent; Maundy Thursday; Seventh Sunday after Epiphany, Year A; Proper 20, Year B

⚟ The first verse, which sums up the whole text of this hymn and is repeated at the end, can be easily learned by younger children. The intimate, moving text could also be beautifully illustrated by young artists.

𝄞 Because of the angularity of the melody, a cantor would be helpful for teaching this hymn. See the section "Using hand gestures to indicate pitch" in chapter 2, "Music Leadership Skills" (page 13). Singing some verses A CAPPELLA in harmony, particularly verses 3 and 5, is quite effective.

? *How are we being "as Christ" when we serve our brothers and sisters?*

Easter

Easter Vigil

Joe Russell, priest and educator, says that the Easter Vigil is the most important service of the Christian year. Even so, this service is only beginning to become commonplace in the Episcopal Church. The Great Vigil of Easter has significant potential for a multigenerational service. There are many wonderful elements — darkness and fire, story and history, water and the rich fragrance of flowers, and the two great sacraments given by Christ to the Church: Holy Baptism and Holy Eucharist. Originally, the catechumens, those to be received into the church on Easter, stayed up throughout the night to prepare for their baptism. (This model could be used with youth and adult candidates for baptism). The Vigil then became an Easter Day sunrise service (still common in many places). It may be held after sunset on Saturday evening.

As "the most important service of the Christian year" the Vigil should make allowances for children to be able to attend. Just as holiday visits to grandparents or attendance at special events allow a relaxing of daily schedules, the Vigil is a special event that offers the community a chance to gather for a real family celebration. Children should be allowed to leave the service periodically (or go to the back of the church) to participate in quiet, planned activities. (See the Good Friday introduction for ideas.) In some churches children wear their pajamas to the service and fall asleep when they become tired! As children grow older, they will look forward to attending the Vigil just as they look forward to attending the midnight service on Christmas Eve.

As the prayer book instructs, there are four parts to this service. It might be a helpful guide to highlight these headings in the bulletin:

The Service of Light

The Service of Lessons

Christian Initiation or the Renewal of Baptismal Vows

The Holy Eucharist

There are several ways that the Vigil may be adapted to include children:

The Service of Light

The Exsultet, sung in semi-darkness lit only by candles, is a profound connection to our liturgical history and our ancestors. Invite the children to move where they can see the action at all times.

The Service of Lessons

The RUBRIC says that "at least two" of the lessons should be read. Alternatively, read several or even all of the lessons, but in briefer, child-friendly "storytelling" PARAPHRASES. Those available in *Godly Play* would be ideal, or storybooks with pictures could be used. Intersperse lively songs, or verses of songs that all can sing. Several possibilities are included in this collection and may be found in the Liturgical Index. The addition of movement — dancing or gestures — is also effective. Prayers could be shortened to a simple statement and response. Consider placing readers in different positions in the church for the various readings.

Christian Initiation or the Renewal of Baptismal Vows

Pre-readers can join in the renewal of vows if they are told that the response to the "will you" questions is "I will with God's help." At the baptism a child may pour the water into the font or lead the prayers. A group of children could sing a song, such as "You have put on Christ" (#122) to welcome those baptized.

To move from baptism to Eucharist, sing a lively song of praise to help everyone "get their wiggles out" and to facilitate the movement of people from around the font to their seats. Ask baptismal families to show their babies off to all in the church. People will then be ready to settle into the most familiar part of this service, the Eucharist.

The Holy Eucharist

In place of the psalm a lively Alleluia (see #18–22) may follow the Epistle and lead immediately to the Gospel. Keep the sermon brief and child-centered. The Prayers of the People may be simplified.

Easter Day

As with the celebration of Christmas, churches often feel strongly about keeping their Easter service unchanged. An important question a church must ask itself is "How can we *both* continue to welcome our regularly attending children *and* make visitors comfortable?" Instead of using old and familiar material as the only means of welcoming newcomers, pay attention instead to how the service is presented. Are bulletins as clear as they can be, containing all the music and readings? Is there a cantor to lead the singing to help newcomers feel comfortable even if they don't know the music? Is the priest doing all he or she can to guide people through the liturgy? Also remember that Easter is an entire season of seven Sundays and its important message should be celebrated with joyous music throughout the season.

C, D

Organ, piano

General

Baptism; Easter Vigil; Trinity Sunday, Year A (v. 1); First Sunday after Epiphany (v. 3); First Sunday in Lent, Year B (v. 3); Third Sunday in Lent, Year A (v. 4)

Water is a central symbol for Christians at any time, especially at the Great Vigil of Easter and at baptism. Just as in the Thanksgiving over the Water in the liturgy for Holy Baptism, this hymn sums up the major stories about water, ending with an oblique reference to the story of the woman of Samaria whom Jesus told about the living water.

This song is complicated for younger children to learn, but each verse could be read to them and the related stories discussed. This hymn could be sung, perhaps by a children's choir, verse by verse throughout the Easter Vigil. An alternate tune for this text is *Ton-y-Botel* (The Hymnal 1982 #527). Once through the tune will require two verses of the text.

? *What's your favorite water story in the Bible?*

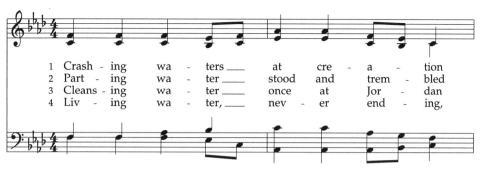

1 Crash - ing wa - ters___ at cre - a - tion
2 Part - ing wa - ter___ stood and trem - bled
3 Cleans - ing wa - ter___ once at Jor - dan
4 Liv - ing wa - ter,___ nev - er end - ing,

or - dered by the Spi - rit's breath, first to wit - ness
as the cap - tives passed on through, wash - ing off___ the
closed a - round the One fore - told, o - pened to___ re -
quench the thirst and flood the soul. Well - spring, Source of

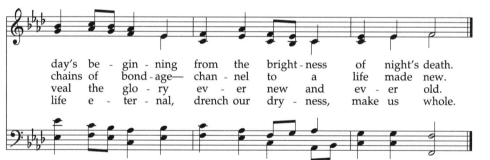

day's be - gin - ning from the bright - ness of night's death.
chains of bond - age— chan - nel to a life made new.
veal the glo - ry ev - er new and ev - er old.
life e - ter - nal, drench our dry - ness, make us whole.

Words: Sylvia G. Dunstan (1955–1993) © GIA Publications, Inc., 7404 S. Mason Ave.,
Chicago, IL 60638 [www.giamusic.com]. All rights reserved. Used by permission.
Music: *Restoration*, melody from *The Southern Harmony*, 1835.
You must contact GIA Publications, Inc. to reproduce these words.

We are on our way

✚ C, D

♪ Organ, piano

✠ General; Liturgy of the Word

📖 Easter Vigil; Second Sunday in Lent, Year A (v. 1); Second Sunday in Lent, Year C (v. 2); Proper 14, Year C (v. 2); Proper 11, Year C (v. 3)

The verses of this song are designed to alternate with the readings printed at the end. Separate verses may be used to coordinate with the readings on Sundays listed above, spread throughout one liturgy, or sung all together.

Since this song as a whole is too complex for the younger children, there are two ways of incorporating them. The youngest children could play a combination of finger cymbals, fixed cymbal, and wind chimes on the first beat of the measure. Older children can play a

pattern throughout, starting on the first beat of the measure on CLAVES, temple blocks, or woodblock.

All ages could learn the first verse only to sing as a refrain with a cantor or choir singing the other verses. After the first reading, the cantor or choir sings the first verse, which is then repeated by all. After the second reading, the cantor or choir sings the second verse, followed by all singing the refrain (first verse). Do the same for verse 3.

? *"We are on our way to the promised land." Is this a message for Abraham, or for us too?*

We are on our way

1 We are on our way to the prom - ised land.
2 A - bra - ham went for a walk with God, who was his friend.
3 I nev - er thought it pos - si - ble, not in a thou-sand years.

We are on our way to the prom - ised land.
God said, "Look up at all the stars— you can - not see their end.
But God per - formed a mir - a - cle and took a - way my fears.

Our God will lead and guide___ us, he will
And can you count the grains of sand on the
He took a - way my bit - ter - ness and

walk a - long be - side___ us, our God will lead and
shore or in a des - ert land? So ma - ny shall your
now I laugh and sing for joy, so dance with me and

guide___ us as we go to the prom - ised land.
chil - dren be— so ma - ny you can - not count."
sing with me; sing a new song of praise and joy.

Reader:
The Lord said to Abraham,
"Leave your country, your people,
and your father's household.
Go to the land I will show you.
I will make you into a great nation,
and I will bless you." *Sing stanza 1*

The Lord took Abraham outside and said,
"Look up at the heavens and count the stars—
if indeed you can count them."
Then he said to him,
"So shall your children be." *Sing stanza 2*

The Lord said to Abraham,
"Your wife Sarah will bear you a son,
and you will call him Isaac.
I will establish my covenant with him
as an everlasting covenant."
The Lord did for Sarah what he had promised.
Sarah became pregnant
and bore a son to Abraham in his old age,
at the very time God had promised him. *Sing stanza 3*

Words: based on Genesis 12:1–2, 15:5, 17:19, 21:1–2, adapted Helen Walter.
Music: Emily R. Brink. Words and Music © 1993 CRC Publications, 2850 Kalamazoo Ave. SE, Grand Rapids, MI 49560 [www.crcpublications.org]. All rights reserved. Used by permission.

B, C, D

Piano, organ, guitar

General

Easter Vigil

This song is about covenant, or the promise made between us and God. It begins with the accounts of God reaching out to humanity in the stories of Noah and of Abraham and Sarah, and in Jesus' birth. In the final verse the singer accepts God's covenant, making promises to God through baptism.

This is a perfect song to sing verse by verse in the Easter Vigil service. Younger children or the whole congregation could sing only the last sentence as a refrain. Be sure to point out that the text changes in the last verse.

? *This song is all about covenant, a word which means promise. What promise has God made to us? What promises can we make to God?*

It rained on the earth forty days

B, C, D

♫ A CAPPELLA, guitar

✠ Liturgy of the Word; moving from one place to another

📖 Easter Day, Evening Service; Easter Vigil

Psalm 136 is constructed as a litany: the leader offers varying petitions or statements to which the congregation responds with a fixed refrain. The twenty-six verses of Psalm 136 recount the salvation history of God's action on our behalf, alternating with the congregational refrain "... for [God's] steadfast love endures forever." Look at this psalm with children and discuss how these stories would have been memorized by our ancestors and handed down from generation to generation. Here is our history in one psalm!

🎵 This song could be sung by cantor or choir alternating with the congregation singing the refrains as marked. Or a cantor could alternate with the choir, singing the refrain in harmony.

? *Can you write other verses for this song about the things that God has done for us, either as found in scripture, or more recently?*

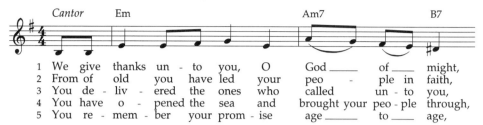

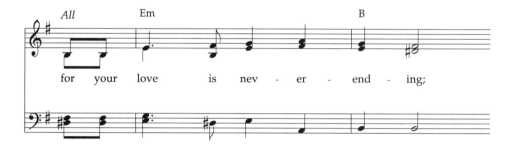

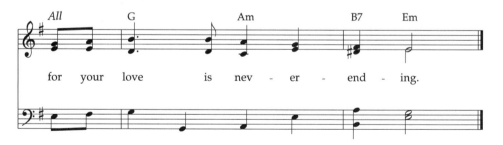

B, C, C*, D

♪ Organic, piano, flute/recorder, finger cymbals, hand drum

✠ Liturgy of the Word; congregational prelude

📖 Easter Day

☗ Chosen to add to the available Easter hymns, this song is one of only a few in this collection that tells a single story. It also highlights the role played by women who surrounded Jesus during his death and resurrection. Both the first verse and folk melody of this hymn were probably created in the fifteenth century, although they didn't appear in print until much later. This is easily the oldest text and tune in this collection. The subsequent verses and accompaniment are newly written.

🎵 The composer has written the text emphases into the rhythm and articulation of the refrain. The SLURRED notes stress the corresponding syllable, as do the half notes at the end of the phrase. To enhance the early music sound, accompany the melody on flute or recorder. Add finger cymbals on the first beat of each measure and a hand drum playing

throughout the verse only.

? *Imagine that you are the first one to see Jesus. What would you tell everyone?*

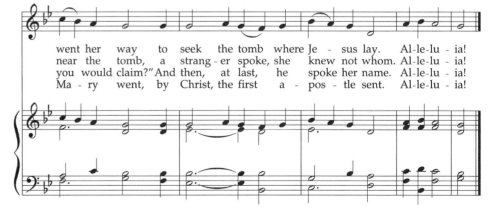

Words: Verse 1 Jean Tisserand (d. 1494); tr. John Mason Neale (1818–1866), alt.
Verses 2–4 Delores Dufner, OSB (b. 1939) © 1994 Delores Dufner (admin. GIA Publications, Inc.,
7404 S. Mason Ave., Chicago, IL 60638 [www.giamusic.com].) All rights reserved. Used by permission.
Music: *O filii et filiae*, melody from *Airs sur les hymnes sacrez, odes et noëls*, 1623; acc. Carl Haywood
(b. 1949) © Carl Haywood. All rights reserved. Used by permission.
You must contact GIA Publications, Inc. to reproduce verses 2–4 of these words.
You must contact Carl Haywood to reproduce this arrangement.

B, C, C*, D

A CAPPELLA, African percussion

Hymn of praise; after communion

Easter Day

Traditional songs in Africa are constructed to be learned by ROTE, and this one is no exception. The presence of verses and a refrain suggest that a soloist or cantor sings the verses with everyone singing the refrain from memory. Although a keyboard accompaniment is provided here, this song is usually sung without it. Traditional percussion accompaniment is expected to give the African flavor. Usually one drum plays a simple downbeat with a second drum adding a more complex rhythm.

Begin with one voice singing the first line. On the second line have another voice join the first in a different octave (such as female, then add male or vice versa). All should sing the refrain in harmony, if possible. One drum should play a

on each measure. A second drum could play

Add an avaga, which is a small iron gong or bell, playing

in each measure against the three beats. The avaga has the sound of a cow-bell struck by a wooden mallet. Shakers round out the ensemble, playing the same two-against-three of the avaga but with a crisp first sound and a shaken second sound.

? *How would you feel if someone you thought was dead turned out to be alive?*

Christ has arisen, alleluia

1 Christ has a - ris - en, al - le - lu - ia.
2 For three long days the grave did its worst
3 The an - gel said to them, "Do not fear.
4 "Go spread the news: he's not in the grave.
5 Christ has a - ris - en to set us free.

Re - joice and praise him, al - le - lu - ia.
un - til its strength by God was dis - persed.
You look for Je - sus who is not here.
He has a - ris - en this world to save.
Al - le - lu - ia, to him prais - es be.

For our re - deem - er burst from the tomb,
He who gives life did death un - der - go,
See for your - selves the tomb is all bare.
Je - sus' re - deem - ing la - bors are done.
Je - sus is liv - ing! Let us all sing;

e - ven from death, dis - pel - ling its gloom.
and in its con - quest his might did show.
On - ly the grave cloths are ly - ing there."
E - ven the bat - tle with sin is won."
he reigns tri - um - phant, heav - en - ly king.

Words: Bernard Kyamanywa (b. 1938), tr. Howard S. Olson (b. 1922) © 1977 Howard S. Olson (admin. Augsburg Fortress, PO Box 1209, Minneapolis, MN 55440-1209 [www.augsburgfortress.org].) All rights reserved. Used by permission.
Music: Traditional Tanzanian.

Refrain

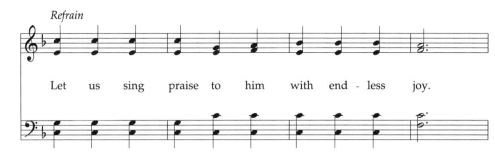

Let us sing praise to him with end - less joy.

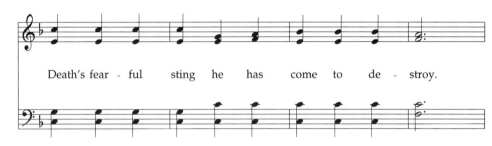

Death's fear - ful sting he has come to de - stroy.

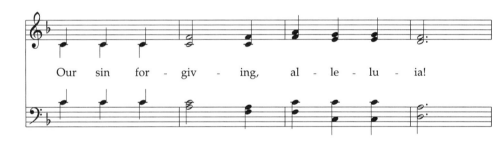

Our sin for - giv - ing, al - le - lu - ia!

Je - sus is liv - ing, al - le - lu - ia!

B, C, D

Organ, guitar, keyboard, drums, clarinet or saxophone

Hymn of praise; offertory; general praise

Easter season

The irresistible sound of this hymn matches the text that urges us to serve and worship God in singing and dancing, in service to those in need, in teaching, and in learning from others. Interesting phrases give new images to encourage us: "Dance, delight and duty," "Teach the way that frees us," and "Seek the children's wisdom."

This hymn is included in the Agape Mass, a setting by David Haas and Marty Haugen. (The more complex version is available from GIA #G3960.) The congregation may sing the refrain and the parts marked "All." An advantage of alternating cantor and congregation in the verses is being able to catch your breath! The TEMPO should be set so that the words are intelligible and easy to sing. This infectiously lively hymn works well with either organ or guitar, keyboard, and drums. Add a wind instrument, such as clarinet or saxophone, on the melody line, and encourage improvisation.

? *Which verse do you like best? Why?*

Sing, O people

Refrain

Sing, O peo - ple, sing our God to - geth - er,

Capo 3: (D) (G/D) (D) (Em7/A)
F Bb/F F Gm7/C

raise your voic - es: sing al - le - lu - ia!

(D) (Em7/A) (D)
F Gm7/C F *Last time*

last time rit.

Verses
Cantor *All*

1 Sing with one an - oth - er: sing the love that gave us breath!
2 Dance the steps of beau - ty: dance the love that gave us breath!
3 Serve all those who suf - fer: serve the love that gave us breath!
4 Teach the way of Je - sus: teach the love that gave us breath!
5 Seek the chil - dren's wis - dom: seek the love that gave us breath!

(D) (G) (D) (Em7/D) (A)
F Bb F Gm7/F C

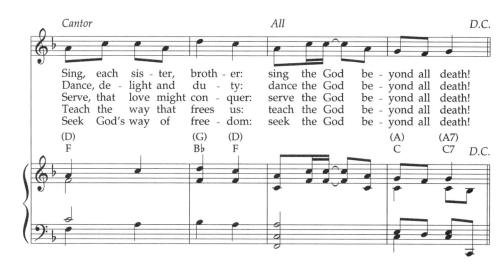

Cantor *All* *D.C.*

Sing, each sis - ter, broth - er: sing the God be - yond all death!
Dance, de - light and du - ty: dance the God be - yond all death!
Serve, that love might con - quer: serve the God be - yond all death!
Teach the way that frees us: teach the God be - yond all death!
Seek God's way of free - dom: seek the God be - yond all death!

(D) (G) (D) (A) (A7)
F Bb F C C7 *D.C.*

The Lord, the Lord, the Lord is my shepherd

102

All, A*, B*

Guitar, A CAPPELLA

Church school and chapel

Fourth Sunday in Lent, Year A; Fourth Sunday of Easter, Years A and B; Proper 23, Year A; Confession of St. Peter

The two songs on the theme of Jesus the Good Shepherd (see also #104) were included in this collection in deference to the *Catechesis of the Good Shepherd* curriculum. The Good Shepherd is a central story for teaching children and deserves good music! The youngest children may sing the refrain only, which contains the central theme, "The Lord is my shepherd and I shall not want." Older children will easily learn the two verses, which PARAPHRASE Psalm 23. The song would be effective as a weekly song for gathering or departure in church school or chapel.

The melody is repeated for both verse and refrain, and the shape is very simple — ABAC. Add a tambourine shake on the first beat of each measure and a triangle on the third beat, finishing with three quarter notes to match the words "shall not want."

? *What would be a modern-day version of the Good Shepherd?*

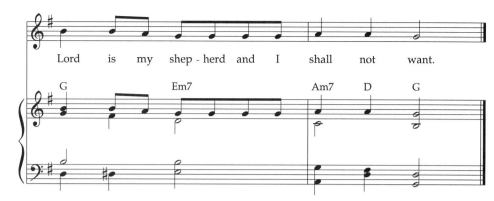

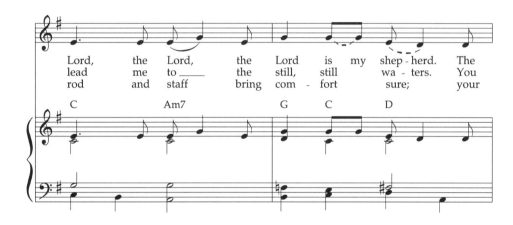

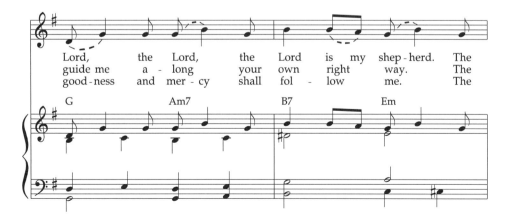

Words and Music: *The Lord Is My Shepherd,* African American Spiritual, harm. Austin Cole Lovelace (b. 1919) © 1986 GIA Publications, Inc., 7404 S. Mason Ave., Chicago, IL 60638 [www.giamusic.com].

Oh, how good is Christ the Lord
Oh, qué bueno es Jesús

B, C, D

Guitar, piano, percussion, A CAPPELLA

Hymn of praise; congregational prelude

Easter season

This song is a wonderful distillation of the themes of Easter into a short, lively memorable song: Jesus died, pardoned my sin, and rose again. Glory be to Jesus! This piece is an ideal one for encouraging non-Spanish speakers to begin learning some of the language even if only the refrain "A su nombre gloria." The words fit to the music well, and the piece is not too fast.

Puerto Rican folk music may be accompanied by bongo drums, GUIRO, guitar, and piano. The drummer should play mostly on the higher pitched smaller drum with the occasional hit on the lower pitched larger drum. A steady pattern

should be played by alternating hands using the pads of the fingers throughout. The GUIRO, a long, hollowed gourd with ridges played by a wooden scraper, should play the pattern

making a long downstroke on the quarter note, with a tap and then a short upstroke on the two eighths.

Pronunciation

Oh, qué bue - no es Je - sús.
*Oh, keh bweh- noh ehs Heh – **soos**.*

Que por mí mu - rió en la cruz.
*Keh poor mee moo – **reeOH**ehn lah croos.*

Mis pe - ca - dos per - do - nó.
*Mees peh - cah - dohs pehr - doh - **noh**.*

A su nom - bre glo - ria.
Ah soo nohm - breh gloh - reeAH.

? *How does knowing that Jesus has pardoned all our sin change our lives?*

Oh, how good is Christ the Lord
Oh, qué bueno es Jesús

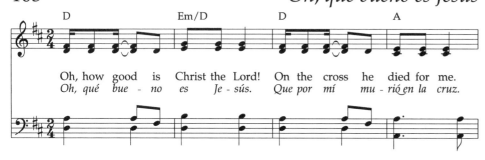

Oh, how good is Christ the Lord! On the cross he died for me.
Oh, qué bue - no es Je - sús. Que por mí mu - rió en la cruz.

He has par - doned all my sin, Glo-ry be to Je - sus.
Mis pe - ca - dos per - do - nó. A su nom - bre glo - ria.

Glo-ry be to Je - sus! Glo-ry be to Je - sus!
A su nom - bre glo - ria. A su nom - bre glo - ria.

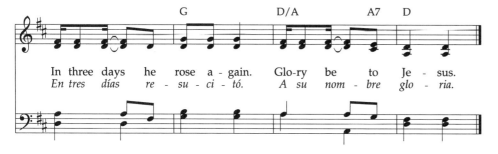

In three days he rose a - gain. Glo-ry be to Je - sus.
En tres días re - su - ci - tó. A su nom - bre glo - ria.

🤸 B, B*, C, D

🎵 Guitar, piano, organ

✠ Church school; children's chapel; during communion

📖 Fourth Sunday in Lent, Year A; Fourth Sunday of Easter, Years A and B; Proper 23, Year A; Confession of St. Peter

🔑 Compare this PARAPHRASE of Psalm 23 to #102. The writer introduces the alternative word "friend" for "shepherd." This is helpful to children who are unfamiliar with the image of shepherd. Show older children this text and Psalm 23 side by side so they can see the paraphrase process. There are other readily available versions of Psalm 23 that you could include, such as #663 and #645 in The Hymnal 1982. These are called metrical psalms because the text of the psalm is written as a paraphrase to fit a poetic meter.

The repeated refrain can be sung by all with a cantor singing the verses. When the cantor completes each verse, the refrain should begin immediately without pause. The text rhythm and accents match those of the music quite well and create a gentle, flowing song. If guitar is used for accompaniment, it should use an arpeggio picking pattern on each chord.

Because the text does not rhyme it might help to write the words on a poster for children to learn.

? *If you were the writer, what word would you choose to paraphrase "shepherd"? What does "Jesus, the shepherd" mean to you?*

Pentecost

Pentecost is the time when the followers of a single man, Jesus, were transformed into a community of faith that would one day be known as Christians. What they learned on that day was that the Holy Spirit would always be with them, even if Jesus was not, and that they had been given the power to do those things they thought only he could do.

"Transformation" is a very popular word in the church, but its close cousin, "change" is not so popular. We see transformation as passive, something done to us by God, whereas we know that change is active — *we* have to take risks. Yet transformation cannot take place unless we are *willing* to change. Jesus' followers could have gone back to their old lives once Jesus left them. They were no longer sure how they should live, and they took a risk staying together, continuing to meet. They were willing to change even though they did not know the form the change would take. When change came, more unexpected and more amazing than anything they had known, they received it gladly, even though those around them thought they were drunk or crazy.

The people who witnessed the miracle of Pentecost said, "In our own languages we hear them speaking about God's deeds of power" (Acts 2:11, NRSV). We need to speak to people in many different languages, literally and figuratively, through different modes and media, if we are to reach out to others. Not only children need this. Many adults are parched for lack of meditative prayer, lively gospel praise, dramatized scripture, liturgical dance, or permission to contribute to the sermon.

Let us dedicate ourselves to transformation by making Pentecost the one time of the year when we attempt the new and different in our worship. Gather a group of creative parishioners to plan worship that includes art, music, poetry, drama, dance, and other gifts they may bring. Draw in the youth, who know more about risk-taking than we do and who often abandon worship because it has become so stultified. Draw in the children, whose creativity is fresh and alive. Assure those who are fearful of change that the spirit of Pentecost suggests something new that may bring in the Holy Spirit transforming us.

We are all children of the Lord

B, B*, C, D

Guitar, A CAPPELLA, piano

Church school and chapel

Pentecost; Epiphany, especially Fourth Sunday after Epiphany, Year A; Propers 10 and 11, Year A; First Sunday after Christmas, Years A, B, and C. For the Mission of the Church

This song has been adapted from an anthem by Natalie Sleeth. Her text sums up the interconnectedness of all generations within the church. It also tells children that they have great value in this one humanity — since it is a family in which all are included "young and old, big and little."

The form of this song is

A B A B1

C C1

A B A B1

Although the beginning music repeats at the end, the words are not identical. This song could be sung weekly in chapel or church school on the Sundays following Pentecost and then performed in church at the end of the academic year.

? *What does it mean to "live in harmony"? How can we be better at it?*

105   We are all children of the Lord

We are all chil-dren of the Lord, young and

old, big and lit-tle. We are all chil-dren of the

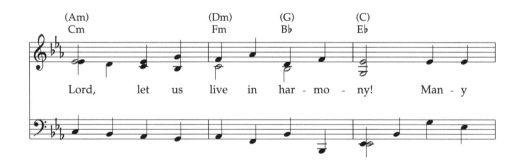

Lord, let us live in har-mo-ny! Man - y

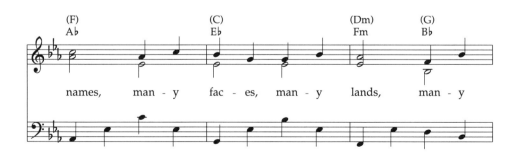

names, man - y fac - es, man - y lands, man - y

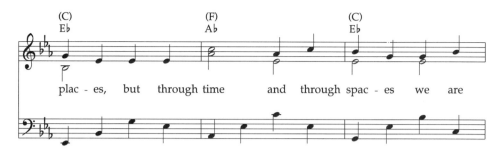

plac - es, but through time and through spac - es we are

one hu - man - i - ty. We are all chil-dren of the

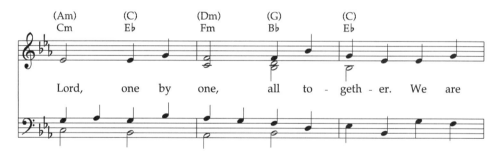

Lord, one by one, all to - geth - er. We are

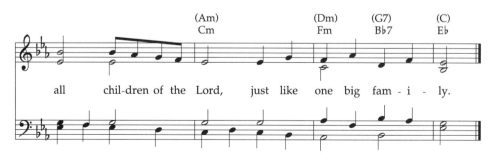

all chil-dren of the Lord, just like one big fam - i - ly.

Words and Music: Natalie Sleeth (1930–1992), adapted from the anthem "Children of the Lord"
© 1976 Hinshaw Music, Inc., PO Box 470, Chapel Hill, NC 27514 [www.hinshawmusic.com].

B, C, D

Keyboard, rhythm and bass guitars, drum kit

Offertory; prayer and healing services; patronal feasts; not appropriate for processions

Pentecost; Baptism; For Social Justice; For the Unity of the Church; For the Mission of the Church; For Peace; Celebration of New Ministry; Rites of Passage

Donna Peña is a beloved Hispanic composer for the Roman Catholic Church. This is one of her best-known bilingual songs. It comes from the rock-inspired traditions of worship music, but its response and refrain, "I say 'yes,' my Lord, in all the good times, through all the bad times" is wonderful congregational music. A more complex arrangement can be obtained from GIA Publishing #5306. www.giamusic.com.

This piece needs a good cantor, preferably one with experience in rock, jazz, or folk styles. The cantor is the storyteller of this song, and the congregation's role is to respond to the story. A rock-style band would support enthusiastic participation in this piece. Plan some congregational rehearsals before you program this for liturgy.

Pronunciation

Verse
Di - go "Si," Se - ñor.
Dee – goh "See," Seh - nyor.

Refrain
Di - go "Si," Se - ñor.
Dee – goh "See," Seh - nyor.

en tiem - pos mal - os, en tiem - pos bue - nos,
ehn tyehm – pohs mahl – ohs, ehn tyehm – pohs bweh – nohs,

Di - go "Si," Se - ñor.
Dee – goh "See," Seh - nyor.

a to - do lo que ha - blas.
ah toh - doh loh kehAH - blahs.

? *What do you want to say "Yes" to God about?*

106   To the God who cannot die

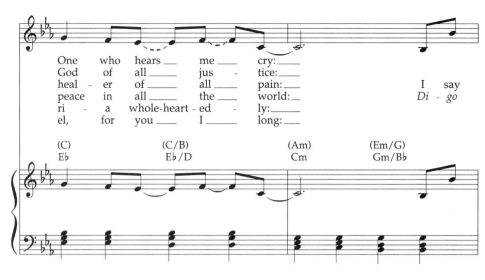

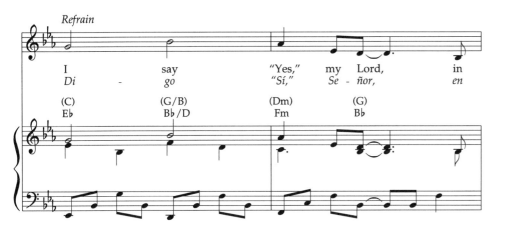

Refrain

I say "Yes," my Lord, in
Di - go "Sí," Se - ñor, en

(C)   (G/B)   (Dm)   (G)
E♭   B♭/D   Fm   B♭

all the good times, through all the bad times,
tiem - pos mal - os, en tiem - pos bue - nos,

(Dm)   (Gm)   (C)   (Em)   (F)   (G)
Fm   B♭   E♭   Gm   A♭   B♭

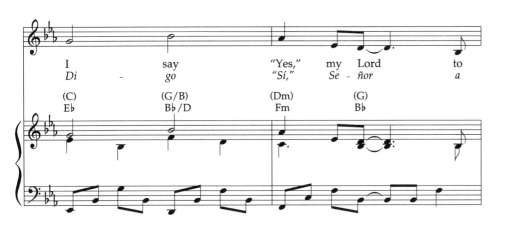

I say "Yes," my Lord to
Di - go "Sí," Se - ñor a

(C)   (G/B)   (Dm)   (G)
E♭   B♭/D   Fm   B♭

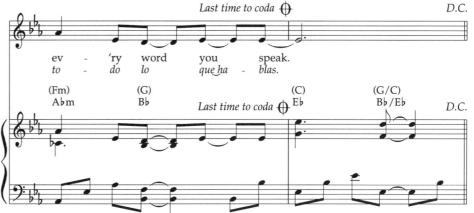

Last time to coda ⊕

ev - 'ry word you speak.
to - do lo que ha - blas.

(Fm)   (G)   (C)   (G/C)
A♭m   B♭   E♭   B♭/E♭
           Last time to coda ⊕   *D.C.*

⊕ *Coda*

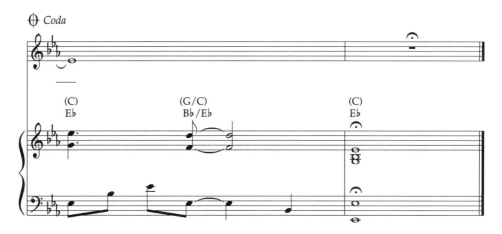

(C)   (G/C)   (C)
E♭   B♭/E♭   E♭

Soplo de Dios viviente
Breath of the living God

ﷺ C, C*, D

♫ Guitar, organ, piano

✠ General; prayer services; beginning of a meeting; retreats

📖 Pentecost; Easter Vigil

This wonderful hymn to the Spirit has a constantly moving melody that illustrates musically the pervasive Breath of God. The tune sounds Latino, like its Argentine text, but it was written by a German! The words draw together the intertwined roles of God, Spirit, and Jesus/Word. This text might be a useful reference when talking to children about the Trinity.

Since Pentecost is a time when we often use differing languages in worship, Anglo congregations may consider having a cantor or soloist sing the verses in Spanish. The word underlay in the English refrain is well done and could then be sung by all. The Spanish words of the refrain could be learned and sung by all as well.

Accompany with a rain stick at the beginning of every two measures to sound like breath — or have children make a gentle "whoosh" noise. The moderate TEMPO should allow the words to sing easily and not sound rushed.

Pronunciation

Refrain

Ven hoy a nues - tras vi - das,
Vehn oy ah nwehs – trahs vee - dahs,

in - fún - de - nos tus do - nes,
een - foon - deh - nohs toos doh – nehs,

So - plo de Dios vi - vien - te,
Soh – ploh deh Dyohs vee - veeEHN – teh

oh San - to Es - pí - ri - tu Cre - a - dor!
oh Sahn – twehs - pee – ree – too Creh – ah – dor!

? *What feels different about a song when you sing it in a different language from the one you speak?*

Come, Holy Spirit, descend on us

So - plo de Dios vi - vien - te, oh San-to Es-pí - ri - tu Cre - a - dor!
Breath of the liv - ing God, our Cre - a - tor Spir - it, e - ter - nal Source.

B, C, D

♪ A CAPPELLA

Congregational prelude; retreat; prayer service

Pentecost; anytime

Through the use of metaphor this prayer song invokes the Holy Spirit's presence
through her different names. Although the cantor's petitions vary, the congregation repeats the same words and music, allowing them to focus entirely on
prayer. The simplicity of this piece makes it ideal to sing during communion
or as an opening for the Prayers of the People on Pentecost. The composer
captures the words "descend on us" by writing harmonies that lead the music
sequentially downward.

Both the tenor and bass parts of this song are relatively simple, but the disso-
nances created by the alto part are challenging. The song could be simplified by
omitting either the alto or the tenor (but not both) without destroying the interesting harmonic movement. When learning all four parts, begin with soprano,
gradually adding the other parts from top to bottom. The cantor phrase may
be sung using the smaller notes only or singing the top notes an octave lower.
Alternatively two cantors could sing the petitions using both pitches.

? *Why do you think we speak of the Holy Spirit as descending, or coming down?*

Cantor(s):
1 Come, Holy Spirit.
2 Come, Breath of Heaven,
3 Come, Word of Mercy,
4 Come, Fire of Judgement,
5 Come, Great Creator,
6 Come to unite us.
7 Come to disturb us.
8 Come to inspire us.
(other invocations ad lib.)

B, B*, C, D

Guitar, piano

Church school and chapel; general

Pentecost, Epiphany

This is a classic children's song that adults should sing occasionally. The text of the first verse is a timeless message we all need to remember. Verse 2 describes a church filled with people of great diversity that includes children. A criterion of membership is to follow Jesus and join others around the world in their belief and commitment. Children could easily illustrate this text in pictures for a large poster.

This song could be sung regularly in children's chapel as a statement of belief. And it could be sung in church with children singing the refrain alone and adults joining in on the verses.

? *Do you ever pray or worship somewhere other than church? What does it feel like?*

I am the church

She sits like a bird

Refrain

I am the church! You are the church!

We are the church to-geth-er! All who fol-low Je-sus,

all a-round the world, yes, we're the church to-geth-er!

1 The church is not a build-ing, the church is not a stee-ple, the
2 We're man-y kinds of peo-ple with man-y kinds of fac-es, all

Repeat refrain

church is not a rest-ing place; the church is a peo-ple!
col-ors and all a-ges too, from all times and plac-es.

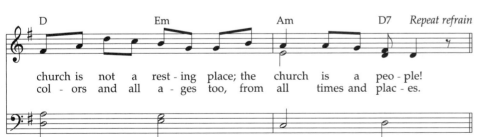

C, D

Piano, guitar, hand chimes

General; offertory

Pentecost

This is one of the finest contemporary hymns, written by John Bell of the Iona Community, perfectly summing up the qualities of the Spirit set to a tune that hovers between folk and contemporary song. The text is full of beautifully descriptive images of the Spirit's qualities described in a timeless way. There are the images of the procreative female: giving birth, brooding over offspring, and nesting in the womb. There are the creative qualities: singing, dancing, and nourishing potential. And finally there are the ecstatic, impulsive qualities: dancing in fire, speaking in tongues, avoiding capture, unable to be silenced or restrained.

Published in 1988, it is an example of a contemporary congregational text that refers to the Holy Spirit as "she." The Hebrew word for Spirit, *ruach*, is a feminine noun. Historically the Spirit was understood to be feminine. This idea is more common in today's world, but this hymn, nevertheless, remains fresh and new in its exploration of the feminine aspect of God, validating female and feminine gifts. If God is perfect, God must encompass and exceed all qualities of both male and female as an indication of gender. Feminine qualities are integrated within the complete Trinity, "one with God in essence, gifted by the Savior."

There is so much to hear in this song that it presents an excellent opportunity for listening as it is sung by soloist or choir The congregation could hum the melody to accompany verses 1 through 3 and join in on the final verse. The chords in the first two measures of the TREBLE CLEF accompaniment could be played on hand chimes. A cello could play the bass clef in the introduction with the verses by a full string quartet.

She sits like a bird

1 She sits like a bird,
2   wings o - ver earth,
3   dan - ces in fire,
4   she is the Spi - rit,

Em   Bm7   Em   Bm7   Em

brood - ing on the wa - ters,   hov - er - ing on the cha - os of the
rest - ing where she wish - es,   light - ing close at hand or soar - ing
start - ling her spec - ta - tors,   wak - ing tongues of ec - sta - sy where
one with God in es - sence,   gift - ed by the Sav - iour in e -

Am   B7   Em

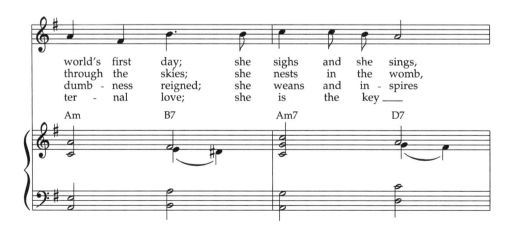

world's first day;   she sighs and she sings,
through the skies;   she nests in the womb,
dumb - ness reigned;   she weans and in - spires
ter - nal love;   she is the key ___

Am   B7   Am7   D7

moth - er - ing cre - a - tion,   wait - ing to give birth to all the
wel - com - ing each won - der,   nour - ish - ing po - ten - tial hid - den
all whose hearts are o - pen,   nor can she be cap - tured, si - lenced
o - pen - ing the scrip - tures,   en - e - my of ap - a - thy and

Gmaj7   Cmaj7   Fmaj7   Am7

Last time

Word will say.   2 She
to our eyes.   3 She
or re - strained.   4 For
heaven - ly dove.

B   Em   Bm7   Em   Bm7   E

Last time

C, D

♪ Organy, piano

✠ Liturgy of the Word; meditation

📖 Pentecost; Baptism; Rites of Passage

Shirley Murray's text evokes images of the Holy Spirit in terms of personal relationship—father, mother, friend, and lover. The text is personal and devotional and as such may be particularly important for those whose relationships with their families have been damaged. The Spirit gives us a perfect model of loving, supportive companionship.

Every hymn has a "voice"—a point of view from which it speaks. The voice of this hymn is personal. Careful planning will be sensitive to the right occasion for this hymn to convey its full meaning.

To establish a forward movement to this hymn, feel it in two beats to a measure. The melody moves mostly by quarter notes. Notice the text where longer notes occur. Also pay attention to the pitch of the final note in the second line and the rising sixth in the next to last measure. In teaching such an interval, ask singers to think of an elevator that has a counterweight going down as the elevator goes up. Think of that balancing downward movement supporting the voice as it goes up. The vowel should not change at all from pitch to pitch. Some of the words on the longer notes, such as "sign" and "I," have vowels that are diphthongs, which means that the vowel is a combination of two sounds: in this case, "ah" and "ee." Most of the sound should be carried by the "ah" closing to the "ee" only in the final moment before moving to the next word ("…sah-aah-een on me").

? *This hymn provides different images of God. How do you imagine God?*

B, B*, C, D

Guitar, A CAPPELLA, organ or piano

Church school or chapel; leavetaking; family blessing; bedtime

Pentecost; Proper 17, Year B (Ephesians reading)

This hymn is PARAPHRASED from part of the hymn attributed to St. Patrick (see The Hymnal 1982 #370). St. Patrick's hymn is a "lorica," or breastplate prayer, to be chanted or sung while dressing or getting ready for battle. This hymn is most like verse 6 of St. Patrick's text, which describes the Celtic way of seeing God weaving in and out, around and through us and our lives — "Christ be with me, Christ within me...."

Read Ephesians 6:10–20 in church school. To dramatize the reading dress children in "the belt of truth," "the breastplate of righteousness," and "the shield of faith."

The melody of this song is very simple; however, the word rhythm varies with each verse in measures two, three, and four. Practice saying the words in rhythm. Younger children could learn the first verse only or sing the last two lines as a refrain/response to a leader who sings the first two lines.

This hymn could also be sung in church or at home when families are setting out on new ventures or moving away. Sing it also when someone feels a need for protection. If you are singing it for one or two people, consider gathering around and laying hands on them as you sing.

? *Ephesians talks of the "armor of God," the "breastplate of righteousness," and the "shield of faith." Can you update these and design the "clothing of God" for today?*

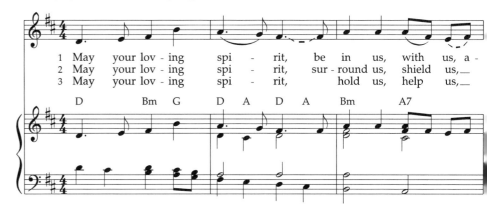

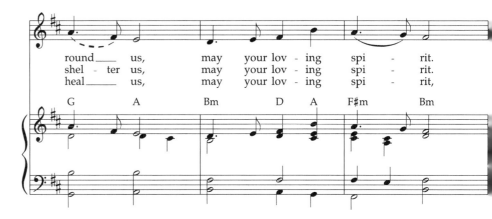

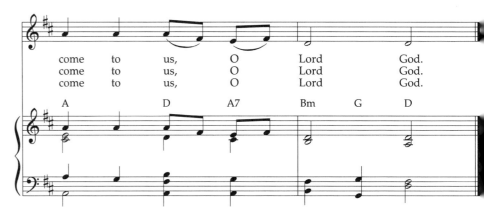

Words and Music: June Baker (b. 1936) © 1995 Stainer & Bell Ltd. and Methodist Church (UK) Division of Education and Youth (admin. Hope Publishing Co., 380 S. Main Pl., Carol Stream, IL 60188 [www.hopepublishing.com].) All rights reserved. Used by permission.
You must contact Hope Publishing to reproduce this selection.

Ascension

The songs in this section show two different aspects of Ascension: the great celebration and the strange and mysterious event. Jesus' ascension is the culmination of his time on earth. He has been crucified. He has risen and shown himself to his disciples over a period of forty days; and now, he must return to God. As the Creed says, Jesus Christ "ascended into heaven and is seated on the right hand of the Father." Now he is with God and with all those who have gone before.

This is a time to reflect on Jesus as both human and divine — to prepare to rededicate ourselves at Pentecost to do his work inspired by the Spirit who brings him close to us once again even though he has returned to heaven. There are two important messages for children: first, that change is part of life and it is easier to understand change if we reflect on what has happened so far. Ascension is a time to be thankful for Jesus' ministry on earth, and await the next part of the story. The disciples were probably afraid that when Jesus left them it was the end of the story, but it was only the beginning of a new story. New beginnings cannot happen without change. The second important message is that Jesus is in heaven with those we love who have died. We have no need to fear death.

B, C, D

Guitar, piano, organ

Liturgy of the Word

Ascension Day

The text of this song is based on Psalm 47, which is appointed for Ascension Day.

This song will appeal to older elementary school children because its fast pace and continual movement provide an exciting but accessible challenge. Younger children can join in on "Clap your hands, all you people," and "Hosanna!" and "Praise him!"

Once the song is learned, it may be sung as a round with as many as four parts (see entrance numbers above the music). When teaching and singing a round, divide the congregation into sections, assigning leaders or small groups of singers to each part for support. A children's choir could sing the song first and then serve as leaders for the congregation as they sing the round. Don't let singers accelerate the TEMPO in their enthusiasm. A round must keep a perfectly steady beat. Once the round is established, sing it several times without accompaniment so that the harmonies can be heard.

? *'Why do you think Jesus went back to God, instead of staying on earth with us?*

113 Clap your hands

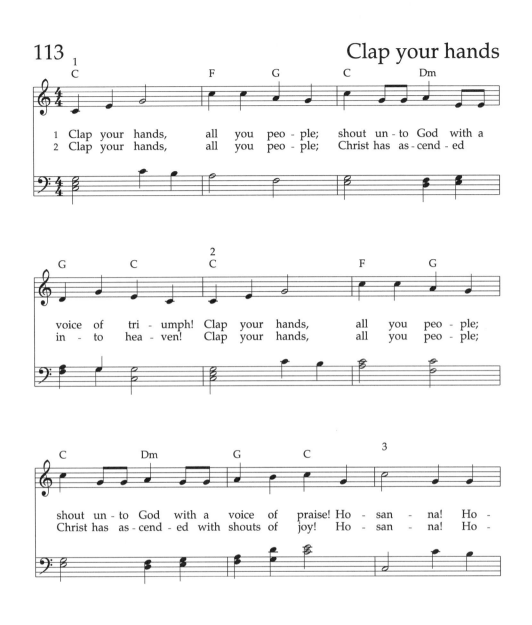

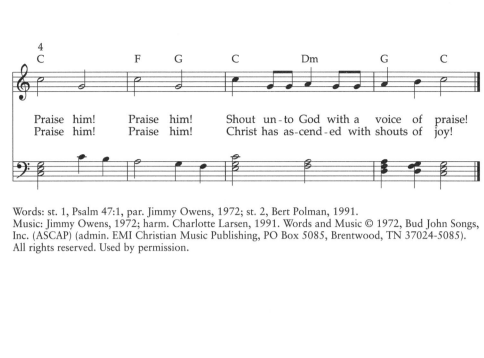

Words: st. 1, Psalm 47:1, par. Jimmy Owens, 1972; st. 2, Bert Polman, 1991.
Music: Jimmy Owens, 1972; harm. Charlotte Larsen, 1991. Words and Music © 1972, Bud John Songs, Inc. (ASCAP) (admin. EMI Christian Music Publishing, PO Box 5085, Brentwood, TN 37024-5085).

B, C, D

Guitar and piano

Liturgy of the Word; retreats; prayer service

Ascension Day; Trinity Sunday, Year C

This white gospel style song proclaims the majesty of Christ being lifted into heaven. The words are based on the call of Isaiah, which came in the form of a vision of God appearing in the Jerusalem temple: "In the year that King Uzziah died, I saw the Lord sitting on a throne, high and lofty, and the hem of his robe filled the temple" (Isa. 6:1, NRSV).

This song is in two parts, "Melody" and "Optional descant." The melody alone can be used in worship, but the descant adds dramatic effect. The descant could be first sung by the choir only or by children with adults singing the melody. As the song becomes well known the descant may be taught to everyone so they can sing the part they prefer. Instruments may be added: cello on the bass line and flute on the descant.

The descant is musically simpler than the melody but requires a good sense of rhythm. The first two short phrases, "We see Jesus," respond to the melody. The descant part sings the word "High" with the melody, but holds it for five beats followed by another punctuating phrase holding "high" for seven beats. A strong leader can conduct these entrances counting off the beats and pointing down for the octave jump on "he is." "The angels cry holy" is sung in nearly parallel harmonies to the end, which soars to a top E for the musical high point. Sing the first "The angels cry, 'Holy' " PIANO and CRESCENDO through to the high E with a DIMINUENDO to the end.

? *Which art do you think would best portray what this song is about? Painting, poetry, dance, or music? Can you create one of these?*

114

We see the Lord

an-gels cry, "Ho-ly." The an-gels cry, "Ho-ly is the Lord!"_____

an-gels cry, "Ho-ly." The an-gels cry, "Ho-ly is the Lord!"

A E   B7   E   A E

Words: based on Isaiah 6:1–3.
Music: Anon.; arr. Betty Carr Pulkingham (b. 1928) © 1971, 1975 Celebration, PO Box 309,
Aliquippa, PA 15001 [www.communityofcelebration.com]. All rights reserved. Used by permission.
You must contact Celebration to reproduce this music.

Trinity

We celebrate the Trinity after we have learned all about Jesus' life, death, and resurrection, and the coming of the Holy Spirit.

Understanding the concept of God the Father, God the Son, and God the Holy Spirit is hard for adults, let alone children. Perhaps the first step is understanding the role that each aspect of the Trinity plays. The recent attributes "creator, redeemer, and sustainer" are very useful. God, who is all-powerful and beyond our human comprehension, made everything, and it is good. Jesus is the image of God and shows us the nature of God. Jesus saved the world to free us from sin and reconcile us to God. The Holy Spirit is the presence of God/Jesus in the world here and now. God's actions and presence are in our past, our present, and our future.

In the liturgy of Holy Baptism, we are asked to affirm our belief in each of the persons of the Trinity (see the Baptismal Covenant, Book of Common Prayer, page 304). Notice also the Thanksgiving over the Water (page 306), which describes the Trinity acting throughout history and accompanying us on our journey of faith. On Sunday we repeat our statement of faith, the Nicene Creed, which also affirms our belief in the Trinity.

👪 C, D

♫ A CAPPELLA, guitar, piano

✠ Congregational prelude; Liturgy of the Word; prayer services

📖 Trinity Sunday; anytime

🎙 The melody of this beautiful and gentle song comes from the Philippines. The words were written by D. T. Niles, who, at the time of his death in 1970, was president of the Methodist Church in Sri Lanka, president of the Christian Conference of Asia, and a president in the World Council of Churches. Each verse focuses on one aspect of the Trinity and could be sung alone and repeated for meditation.

🎼 This hymn should be sung with long LEGATO phrases. The harmonies of this piece are easy and effective. The first two verses feature soprano and alto paired in thirds. The tenor part in the third verse is the most challenging, but offers CHROMATIC interest. The alto rhythm matches the tenor in the second half of the verse, so practice these two moving parts together before adding the melody and bass.

If the four-part arrangement is too complex, continue the soprano and alto thirds for verse 3 and have the men sing a semi-drone on E moving to B in measure seven and back to E in the final measure.

? *Why do you think there are three "persons" or parts of God? How does it help our understanding of God?*

Loving Creator

1 Lov-ing Cre-a-tor, grant to your chil-dren mer-cy and bless-ing, songs ne-ver ceas-ing, grace to in-vite us, peace to u-nite us— Lov-ing Cre-a-tor, par-ent and God.

2 Je-sus Re-deem-er help us re-mem-ber your pain and pas-sion, your re-sur-rec-tion, your call to fol-low, your love to-mor-row— Je-sus Re-dee-mer, our friend and Lord.

3 Spi-rit des-cend-ing, your light un-end-ing, brings hope and heal-ing, is truth re-veal-ing. Dis-pel our blind-ness, in-spire our kind-ness— Spi-rit des-cend-ing, Spi-rit a-dored.

(hum) Spi-rit a-dored.

C, C*, D

♫ Piano, guitar, electronic keyboard, drum kit

✠ Congregational prelude; offertory

📖 Trinity Sunday; anytime

"In the night, in the day" is a fast moving, wordy piece that children will love to learn as a challenge. It includes the memorable phrase, "Creator, Redeemer, Sustainer of life," a good contemporary interpretation of the actions of the three persons of the Trinity.

Learning opportunities for young singers abound in this song. The opening motif has leaps of a fourth, fifth, and sixth from the same note. In SOLFEGGIO terminology in this key the intervals are sol-do, sol-re, and sol-mi. The last phrase of the verse includes both SYNCOPATION and THREE-AGAINST-TWO triplets, a great teaching opportunity. The syncopation adds emphasis to the important or accented words, and the triplets should have a relaxed feel and not be rushed.

Initially this song would be a welcomed performance piece by the children's choir or the older children of the church school. The congregation will readily learn it after hearing the children sing. The piano accompaniment is certainly adequate, and, if available, the contemporary sounds of an electronic keyboard, bass guitar, and drum kit would be icing on the cake! A two-part anthem version of this song is available from Choristers Guild, www.choristersguild.org, #CGA668.

? *Who is the Creator? the Redeemer? the Sustainer?*

In the night, in the day

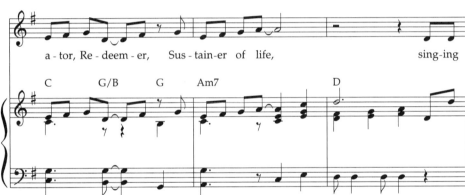

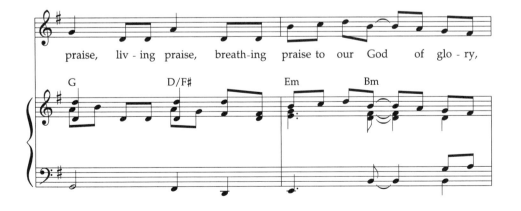

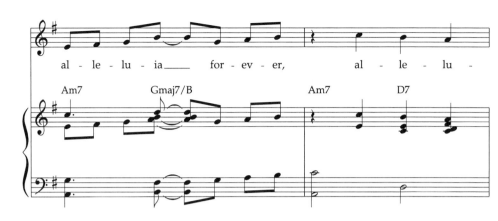

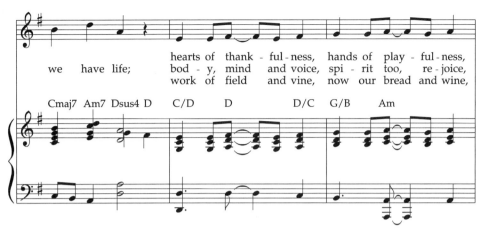

hearts of thank - ful - ness, hands of play - ful - ness,
we have life; bod - y, mind and voice, spi - rit too, re - joice,
work of field and vine, now our bread and wine,

Cmaj7 Am7 Dsus4 D C/D D D/C G/B Am

D.C.

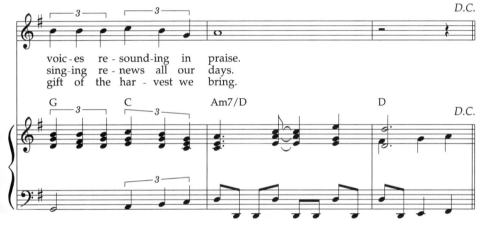

voic - es re - sound - ing in praise.
sing - ing re - news all our days.
gift of the har - vest we bring.

G C Am7/D D D.C.

All, D

A CAPPELLA

Song of Praise; prayer response; opening song for meetings or retreats

Anytime; Trinity Sunday

This short echo piece is a doxology, a form of words ascribing glory to God as Trinity. The text is somewhat similar to the Gloria Patri recited at the end of the psalms in the Daily Office: Glory to the Father, and to the Son, and to the Holy Spirit: as it was in the beginning, is now, and will be for ever. Amen. Some hymns also have a final verse that is a doxology, such as #377 in The Hymnal 1982.

This piece appears to be a simple round, but the second part is changed in the last two phrases, creating a harmony part. The cantor should be careful to sing the C♮ accurately in the sixth measure and contrast it with the C♯ in the next measure.

Most congregations find this song easy to learn and sing in two parts, especially without the printed music. The cantor should sing each short phrase and ask the congregation to immediately repeat it. Then point out the Trinitarian theme as a reminder of the sequence of the words. Sing again, asking the congregation to echo two phrases instead of just one. Repeat once more, singing the entire first part. Once the first part is learned, teach the second part to half the congregation in the same manner. When putting the two parts together, separate each group of singers into two different places physically, for example, left and right of the aisle, front and back of church, or the first floor of the church and the balcony. The piece may be sung several times. Challenge the singers by alternating parts between the two groups.

? *Glory, praise, and love. How are these different? How are they the same?*

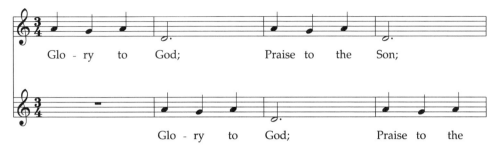

Glo - ry to God;   Praise to the Son;

Glo - ry to God;   Praise to the

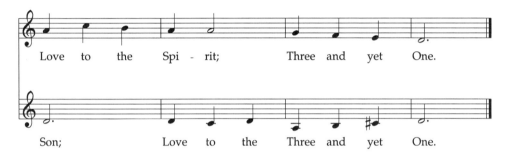

Love to the Spi - rit;   Three and yet One.

Son;   Love to the Three and yet One.

Words: Traditional.
Music: John L. Bell (b. 1949) © 1995 WGRG The Iona Community (Scotland) (admin. GIA Publications, Inc., 7404 S. Mason Ave., Chicago, IL 60638 [www.giamusic.com].) All rights reserved. Used by permission. *You must contact GIA Publications, Inc. to reproduce this music.*

All Saints

A saint is a holy person. The church teaches that people become holy when God's Spirit dwells in them and leads them to holiness. At the festival of All Saints, Christians celebrate all the baptized because at baptism all are given the gift of the Holy Spirit and become members of the communion, or fellowship, of saints. Therefore, All Saints' Day is designated as one of the four days especially appropriate for baptism.

For many children the first experience of death is the loss of a favorite pet. All Saints is an important opportunity to teach children about death — that Christians do not fear it but believe that in death "life is changed, not ended" (Book of Common Prayer, p. 382). Those who have gone before, who are present in prayer, and especially those who accompanied our Christian journey are remembered on All Saints. The collect for All Saints reminds us that we are surrounded "by a great cloud of witnesses" and that together with them, we will "receive the crown of glory that never fades away" (Book of Common Prayer, p. 380).

**᚛ᚚᚚᚚ B, B*, C, D

♩ Piano, organ

✠ Liturgy of the Word; offertory; children's chapel

📖 *Marian feasts:* March 25, May 31, August 15
   St. Joseph: March 19
   The Nativity of St. John the Baptist: June 24; Second Sunday of Advent, Years A, B, and C; Third Sunday of Advent, Year B and C;
   St. Michael and All Angels: September 29
   Francis of Assisi: October 4
   All Saints: November 1
   All Faithful Departed: November 2

⌕ "We sing a song of the saints of God," #293 in The Hymnal 1982, is a much-loved hymn for children, and we need more like it. This hymn, with its alternate verses for various saints, is a good addition. Although it may not seem at first glance an easy one for children to learn, the text of the first and third verses remains the same for each saint's day with verse 2 specific for each saint. The hymn is particularly appropriate for schools in which the regular chapel service may fall on a variety of saint's days. If no verse is given for a desired patron saint, older children may wish to read about the saint and write a new verse. Younger children could illustrate the words for the patron saint on a poster.

𝄞 This lilting Dutch tune uses a repeated motif first seen in the opening measure, a triplet pattern that skips a third. The form of the melody is AABC. It illustrates well the dancing movement of two swinging beats per measure characteristic of pieces in 6/8 time. Be sensitive to a singer's need to breathe at the end of each phrase by keeping the TEMPO moderate but energetic.

? *Do you have a favorite saint or Bible character?*

We sing of the saints

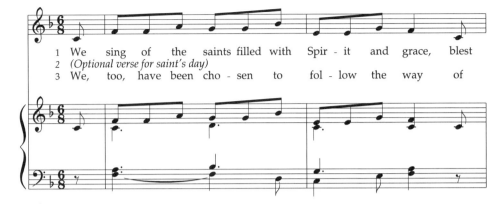

1 We sing of the saints filled with Spir - it and grace, blest
2 *(Optional verse for saint's day)*
3 We, too, have been cho - sen to fol - low the way of

wom - en and men through all time, from each place. God
good - ness and truth in our stud - y and play, we

chose them, the ho - ly, the hum - ble, the wise to
raise up our song, liv - ing saints here be - low, with

spread the Good News of sal - va - tion in Christ.
heav - en - ly saints, as our praise ev - er flows.

Optional Verses for Saint's Days

2 **Feasts of Mary**
A lowly, young woman God's mother would be,
the first true believing disciple was she.
From cradle to cross, she would follow her Son
and share in the life everlasting he won.

Feasts of Joseph
A carpenter, upright and faithful, was called
to care for young Jesus, a child weak and small.
To teach and to guide, to embrace him in love,
reminding him here of the Father above.

Feasts of John the Baptist
A prophet and herald who made straight the way
for Jesus to come, bringing mercy's new day.
He preached to the people to change and repent,
preparing them as the Messiah was sent.

St. Michael and All Angels (September 29)
Of Gabriel, Raphael, Michael we sing,
God's messengers; joyful, glad tidings they bring;
protecting the Church, and announcing the time
when Christ shall return in his glory sublime.

Francis of Assisi (October 4)
Saint Francis was born a rich, noble young man,
but God had in mind a much different plan;
so Francis left status and money behind,
to help many people God's true will to find.

All Saints (November 1)
There are many saints whom we don't know by name,
for God works through people who never find fame.
But, gathered together, they now sing God's might,
with martyrs and prophets, in heavenly light.

All Faithful Departed (November 2)
We honor the mem'ry of those now at rest,
who followed the Gospel, whose lives were so blest;
from fam'lies and friendships, they make heaven seem
more home-like for us, in our prayers and our dreams.

Words: Alan J. Hommerding (b. 1956).
Music: *Zie Ginds komt de Stoomboot*, Traditional Dutch Melody, acc. Karl A. Pölm-Faudré.

Baptism and Rites of Passage

Children are endlessly fascinated with baptism. It involves babies and water and lit candles, and they are allowed to move from their pew to watch this strange and wonderful ritual. Their parents tell them the stories of their own baptism. More importantly of course, baptism is a central ritual, one of the two great sacraments of the church. New songs are included in this collection both to teach children about baptism and to allow them to participate in it more fully. Two of these songs are for children's participation: #120 "I am the light of the world" and #122 "You have put on Christ." The other two songs in the Baptism section are fresh expressions of how the relationship between parents and children informs each other's relationship with God. Children learn about God from their parents and parents learn about God from their children.

Numbers 123–127 are for rites of passage such as confirmation, Rite 13, and other milestones in the lives of children. They are written in different voices: some from the point of view of the person undergoing the changes, some from that of observers of their growth in faith.

C, D

Organ, piano, guitar

As the newly baptized returns from the font; offertory

Baptism

This hymn, written in 1981 by Ronald Cole-Turner, a United Church of Christ minister and professor of theology and ethics, is a wonderful expression of love and gratitude for the gift of a child. The text comments on what parents and the community learn when a child is born. God gives this gift of new life to the family who then dedicates the child to God, promising to nurture the child in God's ways. The community supports the family by promising to share in the guidance and upbringing. A child, in turn, teaches the family and community so much about God's love by being not only God's gift but a gift of themselves.

The form of this traditional Gaelic tune is AABA. Notice the REPEAT SIGN in the second line that repeats the A section before moving on to verse 2, which is the B section and the repeat of the A tune. The high E♭ in the third line is surprising at first, but contributes to the Gaelic character of the tune. Also note the unexpected

rhythm two measures later on the words "expression" and "Parent."

If a familiar tune is desired for this text, use one that corresponds to the hymn's popular 8.7.8.7 METER. There are many alternative tunes available such as *Stuttgart* (#66 in The Hymnal 1982), a well-known eighteenth-century tune, or *Holy Manna* (#580 in The Hymnal 1982), a lively *Southern Harmony* melody.

? *Do you know the story of your baptism?*

Child of blessing, child of promise

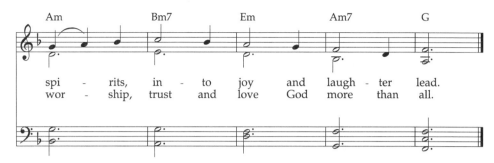

I am the light of the world

All

♪ Guitar, A CAPPELLA

✠ Order of Worship for Evening; Rites of Passage; prayer response

📖 Advent; First Sunday after Christmas (collect); Season of Epiphany; Baptism

In baptism we receive new life and light in Christ and are called to shine as a light in the world as Jesus did. To emphasize the image of this enlightenment the candidate or parents of the candidates may be given a candle lighted from the Paschal Candle (see The Book of Common Prayer, "Additional Directions," p. 313).

Begin teaching this by singing it slowly — the rush of words and SYNCOPATION may be overwhelming, especially for the youngest children. The tied eighth notes in the first full measure may be shortened for a breath.

This song could be used in several different ways: as people move to the font or return to their seats as the parents are given a candle; as an anthem sung by the children of the church for the baptismal candidates; or as a response in the Prayers of the People.

? *What can you do to be a light in the world?*

I am the light of the world, I am the light of the world. Who-

ev-er fol-lows me___ will nev-er walk in the dark, will nev-er

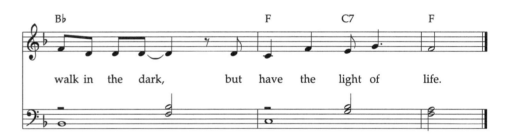

walk in the dark, but have the light of life.

Words: John 8:12.
Music: June Fischer Armstrong © 1991 CRC Publications, 2850 Kalamazoo Ave. SE, Grand Rapids, MI 49560 [www.crcpublications.org]. All rights reserved. Used by permission.

We bring our children

C, D

Piano, cello, and violin

As the baptismal party moves to the font; offertory

Baptism; A Thanksgiving for the Birth or Adoption of a Child

This baptismal hymn is one of a very few that clearly and concisely describes the journey Christians take from baptism and the ongoing recommitment to those vows through the dedication to nurturing children's growth as Christians. Its language is inclusive of the whole community, not just parents, as having responsibility for its children.

The tune, newly composed for this text, expresses musically the sense of journey. The simple, walking accompaniment adds to this movement. The bass line accompaniment could be played by a cello with a violin doubling the melody.

When teaching this hymn for the first time, practice singing the beginning scale from B to G, to hear where the line is going. The tune begins on the third degree of the G major scale pitched a sixth below the TONIC in the melody. The key note is circumvented as a home tone until the final note of each verse. If the initial pitch proves difficult for the congregation to find, the accompanist could add eighth notes, rocking between G above middle C and the beginning pitch (B below middle C) in place of the opening TREBLE CLEF rests.

? *Why do you think we make our promises to God again each time we have a baptism?*

1 We bring our chil-dren, Lord, to - day   as
2 On their be-half and in their name   our
3 Help us in all our ways to show   these

once they did   in   Ga - li - lee,   em -
own com - mit - ment   we   re - new   with
grow-ing souls   your   truth and grace,   till

brace them with your love, we pray,   and
them we die to sin and shame,   with
they shall come them - selves to know   the

1. 2.   3.

bless each home and fam-i-ly.
them we live a - gain in you.
beau - ty of our   Fa-ther's face.

All

♫ Piano or flute, violin, chimes, bells, or xylophone

✠ Immediately following each baptism; at the procession from the font after baptism; Liturgy of the Word

📖 Baptism; Proper 7, Year C

The words of this acclamation are taken from Paul's letter to the Galatians, 3:26–27a: "For through faith you are all sons of God in union with Christ Jesus. Baptized into union with him, you have all put on Christ as a garment" (New English Bible). This is a wonderful image for children and adults to reflect upon. When we are baptized we put on Christ, wearing him as protection and comfort. In children's terms he is both our pajamas and our comfort blanket! In some parishes, after the baptized are submerged in a pool of water or completely drenched with water, they are dressed in a white robe or a baptismal gown.

An appropriate use of this acclamation would be immediately after the baptism of each candidate, especially when there are several, because the prayer over the candidates and the signing with chrism is delayed until all have been baptized. Only one acclamation could be sung for each candidate once the cantor introduces it initially.

The introduction could be played by any two TREBLE CLEF instruments — flute, violin, chimes, bells, or xylophone. The accompaniment of the cantor version uses only four chords and could be arranged easily for hand bells or tuned percussion.

? *What would it be like to "wear" Christ?*

You have put on Christ

122

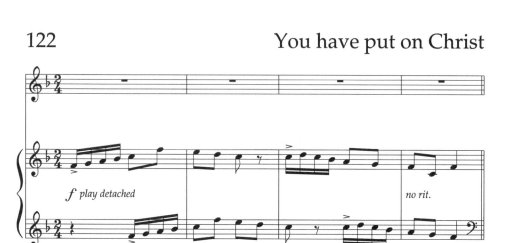

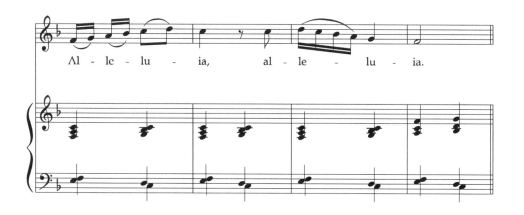

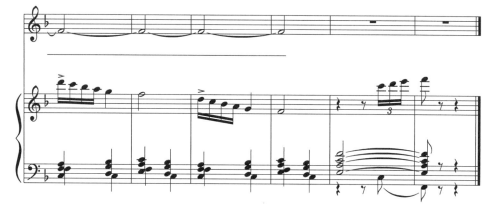

C, D

♫ Organ, piano, hammered dulcimer and bass, A CAPPELLA

✠ Offertory, especially on the First Sunday in Advent or Lent when candidates (catechumens) are enrolled for baptism; as those being commissioned gather following the Creed at Eucharist

📖 Rites of Passage; Baptism; Ordination; Rites of Commissioning (Lay Ministry, Church Planter, Missioner or Mission Team)

⚷ A theme of this hymn is "freedom to believe," the choice people make to be baptized. Being willing to struggle with doubts and examine beliefs rather than accept them unquestioningly sometimes invokes the label "wishy-washy." This hymn celebrates that quality, articulating the tension between faith and doubt, the role of choice, and times of unbelief.

🎼 The hexatonic (consisting of six pitches) tune *Dunlap's Creek* is a shape-note melody from the early nineteenth century. Such tunes were sung without accompaniment but were sung in four-part harmony with a distinctive vocal sound quality. An Appalachian hammered dulcimer would be a compatible accompaniment to unison singing for this tune. It may also be sung to the well-known American folk melody "Land of Rest" (#304, The Hymnal 1982). Since this hymn is written in the first person, some would be more comfortable if it were sung by a soloist or choir on behalf of the candidates. It could also be sung by the candidates themselves.

? *What tensions do you have between faith and doubt?*

1 God, when I came into this life, you called me
2 You give me free - dom to be - lieve; to - day I
3 In all the ten - sions of my life, be - tween my
4 So help me in my un - be - lief and let my

by my name; to - day I come, com -
make my choice, and to the wor - ship
faith and doubt, let your great Spi - rit
life be true: feet firm - ly plant - ed

mit my - self, re - spond - ing to your claim.
of the church I add my learn - ing voice.
give me hope, sus - tain me, lead me out.
on the earth, my sights set high on you.

C, D

♪ Piano

✠ Final hymn; offertory (vv. 1–3)

📖 Rites of Passage; Ordination; Commissioning for Lay Ministries; Commissioning a Church Planter, Missioner, or Mission Team

🗝 This hymn begins with a Trinitarian formula: God has begun the work in us, Christ's (baptismal) mark is on us, and the Spirit will help us follow through. Another theme in this hymn is God's love, which gives us strength to make the vows we say and to resist those sins that hold us back.

🎼 This is not an easy tune for visitors to catch on to, but it is one that will appeal to young people. Teach it to the children's choir, who can teach the congregation before the service. A cantor can help by conducting the unexpected movement of the melody. See in chapter 2: "Using hand gestures to indicate pitch" (page 13). Since this hymn is written in the third person, it would be best sung *to* the candidates.

This could be accompanied in the rock style with electric keyboard and drum kit. An alternate well-known tune is *Puer Nobis* (#124 in The Hymnal 1982).

? *How could knowing that you have the "mark of Christ" help you when faced with a difficult situation?*

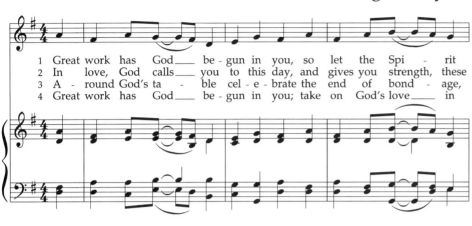

1 Great work has God___ be-gun in you, so let the Spi - rit
2 In love, God calls___ you to this day, and gives you strength, these
3 A - round God's ta - ble cel - e - brate the end of bond - age,
4 Great work has God___ be-gun in you; take on God's love___ in

fol - low through; the mark of Christ___ up - on your brow, bap -
vows to say; take up the faith___ that you were shown, and
sin, and hate: a feast of love___ and vic - to - ry, the
all you do, and may that love___ in you in - crease— now,

tis - mal touch___ re - mem - ber now._____
grow, as - sured___ you are God's own._____
gift of Christ___ who sets us free._____
with God's bless - ing, go in peace._____

C, D

A CAPPELLA, piano, oboe, flute

Prayer service; closing of a meeting or retreat; meditation

Rites of Passage; Ordination; Commissioning for Lay Ministries; Commission-ing a Church Planter, Missioner, or Mission Team

Set in a lush HOMOPHONIC style, this personal prayer for Christ's guidance is a quiet and moving musical devotion. The two eight-measure phrases have six common measures that move in a progressively descending pattern. The style is similar to #108 "Come, Holy Spirit, descend on us," also from the Iona Community. As a meditation, the style is reminiscent of music from TAIZÉ which is sung repeatedly as a MANTRA.

A good high school choir could sing this song with or without piano support. Sing several times in the Taizé style alternating piano with the flute and oboe parts below. Vary the combination of instruments and the dynamic level with each repetition.

?   *Why do we need Christ to both release us and restrain us?*

In love you summon

In love you sum-mon, in love I fol-low, liv-ing to-day for

your to-mor-row. Christ to re-lease me, Christ to en-

fold me, Christ to re-strain me, Christ to up-hold me.

Instrumental parts by Marilyn L. Haskel © 2006

Flute

Oboe

C, D

Organ, piano, A CAPPELLA

Liturgy of the Word

Rites of Passage; Ordination; Commissioning for Lay Ministries; Commissioning a Church Planter, Missioner, or Mission Team

This collection lacked a PARAPHRASE of Psalm 139, which is appointed for use at confirmation and is included in Rite 13 in *Journey to Adulthood*. Hymnwriter Carl P. Daw Jr. was asked if he had written a paraphrase, and he immediately offered this text. The austere and elegant music of David Ashley White captures the essence of the psalm text, which speaks of the mystery of God's intimate knowledge and persistent pursuit of us that began even as we were formed in our mothers' wombs and continues wherever we go. The repeated opening phrase of each verse allows the singer to acknowledge the gift of God's goodness as something awesome and almost unbelievable.

David Ashley White's tune is in the style of an early American folk tune. If sung A CAPPELLA, the hymn would benefit by part singing so that the harmonic movement from G major to E minor is clear. The rhythm should be felt in a large two-beats-per-measure rather than in four.

? *The psalmist seems alternately assured and alarmed by God's constant presence. How do you feel about it?*

One more step along the world I go   127

👫 B, C, C*, D

🎵 Piano, guitar

✠ Times of transition; graduation; end-of-year school events

📖 Rites of Passage

The British composer Sydney Carter has composed many wonderful sacred and folk songs, the best-known being "Lord of the Dance." This song is used for assemblies at the end of the school year in Britain. In this country the need for such rituals has resulted in preschool and elementary school "graduation ceremonies." There are very few songs that mark the various rites of passage that occur throughout childhood. This song allows even the youngest singers to mark the time of transition and acknowledge that God is always present. It could also be sung as a statement of Christian intent at any time of year.

This song contains several variations of dotted pairs (the dotted eighth followed by a sixteenth in measures one, three, seven, and eleven). The eighth/dotted quarter pattern in measures five and six is known as a "Scotch snap," which is characteristic of Scottish dance music and folk songs. It is said to match the irregular rhythm of Scots dialect. Practice clapping these different rhythms with children. The accompaniment is very simple and should remain well in the background of the strong melody.

? *What are you most proud of that you learned in school or church school this year? What new things are you looking forward to learning? What makes these new things easier to learn?*

Creation

In each generation there are subjects about which the children learn more than their parents did. A subject that is of great importance in our children's learning today is the fragility of our ecosystem and our need to protect it or risk losing it. In Christian terminology this is known as one aspect of stewardship: acknowledging the great wonder and beauty of God's creation and our responsibility to care for it. Learning about the oneness of all created life forms will help children develop the strength to acknowledge the corporate sin of regarding financial gain as more important than the protection of the earth. And it will encourage them in their mission to take action.

B, C, D

A CAPPELLA, flute and drum

Celebrations for Earth Day; Liturgy of the Word

Easter Vigil; Trinity Sunday, Year A; anytime

One of the most important contributions of Native American spirituality is the honoring of God as creator and the centrality of reverence for the earth. This austerely beautiful hymn first appeared in a collection entitled *Dakota Hymns* published in 1842. Based on Jeremiah 10:12–13, it is a text born out of the faith of the Dakota people during great tribulation. With great solemnity it acknowledges God's work of creation and the desire for God's presence.

A wooden flute or alto recorder could play the melody with a large reverberant drum playing a steady quarter-note pulse with accents on the second and fourth beats throughout. Native American drums are often large and are played by two or more people simultaneously. A rain stick or a bird call would also be effective additions.

This hymn is ideally suited for dance-like gestures to accompany it. American Sign Language interpreters could teach children to sign the hymn. Liturgical dancers could create interpretive movements as well. This also helps with memorizing the words.

? *What pictures are in your mind when you sing this hymn?*

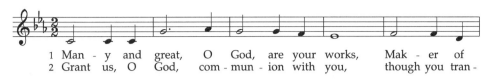

1 Man - y and great, O God, are your works, Mak - er of
2 Grant us, O God, com - mun - ion with you, though you tran -

earth and sky;_____ your hands have set the heav - ens with
scend the stars._____ Come close to us and stay by our

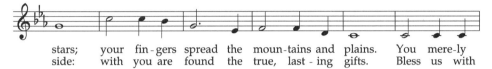

stars; your fin - gers spread the moun - tains and plains. You mere - ly
side: with you are found the true, last - ing gifts. Bless us with

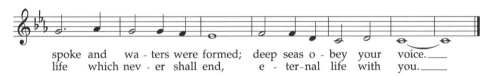

spoke and wa - ters were formed; deep seas o - bey your voice._____
life which nev - er shall end, e - ter - nal life with you._____

Words: American Folk Hymn, para. Philip Frazier (1892–1964); alt. © 1916 Walton Music
(admin. Licensing Associates, 935 Broad St. #31, Bloomfield, NJ 07003 [www.waltonmusic.com].)
All rights reserved. Used by permission.
Music: *Lacquiparle*, Dakota Indian Chant.

B, C, D

Organ, piano, or guitar

Offertory; Liturgy of the Word; Celebrations for Earth Day

Easter Vigil; Trinity Sunday, Year A; anytime

This hymn is first and foremost poetry and time should be taken to read the text before singing it. The verses cover an all-encompassing range of God's creation, including things that we humans judge as both good and bad. This might initiate a discussion about God's role in all of our life, and why God is the God of earthquake and cross as well as of rainbow and empty grave.

A nice addition for variety would be for two flutes to play the TREBLE CLEF accompaniment an octave higher on some of the verses. Note that the melody of verses 1 through 5 ends on the DOMINANT, not the TONIC. To teach children how the composer creates an ongoing melody, sing the last three words on F, E, D, and C instead of the printed notes. This shows how the composer's melody sounds as if it should go on and the F, E, D, C pattern sounds as if it is finished. Then compare the composer's use of the dominant harmony for all endings except the last one, which uses the tonic harmony further emphasizing the continuous sound until the final ending.

?   *Do you have a pet? How can you tell when your pet is happy? sad? loving? grateful? curious?*

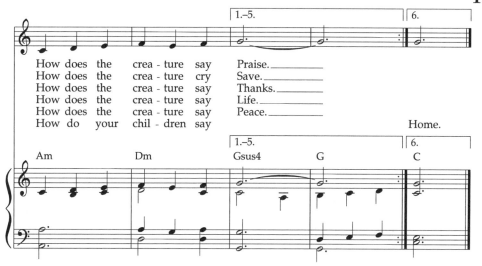

1 God of the sparrow God of the whale God of the swirling stars
2 God of the earthquake God of the storm God of the trumpet blast
3 God of the rainbow God of the cross God of the empty grave
4 God of the hungry God of the sick God of the prodigal
5 God of the neighbor God of the foe God of the pruning hook
6 God of the ages God near at hand God of the loving heart

How does the creature say Awe
How does the creature cry Woe
How does the creature say Grace
How does the creature say Care
How does the creature say Love
How do your children say Joy

How does the creature say Praise.
How does the creature cry Save.
How does the creature say Thanks.
How does the creature say Life.
How does the creature say Peace.
How do your children say Home.

C, D

♫ Piano, strings

✠ Liturgy of the Word; offertory; hymn of praise

📖 Easter Vigil; Trinity Sunday, Year A; anytime

This is a complex text both in language and in form. The shape of the verses is well worth careful study. Each verse begins with four phrases in strong images and lively poetic language naming God's different roles: "nuisance to the Pharaoh," "jeweler of the heavens," "table-turning prophet." The last two phrases of each verse address God directly, drawing a parallel between God's all-encompassing gifts, humanity's need, and the request for God's help.

Each verse has an overall theme. In the first verse God is described as creator. Verse 2 portrays Old Testament images of God's action on behalf of the people of Israel. The third verse describes God in Christ's actions. The fourth verse shows God in the bread and wine.

This new tune was written as a simple frame to enhance the complexity of the text. The tune builds to a climax at the cry of human failure: we are "formless," "sightless," "searching," "hungry." A descending MELISMA carries the request for God's help: "shape us," "lead us," "meet us," "feed us."

♪ The tune emphasizes key words in the text. Shape the phrases accordingly with a little more finesse than you might normally lend to the singing of a hymn. Begin softly at "you are womb," building in volume to the high point in the middle of the next-to-last line. The volume will naturally diminish as the melody descends, but be sure to shape the end of the phrase without fading away.

The two-part accompaniment could be played by a violin or viola with a cello.

? *Can you write another verse for this hymn using the writer's form?*

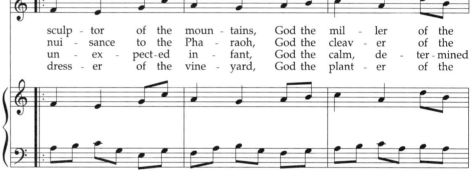

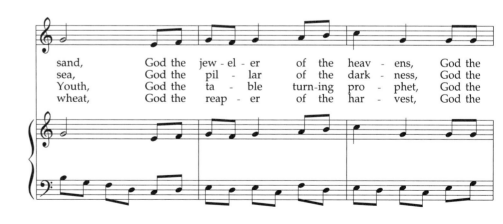

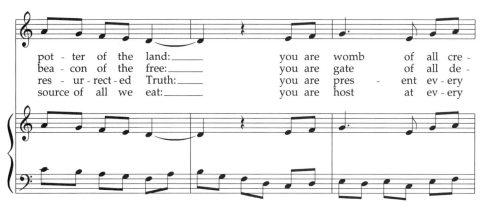

pot - ter of the land:____ you are womb of all cre -
bea - con of the free:____ you are gate of all de -
res - ur - rect - ed Truth:____ you are pres - ent ev - ery
source of all we eat:____ you are host at ev - ery

a - tion, we are form - less; shape____ us now.____
liv' - rance, we are sight - less; lead____ us now.____
mo - ment, we are search - ing; meet____ us now.____
ta - ble, we are hun - gry; feed____ us now.____

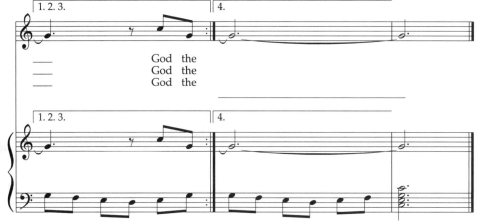

1. 2. 3.   4.
____ God the
____ God the
____ God the

B, C, D

Piano, guitar, drum kit

Liturgy of the Word; offertory; hymn of praise

Third Sunday after the Epiphany, Year C; Last Sunday after Epiphany, Year C; Easter Vigil; Trinity Sunday, Year A; anytime

This song appears in Marty Haugen's *Tales of Wonder: A Musical of Storytelling* (available at www.giamusic.com #G-3387-FS), which includes two other pieces in this collection: Donna Peña's "I Say 'Yes,' My Lord" (#106) and Haugen's arrangement of "When in our music God is glorified" (#140). The original has nine verses, from which the four printed here were selected. Haugen explains that the word *ohana*, which translates as "family," actually means more because at its heart is the root "ha" which could mean "living spirit" or "breath of life."

It is very hard *not* to sing this song with your whole heart and soul. Make sure the accompaniment, whether piano or full rock band, maintains the drive of the rhythm with a TEMPO

♩ = 128

Excellent diction is required to help drive the rhythm and accomplish the wordy text.

? Can you describe, or draw, the picture this song conjures up?

We are a part of all creation

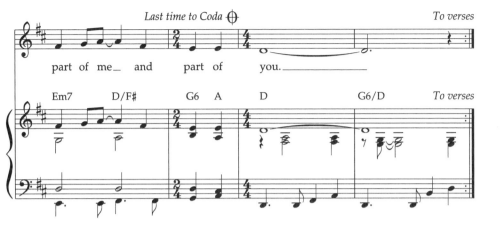

* ohana = great family

B, C, D

♪ Piano or flute and cello

✠ Hymn of praise

📖 Thanksgiving Day; The Martyrs of Japan (February 5)

This Japanese hymn, with contemporary text, is set to the traditional melody *Sakura,* which every Japanese person knows. The melody is often played on a koto (see below), the strings of which have been tuned to the pitches of this melody. Younger children could be taught the repetitive opening and closing phrases of each verse.

The three most characteristic Japanese instruments are the shakuhachi, a wooden flute with only five finger holes; the koto, a large-board zither with thirteen strings that are plucked; and the shamisen, a banjo-like instrument with three strings. A feature of Japanese music is the bending of pitches and the ornamentation of a melody. The flute can accompany the melody line of this hymn with the characteristic pitch bending, if possible. A harp sounds most like the koto, but a cello or guitar playing the bass clef accompaniment PIZZICATO would also be effective.

? *If you were to write a hymn like this one, what few things would you choose to praise God for?*

Praise to God

Capo 2: (Am) (Em) (Am) (Em) (Am)
Bm F#m Bm F#m Bm

1 Praise to God, praise to God, for the green-ness
2 Thanks to God, praise to God, for the gift of
3 Sing to God, sing to God, for the grace of

(Dm) (Am) (Em)
Em Bm F#m

of the trees, for the beau-ty of the flow'rs,
friends in Christ, for the church, our house of faith,
Je - sus Christ, for the love of par - ent God,

(Am) (Dm) (Am) (Em)
Bm Em Bm F#m

for the blue-ness of the sky, for the great-ness of the sea.
for the gift of won - drous love, for the gift of end - less grace.
for the com - fort and the strength of the Spir - it, ho - ly God.

(Am) (Em) (Am) (Em) (Dm) (Em)
Bm F#m Bm F#m Em F#m

Praise to God, praise to God, now and for - ev - er - more.
Thanks to God, thanks to God, now and for - ev - er - more.
Sing to God, sing to God, now and for - ev - er - more.

Praise and Thanks

The summary of the church's teaching, called the "Catechism," gives this brief reason for why we praise God:

Q   Why do we praise God?

A   We praise God, not to obtain anything, but because God's being draws praise from us. (From an Outline of the Faith, "Prayer and Worship," Book of Common Prayer p. 857.)

Marva Dawn also sheds light on why we worship: "True worship arises because God calls us. As an echo, our worship directed toward God is a gift in response to his gifts" (*Reaching Out without Dumbing Down* [Eerdmans, 1995]).

Each Sunday we offer praise to God and recount our salvation history in the eucharistic prayer. We praise God because of all God has done: the creation of the world and our own creation, even when we became disobedient; God's continual action in the lives of the people of Israel, even when we broke the covenant and turned away; the gift of his son Jesus Christ who died for us, even when we continue to do great wrong. The word "Eucharist" means "thanksgiving."

We praise God because God is worthy of praise, not because we expect anything in return. We praise God because in letting go of our sense of self in order to make God the center of our being we experience great joy and even transcendence.

We praise God because it is the natural thing to do, even when, like the psalmist, we are in the midst of great trials. Praise must be offered in the context of real life with its hardships and contradictions or it has no integrity. The words of the burial service anthem reflect this: "... all of us go down to the dust; yet even at the grave we make our song: alleluia, alleluia, alleluia."

Not only do the songs in this section cover many of these themes, but also a great proportion of the songs in the entire collection concern praise. It is natural to express our praise to God in song, because the gifts of music, poetry, our voices, and musical talents are all perfect tools for the expression of praise.

Singing songs of praise at the beginning of our worship is a way to acknowledge that God is at the center of our lives. It also brings us together as a church community and reminds us who we are as we recount the story.

All

♪ A CAPPELLA

✠ Opening song for a retreat or meeting; hymn of praise

📖 Anytime

⛓ This text adapts phrases from different psalms of praise, including Psalm 19 (The heavens declare the glory of God) and Psalm 96 (Sing to the Lord a new song).

🎼 This song sounds rich and complex when sung, but its parts are quite easy to learn. The structure of the melody (top line) is essentially two tunes (A and B), each repeated. A cantor may sing the melody first in the teaching phase, but the tune will soon teach itself so that all may sing. The harmonies are also easily learned. The alto moves almost entirely in parallel thirds with the melody. The single men's part follows predictably the TONIC, SUBDOMINANT, and DOMINANT pitches. In the second half of the song, a D drone is added. When teaching remember to vary the combination of parts. Leaving one part out will reinforce the two remaining and cause the third to be heard more clearly when it is added again. Consider adding the parts one by one or varying the combination of voices in the two sections of the song.

? *In what way would you like God to make you new, and not the same?*

Heaven and earth

Cantor alone, 1st time, 2nd time Sopranos join

Hea-ven and earth, join to wor-ship your Cre-a-tor!

Women

Hea-ven and earth, join to wor-ship your Cre-a-tor!

Men

Hea-ven and earth, join to wor - ship

ma-king all new, leav-ing no-bod-y the same.

ma-king all new, leav-ing no-bod-y the same.
none the same.

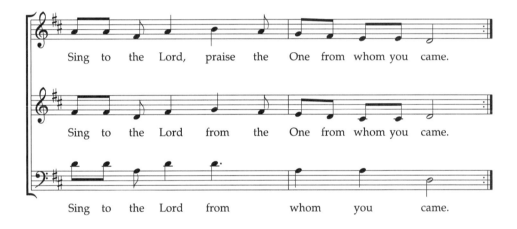

Sing to the Lord, praise the One from whom you came.

Sing to the Lord from the One from whom you came.

Sing to the Lord from whom you came.

Cantor first, then all

Sing a new song to the God who goes be-fore us,

Sing a new song to the God who goes be-fore us,
God be - fore us,

Hum

B, C, C*, D

Piano, guitar, strings

Hymn of praise; Liturgy of the Word; offertory

Proper 21, Year B; Easter Vigil; St. Andrew (November 30)

This PARAPHRASE of Psalm 19:1 by Mexican hymnwriter and composer Carlos Rosas celebrates God's greatness in creation. Note that in the refrain the accents shift every other measure from beats one and four to beats one, three, and five. Sometimes this is notated as a shift between 6/8 and 3/4 and is characteristic of some forms of Spanish music. If the eighth note remains constant, however, a METER change is unnecessary.

The TEMPO of this hymn needs to be lively without running away

$$\text{\textonehalf. = 96–104}$$

Because of the quick TEMPO the music will be felt as alternating between a moderate two beats per measure and a quicker three beats per measure. Teach the children to conduct alternate measures, being mindful of the bass line to keep the tempo steady. The accompaniment could be arranged for strings with violins and violas playing the TREBLE CLEF accompaniment.

Pronunciation

Refrain
Can - te - mos al Se - ñor.
Cahn – teh - mohs ahl Seh - nyor.

? *What is the sound of all creation singing?*

1 Can - te - mos al Se - ñor_____ un
   hi - zo el cie - lo el mar,_____ el
(2 Can-) te - mos al Se - ñor_____ un
   to - da la crea - ción_____ pre -
1 O   sing   un - to   the   Lord_____ a
   made   the   sky   and   sea,_____ the
(2 O) *sing   un - to   the   Lord_____ a*
   a - tion   shouts   to   all_____ that

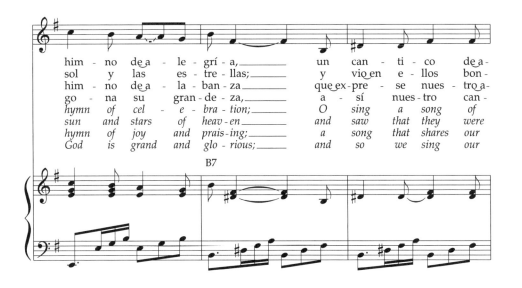

him - no de a - le - grí - a,   un can - ti - co de a -
sol   y   las   es - tre - llas;_____ y vi o en e - llos bon -
him - no de a - la - ban - za_____ que ex - pre - se nues - tro a -
go   na   su   gran - de - za,   a - sí nues - tro can -
hymn   of   cel - e - bra - tion;   O   sing   a   song   of
sun   and   stars   of   heav - en_____ and   saw   that   they   were
hymn   of   joy   and   prais - ing;   a   song   that   shares   our
God   is   grand   and   glo - rious;_____ and   so   we   sing   our

mor_____ al na - cer el nue - vo dí - a;_____ El
dad,_____ pues sus o - bras e - ran   be - llas.____
mor,_____ nues - tra fe y nues - tra es - pe - ran - za:_____ Hoy
tar va a - nun - cian - do su be   lle - za.____
love,_____ ev - 'ry day a new cre - a - tion;_____ God
good;_____ all cre - a - tion sings in   splen - dor:____
love,_____ our faith and hope - ful wait - ing.____ Cre -
song_____ to the God of grace and   beau - ty:____

Estribillo / Refrain

A - le - lu - ya!____ A - le - lu - ya! Can -
Al - le - lu - ia!____ Al - le - lu - ia! O

te - mos al Se - ñor.____ A - le - lu - ya!
sing un - to the Lord.____ Al - le - lu - ia.

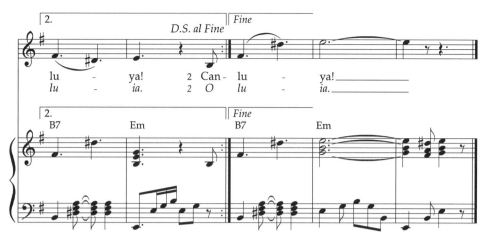

Words: based on Genesis 1; Psalm 19:1; Carlos Rosas, 1976, tr. C. Michael Hawn.
Music: Carlos Rosas, 1976, arr. Arturo González.

134

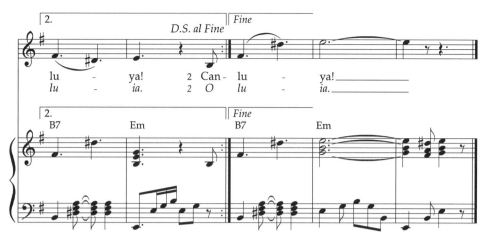

Words: based on Genesis 1; Psalm 19:1; Carlos Rosas, 1976, tr. C. Michael Hawn.
Music: Carlos Rosas, 1976, arr. Arturo González.
Spanish text and melody © 1976 Resource Publications, Inc., 160 E. Virginia St. #290, San Jose, CA 95112-5876 [www.rpinet.com]. All rights reserved. Used by permission.
Tr. and arr. © 1999 Choristers Guild, 2834 W. Kingsley Rd., Garland, TX 75041-2498 [www.choristersguild.org]. All rights reserved. Used by permission.
You must contact Resource Publications, Inc. to reprint this Spanish text or melody.

C, C*, D

Organ, piano

Hymn of praise; hymn after communion; patronal festivals

Anniversary of the Dedication of a Church; anytime

This hymn praises God for all the aspects of our weekly worship: the place in which we worship, the people who serve, God in the Word, Christ in the Sacraments, and the Spirit who acts within us. In the final verse we are reminded that we praise God through songs and words of praise, but also through our willing service: "Though praise ends, praise is begun where God's will is gladly done" (v. 5).

The refrain of this hymn is not a separate entity but flows from the verse, just as "God's goodness" flows from the third "Hallelujah." To keep the phrase moving, breathe after the second "Hallelujah." Young children will find the B on the first "Hallelujah" too low. The range of the hymn is limited, so consider transposing the hymn up to F or even G major.

? *Can you think of some examples of "food for body, soul, and mind" in God's word (scripture)?*

B, C, D

Piano, electronic keyboard, guitar, and drums

Liturgy of the Word; communion

Proper 14, Year B; Fourth Sunday in Lent, Year C; St. Mary the Virgin (August 15)

This wonderful song is based on Psalm 34, using verse eight as the refrain. The psalmist is so familiar with the goodness of God that these blessings become as familiar to him as what he perceives through the senses (taste). The taste of chocolate cannot be described adequately with words; one understands the essence of chocolate by tasting it. If you find it good, you want to tell others about it. And so it is with God.

The accompaniment for this song is very simple and could be played by a capable young pianist. The bass line could be played by a young pianist on an electronic keyboard, by a cellist, or by an electric bass player. Use the first four measures as an introduction, extending the first chord in measure four for the four beats. The verses should be practiced strictly in rhythm at first, but as they become better known, the timing can be relaxed a little, so the focus can be on the natural rhythm of the words.

A version of this piece with SATB chorus and instrumental parts is available from www.giamusic.com #6076.

? *What does "the goodness of the Lord" taste like and look like?*

136   Taste and see

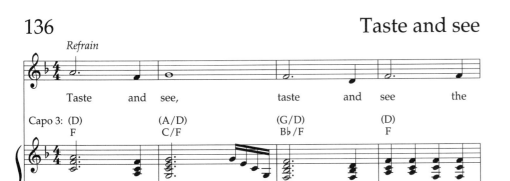

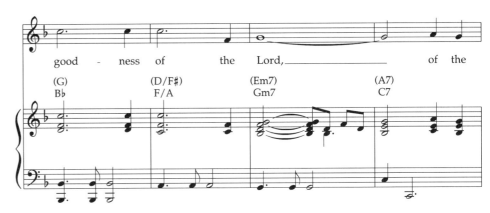

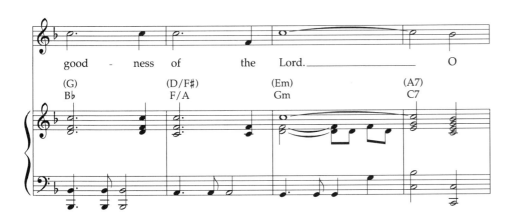

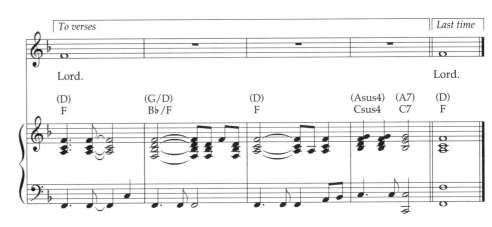

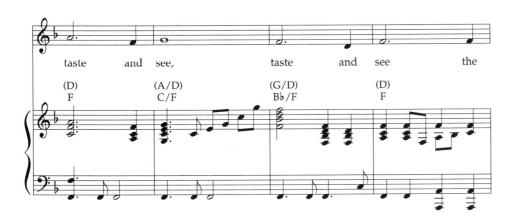

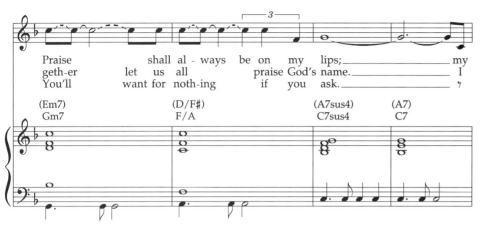

Praise shall al-ways be on my lips;_____ my
geth-er let us all praise God's name._____ I
You'll want for noth-ing if you ask._____

(Em7)   (D/F#)   (A7sus4) (A7)
Gm7   F/A   C7sus4   C7

soul_____ shall glo-ry in the Lord_____ for
called_____ the Lord who an - swered me;_____ from
Taste_____ and see that the Lord is good;_____ in

(D)   (F#7) (F#/A#) (Bm) (Bm7/A)
F   A7   A/C#   Dm   Dm7/C

D.C.

God_____ has been so good to me._____
all_____ my trou-bles I was set free._____
God_____ we need put all our trust._____

(Gadd9)   (D/F#)   (Em)   (A7)
Bbadd9   F/A   Gm   C7   D.C.

All, A*

♪ A CAPPELLA, guitar, piano

✠ Church school; children's chapel; prayer

📖 Anytime

This simple song could be the one song of thanks and praise you teach to the youngest children.

Children can be asked what they would like to thank God for — in one or two syllables (to fit into the space of the printed word "life") — and you can take turns singing each child's verse.

? *Why do we thank God every day?*

We thank God

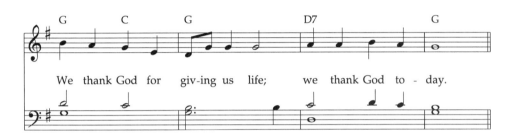

We thank God for giv-ing us life,* giv-ing us life, giv-ing us life.

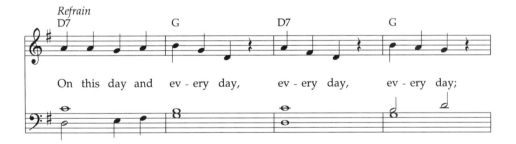

We thank God for giv-ing us life; we thank God to - day.

Refrain

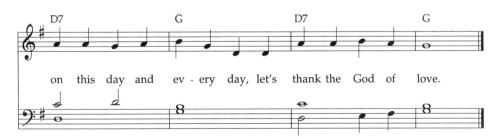

On this day and ev-ery day, ev-ery day, ev-ery day;

on this day and ev-ery day, let's thank the God of love.

* Additional stanzas: love, faith, hope, joy, Mom, Dad, and so on.

Words and Music: Kathleen Hart Brumm © 1988 in *Sixteen Scripture Songs for Small Singers*, Brummhart Publishing Co., 1708 Blooming Grove Dr., Rensselaer, NY 12144 [www.hometown.aol.com/khbising2]. All rights reserved. Used by permission.

B, C, D

A CAPPELLA

Liturgy of the Word; hymn of praise

Easter Day, Evening Service; Thanksgiving Day; anytime

The psalm on which this song is based was known in late Judaism as the "Great Hallel," and it was probably used at the time of the autumn harvest festival. Psalm 136 is a litany psalm, which means that the first half of the verse was sung by the cantor and the response "for God's love endures forever" was sung by the congregation. The complete psalm gives thanks to God the creator, God the deliverer of the people of Israel, in Egypt, in the wilderness, and in the later time of Judges. This psalm PARAPHRASE from Taiwan maintains both the structure and content. Discuss the meaning of the words "steadfast" (never-ending, unchanging) and "endures" (lives on, lasts forever) with young children.

This song comes from the Amis, who are the largest tribe of indigenous people in Taiwan. The melody is PENTATONIC with solo verses and harmonized responses. Note that although the harmonies change slightly each time, the melody remains the same. In typical Amis style the end of each harmonized phrase becomes unison for the last four notes. The vocal sound of these aboriginal people is high-pitched and thin to Western ears. Harmonies could be doubled with either xylophones or METALLOPHONES. Small finger cymbals could be added on the third beat of each measure.

? *Is there a difference between God's love and the love of people?*

O give thanks to the Lord

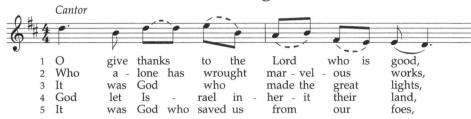

Cantor

1 O give thanks to the Lord who is good,
2 Who a - lone has wrought mar - vel - ous works,
3 It was God who made the great lights,
4 God let Is - rael in - her - it their land,
5 It was God who saved us from our foes,

All

For God's stead-fast love en - dures for - ev - er.

For God's love en - dures for - ev - er.

All

For God's stead-fast love en - dures for - ev - er.

For God's love en - dures for - ev - er.

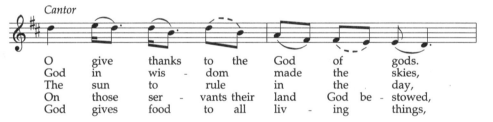

Cantor

O give thanks to the God of gods.
God in wis - dom made the skies,
The sun to rule in the day,
On those ser - vants their land God be - stowed,
God gives food to all liv - ing things,

All

For God's stead-fast love en - dures for - ev - er.

For God's love en - dures for - ev - er.

Cantor

O give thanks to the Lord of lords.
Who fixed the earth firm - ly on the seas.
The moon and stars in the night.
God re - mem-bered us in our dis - tress.
To the God of heav'n give thanks.

☛ D

♫ Piano, organ

✝ Offertory; final hymn

📖 All Saints; Anniversary of the Dedication of a Church; Founding of a Church; Proper 12, Year A; patronal feasts

This hymn was commissioned by Christ Church, Needham, Massachusetts, for its parish centenary. The church wanted a text that was appropriate both for that event and also for continual use. It was to be set to a common METER that could be sung to other well-known tunes. The tune *Cederholm* was written for another text, but was later paired with this one and named for the Rt. Rev. Roy F. (Bud) Cederholm, bishop of Massachusetts, who was the rector of Christ Church at the time. Patrick Michaels is the musician at the Episcopal Divinity School and St. James's Episcopal Church, Cambridge, Massachusetts.

As mentioned above, this text may be sung to other tunes with the METER 87.87.D. The hymn has a repeated rhythmic pattern that provides an anchor for this lively tune. Each phrase, whether short or long, begins with a

pattern. Clapping on the first beat of every other measure will help with learning. Also work on clarity of diction to keep the SYNCOPATION sharp.

? *Can you write a poem, or draw a picture, that expresses all the good things about your church?*

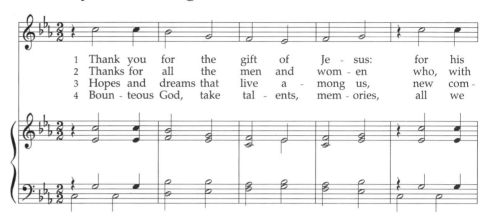

1 Thank you for the gift of Je - sus: for his
2 Thanks for all the men and wom - en who, with
3 Hopes and dreams that live a - mong us, new com -
4 Boun - teous God, take tal - ents, mem - ories, all we

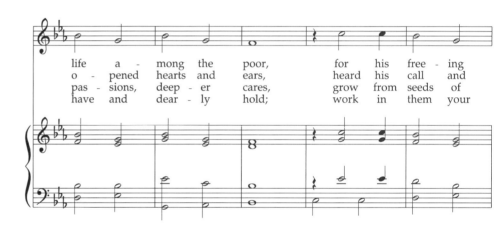

life a - mong the poor, for his free - ing
o - pened hearts and ears, heard his call and
pas - sions, deep - er cares, grow from seeds of
have and dear - ly hold; work in them your

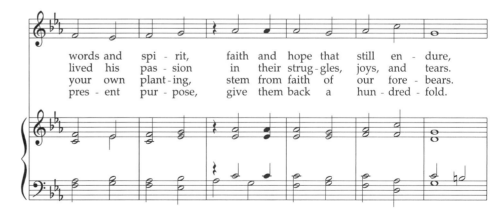

words and spi - rit, faith and hope that still en - dure,
lived his pas - sion in their strug - gles, joys, and tears.
your own plant - ing, stem from faith of our fore - bears.
pres - ent pur - pose, give them back a hun - dred - fold.

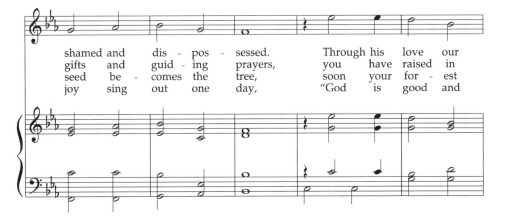

for the love he felt and nur-tured in the
Through their touch-ing, speak-ing, teach-ing, plen-teous
So the past re-news the pres-ent, soon the
So your peo-ple born to-mor-row may with

shamed and dis-pos-sessed. Through his love our
gifts and guid-ing prayers, you have raised in
seed be-comes the tree, soon your for-est
joy sing out one day, "God is good and

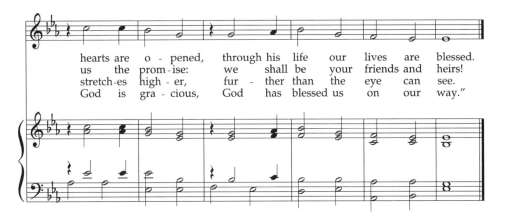

hearts are o-pened, through his life our lives are blessed.
us the prom-ise: we shall be your friends and heirs!
stretch-es high-er, fur-ther than the eye can see.
God is gra-cious, God has blessed us on our way."

♔ B, C, D

♪ Organ, piano, flute, electronic keyboard, guitar, drums

✠ Hymn of praise; closing hymn; hymn festivals

📖 Commissioning for Lay Ministries (musicians)

⚷ There are not very many hymns that speak of music as another language in which to praise God, and this wonderful text deserves an alternative tune (see #420 in The Hymnal 1982). This version from Marty Haugen's musical *Tales of Wonder* works well as a congregational hymn. The angular tune is easier than it might seem at first glance. The composer has used repetition well in creating a lilting tune that is fun to sing. The first half of each phrase of the verses is nearly identical, and the three alleluias are musically predictable acclamations.

𝄞 Marty Haugen has written a joyous song that could be easily introduced by a middle or high school choir singing the parts printed here. An easy soprano descant is printed here for the first eight measures of the final verse. Sopranos should join the melody following the descant. The small notes in the final four measures may be played by a C instrument, such as a violin or a flute playing an octave higher. A full anthem arrangement is available from www.giamusic.com, #G-3335.

❓ *Can you share an experience of being moved "to a more profound Alleluia" through music in worship?*

1 When in our mu-sic God is glo-ri -
2 How of - ten, mak - ing mu - sic, we have
3 So has the Church, in lit - ur - gy and
4 And did not Je - sus sing a psalm that
5 Let ev - ery in - stru - ment be tuned for

G   C/G   Gmaj7   C/G   G   C/G

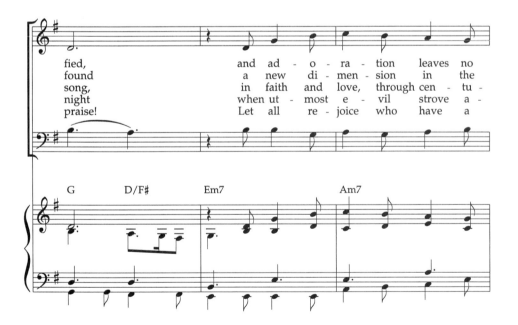

fied,   and ad - o - ra - tion leaves no
found   a new di - men - sion in the
song,   in faith and love, through cen - tu -
night   when ut - most e - vil strove a -
praise!   Let all re - joice who have a

G   D/F#   Em7   Am7

room   for   pride,   It is as
world   of   sound,   as wor - ship
ries   of   wrong,   borne wit - ness
gainst   the   Light?   Then let us
voice   to   raise!   And may God

F   Cmaj7   Am7/D   D   G/B

though the whole cre - a - tion cried:
moved us to a more pro - found
to the truth in ev - ery tongue: Al - le - lu -
sing, for whom he won the fight:
give us faith to sing al - ways:

Am7   Em7   A7

Descant for the first eight measures of the final verse.

Al - le - lu - ia! Al - le - lu - ia!

Al - le - lu - ia! Al - le - lu - ia!

ia! Al - le - lu - ia! Al - le - lu - ia! _____

Last time

All, A*

♪ A CAPPELLA, guitar, hand chimes

✠ Mother's Day; children's chapel

📖 Second Sunday in Lent, Year C; St. Stephen (December 26)

The various examples in this text of the female of the species caring for her young teach children about the nature of God. God is like a parent who nurtures and cares for us. In Luke 13:34 and in Matthew 23:37 Jesus agonizes over Jerusalem and describes himself using a simile of the mother hen gathering her brood under her wings. Take the opportunity to teach children that God can be described using examples of the good things that we know. God can be like our mother or our father or a breath of fresh air.

This simple tune is ideal for young children. The melody consists of the repetition of the opening pattern of thirds and stepwise movement. Invite the children to invent gestures for each animal or draw pictures to hold up for each verse.

The melody may be accompanied by only two chords played on hand chimes: F and C7. In the next-to-last measure use a C7 on the third beat instead of the printed Dm and B♭9.

? *Can you make a list of all the ways in which God is like a mother?*

1 Moth-er hen, moth-er hen, guards her ba-bies with her wings,
2 Moth-er bear, moth-er bear, guards her ba-bies with a growl,
3 Ea-gle mom spreads her wings, keeps her ba-bies free from harm,
4 Moth-ers all show their love like our God in heaven a - bove,

Moth-er hen, moth-er hen, God is like a__ moth-er hen.
Moth-er bear, moth-er bear, God is like a__ moth-er bear.
Ea-gle mom spreads her wings, God is like an__ ea-gle mom.
Thank you, God, for the care of lov-ing moth-ers__ ev-ery-where.

B, C, D

Organ, piano

Offertory; communion

Trinity Sunday; Eighth Sunday after Epiphany, Year A; Proper 3, Year A

The poet Jean Wiebe Janzen based this text on the writings of Julian of Norwich. In her *Revelations of Divine Love,* Julian speaks of "God Almighty" as our natural father and "God all-wisdom" as our natural mother. She also writes that a mother can give her child milk, but our mother, Jesus, can feed us with himself. Each verse of her text describes aspects of the Trinity.

Composer Sharon Hershey has written a kind of gentle lullaby for this contemporary text. Demanding no more than unison singing, the printed descant could be sung by the choir or played on a melodic instrument such as a flute, oboe, or violin.

?   *What kinds of things does God do that are mother-like?*

142 Mothering God

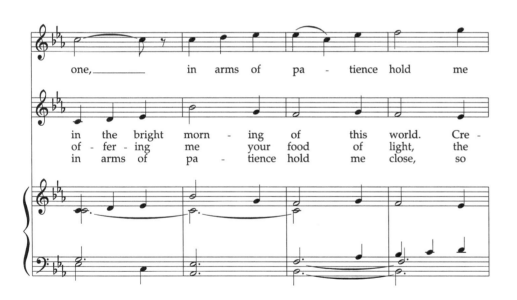

know._____ Moth - er -ing God_____ Moth - er -ing God.

know._____ Moth - er -ing God.

Healing and Assurance

Adults and parents sometimes think that children live a golden life without suffering, but of course this is not true. Children suffer from mistreatment, poverty, illness, bereavement, and despair. Because they are learning how to cope in the world, they also may suffer greatly from events that adults have learned to accept, such as moving to a new house, having difficulties at school, or experiencing an argument with a friend. Learning that God is always with us during any crisis in life is a central part of the journey of faith. God will not always solve the problem, and sometimes God's solution is not the one we would expect. As we travel through our difficulties God's presence will give us strength and comfort.

These songs are not just for times of trial. Even in the best of times, we need to step away from our "busy-ness" (and children's lives these days are almost as overscheduled and stressed as ours) and meditate on God's care for us. When hard times come, we will have the words and music of comfort in our hearts.

B, C, D

Piano, guitar, C instrument

Liturgy of the Word; offertory

Trinity Sunday, Year A; Rites of Passage

This song bridges the gap between children's and adult music; it has a beautiful simplicity, but it is not simplistic, and adults, as well as children, will find a great comfort in it. The text is congruent with Matthew 28:20, in which Jesus tells his disciples that he is with them always to the end of the age. The text is also parallel to Psalm 139, "Where can I go then from your Spirit?"

The words "for the Lord is near, everywhere I go" repeat at the end of each verse. Young children could learn the entire last line with the simple but changing phrases immediately before this refrain — verses 1 and 4 are the same. The instrumental descant could be played by an oboe, violin, or a flute playing an octave higher.

? *Do you ever talk to God at night if you are afraid?*

Everywhere I go

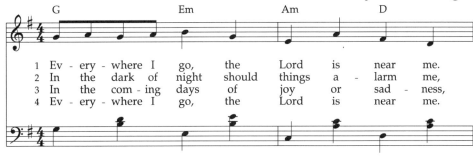

1 Ev - ery - where I go, the Lord is near me.
2 In the dark of night should things a - larm me,
3 In the com - ing days of joy or sad - ness,
4 Ev - ery - where I go, the Lord is near me.

Descant for C instrument

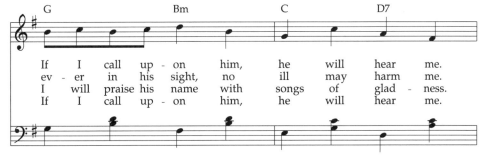

If I call up - on him, he will hear me.
ev - er in his sight, no ill may harm me.
I will praise his name with songs of glad - ness.
If I call up - on him, he will hear me.

Nev - er will I fear, for the Lord is near, ev - ery - where I
I will be of cheer, for the Lord is near, ev - ery - where I
For to me it's clear that the Lord is near, ev - ery - where I
Nev - er will I fear, for the Lord is near, ev - ery - where I

go. _____   go.

One, two, three, Jesus loves me

A*

A CAPPELLA, guitar, piano

Church school, children's chapel, camp

Anytime

Here is a "first church song" for children just old enough to speak, which can also be sung at home with parents.

The melody of this song is very simple; one phrase is repeated with slight variations, and it bears a definite resemblance to the first line of "Twinkle, Twinkle Little Star."

Some simple actions for this song:

Jesus loves me:	*point to yourself*
Jesus loves you:	*point to everyone in the circle*
He loves you more:	*wrap your arms around yourself in a hug and rock from side to side*
Going to heaven:	*open hands in an arc overhead.*
Truly divine:	*clasp hands over heart*
. . . sing it again:	*roll hands around one another*
There's no time:	*wave finger in "no" gesture*

To indicate numbers hold up closed hands with fingers toward the children. Raise the little finger of the right hand for "one," moving through all ten fingers right hand to left (seen as left to right by the children). Lift up fingers for each number, bringing them back down when numbers are repeated. Explain that heaven will be "truly divine" because "divine" means "God-like."

Children really enjoy changing the ending. Let them choose to keep going a few times before singing the ending line.

? *What do you think heaven is like?*

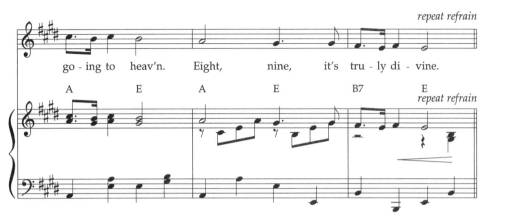

go - ing to heav'n. Eight, nine, it's tru - ly di - vine.

3 Nine, ten, it's time to end; but in - stead we'll

sing it a - gain. there's no time to sing it a - gain.

In you our hearts find rest

145

All

♫ A CAPPELLA

✠ Prayer services; healing; retreat and camp

📖 Eighth Sunday after Epiphany, Year A; Proper 3, Year A

Not many TAIZÉ pieces have been included in this collection because they are so easily found elsewhere (*see* #825–832 in *Wonder, Love, and Praise,* Church Publishing), but this piece is not as familiar as many. The quiet, meditative text matches the nature of Taizé music quite well. These short pieces are designed for repeated singing so that prayer can be an internal process.

This piece is simply one phrase repeated. Rehearse sopranos and basses first, then add alto and tenor.

? *What does the phrase "our hearts find rest" mean to you?*

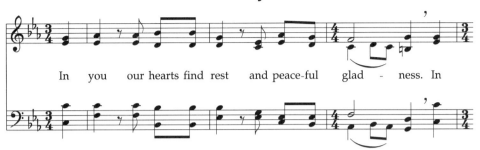

In you our hearts find rest and peace-ful glad - ness. In

you our hearts find rest and peace-ful glad - ness.

Words: *Psalm 62.*
Music: Jacques Berthier © by Les Presses de Taizé (France) (admin. GIA Publications, Inc., 7404 S. Mason Ave., Chicago, IL 60638 [www.giamusic.com].) All rights reserved. Used by permission.
You must contact GIA Publications, Inc. to reproduce this music.

B, C, D

A CAPPELLA

Prayer services; healing; retreat; camp; closing song

Anytime; Burial (Committal)

This is another example of a Celtic "breastplate" or "lorica" hymn (see #112 "May your loving spirit"). God, Christ, and Spirit are called to surround us with protection. The phrase "lead you through darkness into the light" reminds us that God's protection doesn't remove the dark times, but accompanies us as we travel through them.

This song is one repeated phrase with only a slight change at the end. The moving tenor and bass parts are not difficult. (Note the A♭ pitch in the bass part in measure eight). Soprano and alto move almost entirely in parallel thirds. Rehearse women first and then tenor and bass before singing altogether. Depending on the occasion, the word "us" may be more appropriate than "you" throughout.

? *What could you write this text on that would fit into your pocket or backpack?*

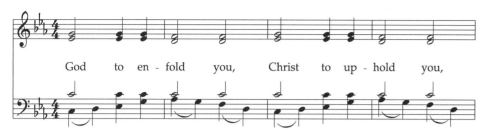

God to en-fold you, Christ to up-hold you,

Spi - rit to keep you in hea - ven's sight;

so may God grace you, heal and em - brace you,

lead you through dark - ness in - to the light.

D*

♪ Guitar, piano

✠ Prayer services, retreat, camp

📖 Second Sunday in Lent, Year B; Proper 13, Year A; Proper 27, Year C

⚷ One of the beauties of this song is that while God is referred to in masculine terms, the central image is of gentleness. At the best of times, God's constant presence and love keeps us on the right path. At other times we might stray from God, but God will be waiting for us to turn back and offering us mercy, not judgment.

♪ The TEMPO of this song should be in a gentle two but not dragging.

♩ = 80

? *How does the image of "gentleness" affect our vision of God?*

Oh, the love of my Lord

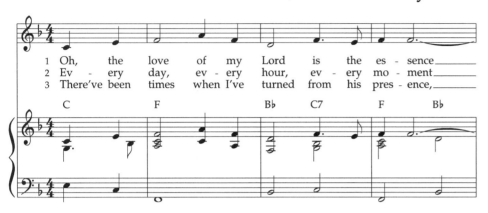

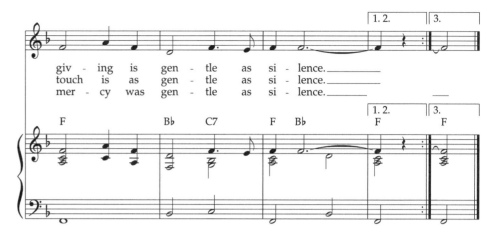

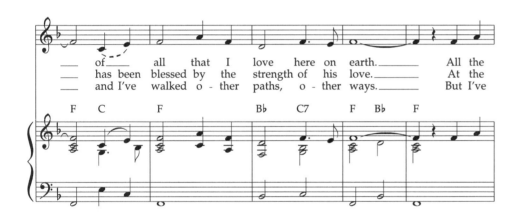

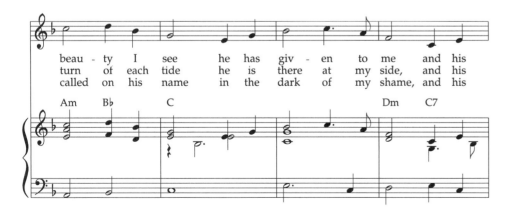

D

♪ A CAPPELLA, piano

✠ Healing services; prayer services

📖 Pentecost; Commissioning for Lay Ministries; Proper 15, Year A; Proper 18, Year B; Sixth Sunday after Epiphany, Year B

🗝 African American church music often relies upon a gifted gospel piano player; however, some songs can be arranged for A CAPPELLA singing, as seen here. The melody may also be sung alone with the harmonies played by a piano. This song has a different approach from the others in this section. It is a passionate plea for God's presence that is vibrant and moving.

There are really two parts to this song: the bass, and the three harmony parts printed on the TREBLE CLEF, which function as one voice. Male singers should be strong and capable of singing with confidence. This song should move forward in a moderate two beats per measure, allowing for its wordiness.

♩ = 72

Repeat the first section, changing the words as suggested, or add your own. The coda (last eight measures) provides a natural cool-down of the excitement of the song. Gradually become softer throughout the first four measures of the coda, and then become gradually louder throughout the last four measures.

? *Do you imagine God as being above — or somewhere else?*

Lord, my soul is thirsting

Additional verses ad libitum:
Lord, my soul is thirsting for a cleansing today.
. . . for your spirit today.
. . . for your healing today.

D

♪ A CAPPELLA, violin, flute, and tambour

✠ Liturgy of the Word

📖 Sixth Sunday of Easter, Year C; Seventh Sunday of Easter, Year C (Revelation); Lent; Season of Epiphany

This text was first collected by Baptist pastor Joshua Smith of New Hampshire in *Divine Hymns or Spiritual Songs*, first published in 1784 and continuing through eleven editions. Although anthem versions of this text are often sung at Christmas, this hymn may be used at any time. The imagery of Christ as an apple tree in this text is very compelling particularly for those who live and work in agricultural areas. Encourage children to draw illustrations for each verse.

This song may be sung unaccompanied or with flute or violin doubling melody. A tambour or other small drum could play

in each measure. For variety, this song may also be sung as a four-part round at a two-measure interval. All parts should alter the next-to-last note from E to G. The final voice may sing the ending as written.

? *Consider all of creation. What else might you see as being like Jesus?*

1 The tree of life my soul hath seen, la-
2 His beau-ty doth all things ex-cel: by
3 For hap-pi-ness I long have sought, and
4 I'm wear-y with my form-er toil, here
5 This fruit doth make my soul to thrive, it

den with fruit and al-ways green. The
faith I know but ne'er___ can tell: the
plea-sure dear-ly I___ have bought: I
I will sit and rest___ a-while: un-
keeps my dy-ing faith___ a-live; which

trees of na-ture fruit-less be, com-
glo-ry which I now___ can see in
missed of all: but now___ I see 'tis
der the shad-ow I___ will be of
makes my soul in haste___ to be with

pared with Christ, the ap - ple tree.
Je-sus Christ, the ap - ple tree.
found in Christ, the ap - ple tree.
Je-sus Christ, the ap - ple tree.
Je-sus Christ, the ap - ple tree.

Words: Anon., from a collection of Joshua Smith, New Hampshire, 1764.
Music: Fiona Vidal-White © Fiona Vidal-White. All rights reserved. Used by permission.

Peace and Justice

The human condition is that we are created in an ideal and normative covenant relation with one another, with nature, and with God, and that this covenant is broken; salvation is the repair of the covenant.
— Robert Cummings Neville, *A Theology Primer*

Then one of the lawyers . . . came forward and asked him, "Which commandment is first of all?" Jesus answered, "The first is, 'Hear, O Israel: the Lord our God is the only Lord; love the Lord your God with all your heart, with all your soul, with all your mind, and with all your strength.' The second is this: 'Love your neighbor as yourself.' There is no other commandment greater than these." (Mark 12:28–31 NEB)

Why is the pursuit of peace and justice an essential part of the Christian life? Because the covenant with God, as described in the passage from Mark above, is not just personal. If God is the Supreme Being, the covenant must encompass every aspect of life. If one tiny part of the covenant is broken, then the whole covenant is broken. Jesus' story of the Good Samaritan, in answer to the question "Who is my neighbor?" makes this clear. My neighbor is not only the person I know, whose concerns I care about. My neighbor is anyone who is in need. We could extrapolate from this that, since humans live in a physical environment and are seriously affected by harm done to the earth, the earth is also "a neighbor in need." If we believe that the covenant must encompass every part of life, we must acknowledge that we have learned, at significant cost, that all aspects of the environment are linked. Treating the earth as something from which we can "take" while giving nothing back does irreparable damage both to the earth and to our covenant with God.

The church has struggled for centuries with the concept of justice, often failing as an institution to grasp it as an issue of our communal existence. It has been left to one or more inspired individuals to act as prophets. Dr. Martin Luther King Jr., for example, summed up the idea of the interrelation of all life in a passage from his letter from Birmingham Jail:

Moreover, I am cognizant of the interrelatedness of all communities and states. I cannot sit idly by in Atlanta and not be concerned about what happens in Birmingham. Injustice anywhere is a threat to justice everywhere. We are caught in an inescapable network of mutuality, tied in a single garment of destiny. Whatever affects one directly, affects all indirectly.

Being on the side of justice is often difficult. It takes courage and the willpower to constantly reexamine motives in light of Christian beliefs. As people committed to doing the will of God, Christians evaluate their actions because they participate in bringing the kingdom of God to earth.

War is the most dramatic destroyer of the fabric of covenant. Those who declare war mark their neighbors as the enemy, denying that they are human and that their lives have value. Hatred and killing are sins that bring destruction of every kind: environmental, physical, communal, familial. Longing for peace is a Christian state of mind. Striving for peace in a nonviolent way, even as war continues, Christians vow to love even those who are engaged in war.

Hatred and greed are learned responses. Children and youth may not have learned to combat these evils and need the church to be actively engaged in such issues. The songs in this section, if used regularly, will help with the Christian formation of children and youth and give them a voice for peace and justice, about which they care deeply.

Peace among earth's peoples

D

Piano, organ

Prayer services; meditation; Liturgy of the Word

The Epiphany; Advent, especially First Sunday of Advent, Year A; Third Sunday of Easter, Year B (Micah); For Peace; Lent

This prayer for peace also issues a call to repent of all that contributes to conflict: "flaunting lawless powers," "greed," "covetously plotting," "lust." Teaching older children about these evils can be related to them through the phrase "Wars are caused by wanting what is not ours" (v. 2). The tenth commandment is "You shall not covet anything that belongs to your neighbor" (see The Book of Common Prayer, Decalogue II, p. 350).

Complex themes in this text are musically set to this PENTATONIC simple tune that is also simple in form — AA2BA2. Include this hymn as the centerpiece in an informal liturgy for peace, singing a verse at a time throughout the service.

? *Have you ever longed for something that someone else had? How do we do this on a national or global scale?*

1 Peace a-mong earth's peo - ples___ is like a star
2 Wars are caused by want - ing___ what is not ours.
3 Cov-et-ous-ly plot - ting,___ we do not pray,
4 From our war-ring sens - es___ we seek re - lease!
5 Peace a-mong earth's peo - ples___ is like that star

beam-ing just a - bove us,___ so near, so far.
Why must we keep flaunt - ing___ our law - less powers?
ask - ing our Pro - vid - er___ to light our way.
then all earth - ly con - flicts___ might al - so cease.
lead - ing to a man - ger,___ so near, so far.

Though out of grasp, we long to clasp it:
We act in lust rath - er than trust that
Is it not greed rath - er than need that
Can we not share one com - mon prayer with
Some saw the light; some were in fright, but

peace a - mong earth's peo - ples,___ so near, so far.
God who an - swers want - ing___ will an - swer ours.
tempts us in - to plot - ting___ when we should pray.
all of this earth's peo - ples___ to know world peace?
all for peace were long - ing,___ just as we are.

👥 C, D

🎵 Piano, organ, guitar

✠ Prayer services; meditation

📖 The Epiphany; Advent, especially First Sunday of Advent, Year A; Third Sunday of Easter, Year B (Micah); For Peace; Lent

This is the oldest "new" hymn in this collection, dating from 1955. Its theme, however, has never been more appropriate. The essential message, "Let there be peace on earth and let it begin with me," is one of commitment and empowerment. Carefully select the time this song is to be used. The surrounding liturgy should evoke a deep fervor from the singers because without it the song becomes a sentimental popular song from a different era.

Because this hymn mentions God only, it might be appropriate for interfaith gatherings.

Rather than emphasize the swinging, waltz rhythm of the 3/4 meter, feel this song in six-beat "measures" with the strong pulse on every other three-beat measure. The musical indications for repeats and adding the coda at the end can make this hymn difficult to follow for some. There are essentially three verses and then the ending (coda). This may be described as follows:

Verse 1   "Let there be peace on earth" through to "meant to be"

Verse 2   "With God" to "perfect harmony" (then return to beginning)

Verse 3   "Let peace begin with me" to solemn vow"

Ending   "to take each moment" to end.

Ideally, the song could be memorized. Smaller children can participate by learning the phrase "With God as creator"...to "...harmony," and the last line, "let there be peace on earth...begin with me."

❓ *"Let there be peace on earth and let it begin with me." What does this inspire you to do?*

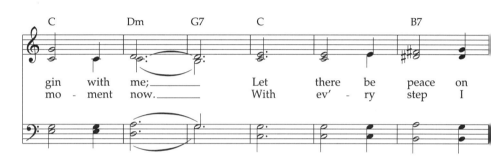

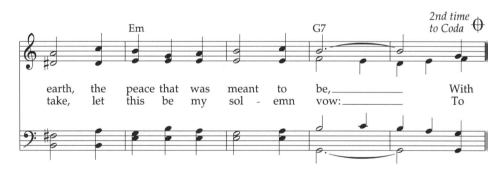

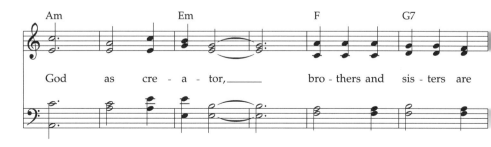

Peace before us

All

Piano, guitar, or A CAPPELLA

Sung prayer with or without petitions; prayer at home before a new challenge; closing of a retreat or camp; meditation

The Epiphany; Advent, especially First Sunday of Advent, Year A; Third Sunday of Easter, Year B (Micah); For Peace; Lent; Burial

This beautiful song is suited to many situations. It can be a gentle sung prayer, a prayer of healing after disaster, a prayer for protection before a challenge, or a simple children's song. Gestures could be added indicating each direction. This also helps in remembering the words in order. A single verse could be sung standing in a circle with hands held in the ORANS position. Ask children to choose a first word for each verse.

This piece could be arranged for two cellos on bass clef parts and a flute on top treble line of the introduction and interlude between verses. Make sure that the "ee" vowel of the word "peace" is the sustaining sound (avoid sssssss's)

What does it feel like to have peace, love, light, and Christ all around?

Peace before us

peace   o - ver us, let all a - round us be   peace._____
love   o - ver us, let all a - round us be   love._____
light   o - ver us, let all a - round us be   light._____
Christ o - ver us, let all a - round us be   Christ._____

1 Peace be - fore us,   peace be - hind us,
2 Love be - fore us,   love be - hind us,
3 Light be - fore us,   light be - hind us,
4 Christ be - fore us,   Christ be - hind us,

peace   un - der our feet._____   Peace with - in us,
love   un - der our feet._____   Love with - in us,
light   un - der our feet._____   Light with - in us,
Christ un - der our feet._____   Christ with - in us,

peace._____   6 Let all a - round us be   peace._____

5 Alleluia, alleluia, alleluia.
  Alleluia, alleluia, alleluia.

6 Peace before us, peace behind us,
  peace under our feet.
  Peace within us, peace over us,
  let all around us be peace. *(three times)*

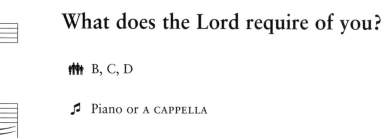

🚶 B, C, D

🎵 Piano or A CAPPELLA

✠ Prayer services; Liturgy of the Word

📖 Fourth Sunday after Epiphany, Year A; For Social Justice; Baptism; Rites of Passage; Ordination; Commissioning for Lay Ministries

☍ Micah 6:6–8 is the basis for this hymn text. Micah, along with Amos, Hosea, and Isaiah, is one of the key Hebrew scriptures about righteous living. In the beginning of the text, the prophet wonders what action, what gift should be given to God. Verse 8 is a simple and succinct list of all that is required of those who profess belief.

♪ Children will find the top line, the first part, of this song the easiest with its descending stepwise movement through the B♭ major scale. Parts two and three may be added once this is learned. The song may be sung by separate groups on each part or by the entire congregation progressing through each part as in a round. Each part may be sung in any octave. Remember that variety is important. A part may be hummed, shaped dynamically from soft to moderately loud to soft again, or omitted for one cycle.

? *Which of these three requirements is most meaningful to you? Why?*

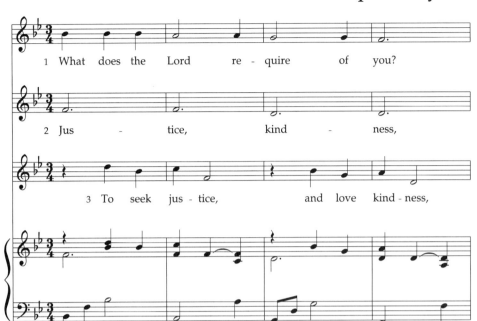

1 What does the Lord re-quire of you?

2 Jus - tice, kind - ness,

3 To seek jus - tice, and love kind - ness,

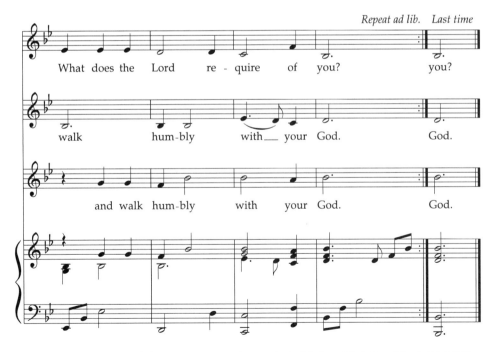

Repeat ad lib. Last time

What does the Lord re-quire of you? you?

walk hum-bly with_ your God. God.

and walk hum-bly with your God. God.

C, C*, D

♪ Piano, guitar, trumpets, percussion

✠ Multicultural liturgies; hymn of praise; in place of "Holy, holy, holy Lord" (see below)

📖 For Social Justice; anytime

In contemporary usage in Latin American countries the service music for the liturgy captures more the essence of the traditional text rather than adhering to a proscribed set of words. This text is a Sanctus (Holy, holy, holy Lord) and comes from *La Misa Popular Salvadoreña,* a Mass setting using local folk tunes commissioned from Salvadoran composer Guillermo Cuéllar by Archbishop Oscar Romero. Romero was assassinated in 1980 as he celebrated the Eucharist. The Sanctus echoes the liberation theology that developed in the crucible of Roman Catholic Latin America during and after Vatican II. It holds that the gospel calls us to free people from political, social, and economic oppression.

The Sanctus text is made contemporary and relevant to its singers by using traditional musical idioms and including references to a God "who lives with us in our struggles" and the "good news of God's salvation and liberating hope." It is included in the Peace and Justice section of this collection because of the text of the verses. It is important for Anglos who sing this to understand that, as "First World" oppressors, one sings it to stand in solidarity with those who are oppressed and to work for their liberation.

Although notated throughout in 3/4 this Latin American rhythm alternates between the feel of 6/8 and 3/4. Throughout it is the bass line, firmly in 3/4, that holds the polyrhythm together. Above all this is dance music. Children enjoy learning the "math equation" for this:

Keeping the eighth note constant, helps singers feel the contrast between the "lazy swinging" two of 6/8 moving immediately to the "busy striding" three of the 3/4. Conducting beat patterns of two alternating with three will help to illustrate. For a challenge try walking while stamping your feet for the first beat of each group and clapping for the weaker beats.

Salvadoran music is influenced by the music of Africa, Cuba, and Mexico and by its early history of military bands. Two trumpets could play the introduction in thirds (top two notes) moving to sixths on the last two measures. Various hand percussion instruments could also be added throughout—shakers, a GUIRO, hand drum, and CLAVES. If the piano is used it could play percussive patterns in the chords indicated that heighten the rhythm described above rather than the printed notation.

Pronunciation

Refrain

San - to, san - to es   nues - tro Dios,
Sahn – toh, sahn – twehs   nwehs - troh Dyohs,

Se - ñor de to - da la tie - rra,
Seh – nyor deh toh - dah lah teeEH – rrah,

Se - ñor de to - da la his - to - ria
Seh- nyor, deh toh - dah lice - to - reeAH.

? *What stories do you know about Jesus paying attention to poor people?*

154 ♩ = 108–120

Santo *Holy*

Fine

Estribillo / Refrain

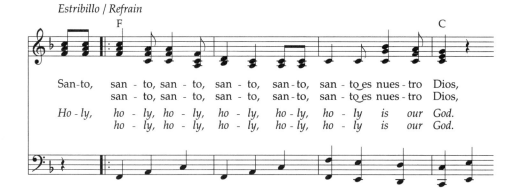

San-to, san-to, san-to, san-to, san-to, san-to es nues-tro Dios,
san-to, san-to, san-to, san-to, san-to es nues-tro Dios,
Ho-ly, ho-ly, ho-ly, ho-ly, ho-ly, ho-ly is our God.
ho-ly, ho-ly, ho-ly, ho-ly, ho-ly is our God.

Se-ñor de to-da la tie-rra, san-to, san-to es nues-tro
Se-ñor de to-da la his-to-ria, san-to, san-to es nues-tro
You are Lord of all the na-tions, ho-ly, ho-ly is our
You are Lord of all of his-t'ry, ho-ly, ho-ly is our

Estrofas / Verses

Dios.   San-to,   Dios.   Que a-com-pa-ña a nues-tro
God.   *Ho-ly,   God.*   Ben-di-tos los que en su
                     The Com-pan-ion of our
                     Bless-ed be those who in

pue-blo,   que   vi-ve en nues-tras lu-chas; del
nom-bre   el   e-van-ge-lio a-nun-cian, la
peo-ple   who   lives with us in strug-gles; Cre-
God's name   de-clare the right-eous Gos-pel, good

u-ni-ver-so en-te-ro   el   ú-ni-co Se-ñor.
bue-na y gran no-ti-cia   de   la li-be-ra   -ción.
a-tor of the cos-mos,   the   on-ly Son of God.
news of God's sal-va-tion   and   lib-er-at-ing   hope.

to the
beginning

Words: Guillermo Cuéllar, tr. C. Michael Hawn.
Music: Guillermo Cuéllar, arr. Raquel Mora Martinez © 1988 GIA Publications, Inc., 7404 S. Mason
Ave., Chicago, IL 60638 [www.giamusic.com]. All rights reserved. Used by permission.
You must contact GIA Publications to reproduce this selection.

Come now, you blessed

D

♪ Piano, guitar, cello

✠ Liturgy of the Word; meditation for organizational meetings

📖 Proper 29, Year A; For the Mission of the Church; For Social Service

In Matthew 25:31–46 Jesus describes the Last Judgment, when the Son of Man comes into the kingdom of God and separates the sheep from the goats. He then goes on to explain that whenever we help another, we are helping him. This hymn recounts that text and ends with a prayer that helps the singers voice the desire that they will recognize Christ in "the faces of need" responding with love "in word and in deed."

To heighten the dialogue between Jesus and his followers in the first three verses, assign different groups, such as choir and congregation, each of the roles. All should sing the final verse. The accompaniment is very simple and could be played by a young musician on piano with the bass line doubled by a cello.

? *What can we do that will help us recognize "the faces of need?"*

1 "Come now, you bless-ed, eat at my ta-ble,"
2 When did we see you hun-gry or thirs-ty?
3 "When you gave bread to the earth's hun-gry chil-dren,
4 Christ, when we see you out on life's road-ways,

said Je-sus Christ to the right-eous a-bove.
When were you home-less, a strang-er a-lone?
when you gave shel-ter to war's ref-u-gees.
look-ing to us in the fac-es of need,

"When I was hun-gry, thirs-ty, and home-less,
When did we see you sick or in pris-on?
When you re-mem-bered those most for-got-ten,
then may we know you, wel-come and show you

sick and in pris-on, you showed me your love."
What have we done that you call us your own?
you cared for me in the small-est of these."
love that is faith-ful in word and in deed.

At Home

Even the very best Christian education program is but a small part of a child's Christian formation. It is the parents who see how children absorb what they learn in church, and how they put it to use. The parents must teach children how to rely on their formation to make faithful decisions as they interact with others away from home and church. It is therefore essential that parents be co-teachers with church leaders in their children's religious training. Christian belief is not an academic subject, but a practical one. The initial steps in the spiritual journey are taken by first learning how to love siblings long before learning how to love a "Samaritan neighbor," and by visiting a lonely next-door neighbor before fully understanding the baptismal covenant.

Encourage parents to use songs, especially in this section, to create rituals in the home such as prayer before meals and bedtime; blessings; preparation for important events; petitions for healing and protection; and service to others. What is learned in church has no meaning unless it has value outside church.

👫 D

🎵 A CAPPELLA

✠ Offertory; at the Breaking of the Bread; blessing over food

📖 Maundy Thursday; For Social Justice; For the Mission of the Church

🗝 In response to the Devil's first temptation in the wilderness, Jesus quotes Deuteronomy 8:3: "Man cannot live on bread alone; he lives on every word that God utters" (see Matt. 4:4, Luke 4:4).

This song from Argentina brings a social conscience to our grace over food. We ask God to bless our bread, to feed the hungry with bread, and to give the well-fed a hunger for justice. If we are God's people, we must be called to action when we are able to eat enough while others have too little.

🎼 This gentle prayer is perhaps best sung unaccompanied in harmony but is also effective in unison and accompanied by piano. The first phrase may be sung by a cantor. The English translation could be sung by slightly changing the rhythms and being sensitive to word accents.

Pronunciation

Ben - di - ce, Se - ñor, nues - tro pan,
Behn - dee - seh, Seh - nyor, nwehs – troh pahn,

y da pan a los que tien - en ham - bre
ee dah pahn ah lohs keh teeEHN – ehn ahm - breh

y ham - bre de jus - ti cia a los que tien - en pan.
yahm - breh deh yoos – tee seeAH lohs keh teeEHN – ehn pahn.

Ben - di - ce, Se - ñor, nues - tro pan,
Behn - dee - seh, Seh - nyor, nwehs – troh pahn,

❓ *Why do people need both bread and justice?*

Ben - di - ce, Se-ñor, nues-tro pan,   y da pan a los que tien - en

ham - bre   y ham-bre de jus - ti - cia a los que tien - en

pan.   Ben - di - ce, Se - ñor, nues - tro pan.

Translation
May the blessing of God be on our bread and
give bread to those who are hungry;
and a hunger for justice to those who are fed.

Oh, come, Lord Jesus

B, C, D

A CAPPELLA, piano, or guitar

Blessing over food at home, for potluck suppers, or at camp

The tune used for this table grace is generally known as the Tallis Canon and
is most widely associated with the evening text by Bishop Ken, "All praise
to thee, my God, this night." Tallis was a composer of church music in the
sixteenth century who served four different English monarchs. The simplicity
of the melody and the possibility of singing it in CANON have assured its place
in the sacred music of many centuries.

The melody moves entirely in quarter notes and should be felt in a stately two
beats per measure. The tune may be sung in canon by as many as eight parts
with each consecutive voice entering at the interval marked by the number two.
The parts written in this harmonization are simple and could be learned easily
by a high school choir. The tenor voice is in canon with the soprano, and the
bass and alto move together rhythmically.

? *What would you do if Jesus came as a guest to your house?*

Oh, come, Lord Jesus

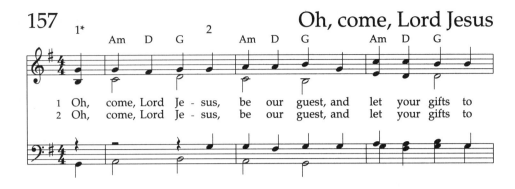

1 Oh, come, Lord Je - sus, be our guest, and let your gifts to
2 Oh, come, Lord Je - sus, be our guest, and let your gifts to

us be blest. Oh, may there be a good - ly share on
us be blest. Come deep with - in our hearts to dwell, that

ev - 'ry ta - ble ev - 'ry - where._____
we may all your good - ness tell._____

* May be sung as a round.

All night, all day

B, C, D

A CAPPELLA, guitar, or piano

Prayer at bedtime at home, retreat, or camp.

This well-known spiritual is perfect for children's evening prayers. Children often believe in "monsters under the bed." Counter them by singing about the presence of protecting angels. The sentiment is similar to the traditional children's prayer:

> Matthew, Mark, Luke, and John,
> Guard the bed I lie upon.
> Four pillars round my bed;
> Four angels round my head.
>
> One to watch, one to pray,
> And two to keep me till the day. Amen.

It is common practice in African American hymnody to alter the rhythm while singing rather than to adhere strictly to the printed pattern. For example, the even eighth-note rhythms, as in the third measure, would be changed to a swinging dotted eighth and sixteenth pattern. Also, "me, my Lord." is usually sung with an eighth and dotted quarter substituted for the first two quarter notes. For variety alternate a song leader and children on each phrase with the leader singing the first two measures and the children responding "...angels watching over me, my Lord" each time.

? *Can you draw a picture of angels watching over you to put on your bedroom wall?*

All night, all day

All__ night, all__ day, an-gels watch-ing o-ver me, my Lord.

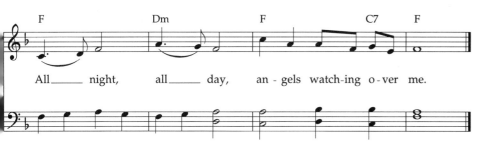

All__ night, all__ day, an - gels watch-ing o-ver me.

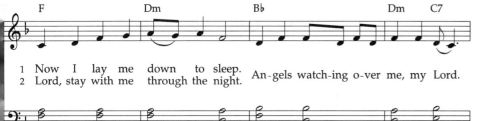

1 Now I lay me down to sleep. An-gels watch-ing o-ver me, my Lord.
2 Lord, stay with me through the night.

Repeat refrain

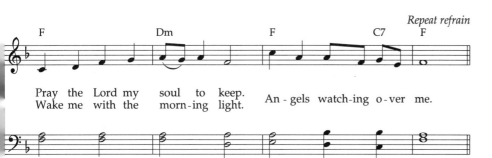

Pray the Lord my soul to keep. An - gels watch-ing o-ver me.
Wake me with the morn-ing light.

C, D

♪ A CAPPELLA, piano, guitar

✠ Evening Prayer; evening meetings; retreats

This is a bedtime song for adults. Like the grace "Bendice, Señor, nuestro pan" (#156), it moves beyond prayer for ourselves to thinking about the needs of others. Mundane events ("lights of the city," "little ones sleeping," "food on the table") become the biddings that prompt an awareness of Christ's presence. The final verse sets this prayer in the context of an evening parish meeting and would be appropriate before a vestry or committee meeting, a youth group gathering, or an educational program. Older children will find this a meaningful song at home or at camp.

David Haas has written a compact tune within the span of an octave (D to D) around the key note G. The first half of the melody is marked by ascending three-quarter-note patterns and the second half by descending three-quarter-note patterns. The rocking bass clef accompaniment is a quiet and comforting sound that could be duplicated by a guitar player finger-picking the pattern rather than using a strum.

? *Why should we reflect on others as we finish our day?*

Now it is evening

1 Now it is eve - ning: lights of the cit - y
2 Now it is eve - ning: lit - tle ones sleep - ing
3 Now it is eve - ning: food on the ta - ble
4 Now it is eve - ning: here in our meet - ing

bid us re - mem - ber Christ is our Light.
bid us re - mem - ber Christ is our Peace.
bids us re - mem - ber Christ is our Life.
may we re - mem - ber Christ is our Friend.

Man - y are lone - ly, who will be neigh-bor?
Some are ne - glect - ed, who will be neigh-bor?
Man - y are hun - gry, who will be neigh bor?
Some may be stran - gers, who will be neigh-bor?

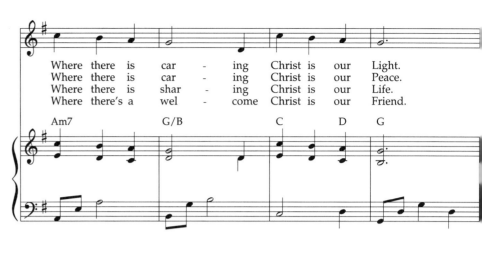

Where there is car - ing Christ is our Light.
Where there is car - ing Christ is our Peace.
Where there is shar - ing Christ is our Life.
Where there's a wel - come Christ is our Friend.

Copyright Information

Acknowledgment

Every effort has been made to determine the owner and/or administrator of copyrighted material in this book and to obtain the necessary permission. After being given written notice the publisher will make the necessary correction(s) in subsequent printings.

Permission

The publisher gratefully acknowledges all copyright holders who have permitted the reproduction of their materials in this book. We especially thank those who have consented to allow Church Publishing to issue one-time, not-for-profit use free of charge. You must contact Church Publishing in writing to obtain this permission (see phone, fax, e-mail and web below). Certain selections will note those copyright holder(s) who require that you contact them directly to obtain permission to reprint their materials.

For extended or for-profit use of copyrighted materials in this book, you must write directly to the copyright holder(s). Contact Church Publishing for information. Phone: 1-800-223-6602; Fax: 1-212-779-3392; e-mail: copyrights@cpg.org; web: www.churchpublishing.org; Mailing: 445 Fifth Avenue; New York NY 10016.

Many copyright holders now use a licensing agency and if they have they will send you to the agency for reprint permissions. Here are the addresses of two popular licensing agencies:

OneLicense.net
7343 S. Mason Avenue
Chicago IL 60638
1-800-663-1501
1-708-458-5900
Fax 1-708-458-4940
www.onelicense.net

Christian Copyright Licensing Int'l.
17201 NE Sacramento Street
Portland OR 97230
1-800-234-2446
1-503-257-2230
Fax 1-503-257-2244
www.ccli.com

Abingdon Press – see *T.C.C.*

Amity Music Corp.
1475 Gaylord Terr.
Teaneck, NJ 07666
201-833-4808
(F) 201-833-4808

Augsburg Fortress
PO Box 1209
Minneapolis, MN 55440-1209
www.augsburgfortress.org
800-421-0239
(f) 800-722-7766

Birdwing Music(ASCAP) – see *E.M.I.*

Boosey & Hawkes, Inc.
35 E. 21st St.
New York, NY 10010
www.boosey.com
212-358-5350

Brummhart Publishing Co.
1708 Blooming Grove Dr.
Rensselaer, NY 12144
www.hometown.aol.com/khbising2
518-286-1837

Bud John Songs – see *EMI*

Celebration
PO Box 309
Aliquippa, PA 15001
www.communityofcelebration.com
724-375-1510
(f) 724-375-1138

Choristers Guild
2834 West Kingsley Rd.
Garland, TX 75041-2498
www.choristersguild.or
972-271-1521
(f) 972-840-3113

Christian Conference of Asia
96 Pak Tin Village Area 2
Mei Tin Road, Shatin NT
Hong Kong SAR, CHINA
www.cca.org.hk/info/infoframe.htm

Church of Scotland, The – see *Oxford*

Concordia Publishing House
3558 S. Jefferson Ave.
St. Louis, MO 63118-3968
www.cph.org
314-268-1000

Copyright Company, The – see *T.C.C.*

CRC Publications
2850 Kalamazoo Ave. SE
Grand Rapids, MI 49560
www.crcpublications.org
616-224-0819

Desert Flower Music
PO Box 1476
Carmichael, CA 95809
www.strathdee_music.com

E.M.I. Christian Music Publishing
PO Box 5085
Brentwood, TN 37024-5085

GIA Publications, Inc.
7404 S. Mason Ave.
Chicago, IL 60638
www.giamusic.com
800-442-1358 x 56
(f) 708-496-3828

Hal Leonard Corp.
PO Box 13819
Milwaukee, WI 53213
www.halleonard.com

Harvestcross Productions
258 School La.
Springfield, PA 19064

Hinshaw Music, Inc.
PO Box 470
Chapel Hill, NC 27514
www.hinshawmusic.com
919-933-1691
919-967-3399

Hope Publishing Co.
380 S. Main Pl.
Carol Stream, IL 60188
www.hopepublishing.com
800-323-1049
(f) 630-665-2552

Hymn Society, The – see Hope

Integrity Music
1000 Cody Rd.
Mobile, AL 36695
www.integritymusic.com
800-533-6912

Iona Community (Scotland) – see GIA

Jann-Lee Music – see MCCG

Jenkins, W. L. – see Westminster John Knox Press

Licensing Associates
935 Broad St. #31
Bloomfield, NJ 07003
www.waltonmusic.com
919-929-1330
(f) 919-929-2232

Lumko Institute, The
PO Box 5058
Delmenville, South Africa
www.catholic-johannesburg.org.za

Malaco Music Group
PO Box 9287
Jackson, MS 29386
www.malaco.com
601-982-4522
(f) 601-982-4528

Malted Milk Music
575 Riverside Dr. #51
New York, NY 10031-8545
212-368-7117

Mayhew, Ltd., Kevin
Buxhall, Stowmarket
Suffolk IP14 3BW, UK
www.kevinmayhew.com
01-449-737-978
01-449-737-834

Methodist Church (UK) – see Hope Publishing Co.

MCCG
145 Attorney St.
New York, NY 10002
212-473-6702
(f) 212-473-6708

OCP Publications (Oregon Catholic Press)
5536 NE Hassalo
Portland, OR 97213
www.ocp.org
800-548-8749
(f) 800-462-7329

Oxford University Press
198 Madison Ave.
New York, NY 10016-4314
www.oup.com/us
212-726-6000

Pilgrim Press, The
700 Prospect Ave.
Cleveland, OH 44115-1100
www.thepilgrimpress.com
800-537-3394

Presses de Taizé (France) – see GIA Publications, Inc.

Resource Publications, Inc.
160 E. Virginia St. #290
San Jose, CA 95112-5876
www.rpinet.com
408-286-8505
(f) 408-287-8748

Savgos Music – see Malaco

Scripture in Song – see Integrity Music

Selah Publishing Co.
4143 Brownsville Rd., Suite 2
Pittsburgh, PA 15227-3306
www.selahpub.com
800-852-6172
(f) 412-886-1022

Stainer & Bell Ltd. – see Hope

Taizé (France), Presses de – see GIA

T.C.C. – The Copyright Co.
1026 16th Ave. South
Nashville, TN 37212
www.thecopyrightco.com
615-321-1096

United Church Press
Cleveland, OH
www.unitedchurchpress.com

United Methodist Publishing House
see T.C.C. – The Copyright Co.

Walton Music – see Licensing Associates

Westminster John Knox Press
100 Witherspoon St.
Louisville, KY 40202-1396
www.ppcbooks.com
800-227-2872
(f) 800-541-5113

WGRG (Wild Goose Resource Group) – see GIA Publications, Inc.

Word of God Music – see T.C.C.

World Council of Churches
475 Riverside Dr.
New York, NY 10027

World Library Publications, Inc.
3708 River Rd.
Franklin Park, IL 60131-2158
www.wlpmusic.com
800-566-6150
(f) 888-957-3291

Glossary

A cappella: unaccompanied

Antiphonal: sung by two groups answering responsively

Bodhran: Irish hand drum played with a small stick called a tipper

Call and response: a style of singing in which a leader sings a phrase and the singers repeat it

Canon: a song that may be sung simultaneously by additional voices entering at fixed intervals of pitch and time after the first

Canticle: a non-metrical song usually found in scripture and appointed to be sung at church services

Cantor: a leader of song who teaches and nurtures the community's song

Chromatic: a melody or harmony part that is characterized by many half-steps or semi-tones

Claves: two wooden sticks about an inch in diameter made of resonant wood and struck together

Crescendo: becoming gradually louder

Diatonic: based on the seven tones of five whole steps and two half steps of the major or minor scales of Western music

Diminuendo: becoming gradually softer

Dominant: the fifth degree or pitch in a DIATONIC scale, or the chord built on that pitch. The pitch G is the dominant of the C major scale.

Fermata: a musical mark (a dot inside a half circle) above or below a note that means to hold it longer than its normal length; sometimes called a "bird's eye" because of its appearance

Guiro: an oblong, hollow wooden instrument with ridges that is scraped with a metal comb or wooden stick

Homophonic: a single melodic line accompanied by harmony parts moving in the same or similar rhythm

Key signature: the sign following the clef on a musical staff that indicates the tonal center of the music; may consist of either sharps or flats

Legato: smooth, flowing

Mantra: a brief repeated phrase or song used in prayer to free the rational mind for prayer and discernment

Marcato: marked, accented

Melisma: several pitches sung to one syllable or word

Metallophone: a musical instrument consisting of a hollow wooden box with tuned metal bars laid across the top that are struck by padded mallets

Meter: the numeric indication on hymns that describes the number of syllables in each poetic phrase; 8.7.8.7 means that there are eight syllables in the first phrase, seven in the second, eight in the third, and seven in the fourth

NEB: the New English Bible version of the scriptures

NRSV: the New Revised Standard Version of the scriptures

Orans position: an ancient and traditional posture of prayer, the worshiper standing with arms outstretched and palms uplifted

Ordinary: the parts of the liturgy that are unchanged from day to day, such as the Lord, have mercy; Glory to God; Holy, holy, holy Lord; and the Lamb of God

Orff instruments: various kinds of percussive instruments used by the German composer and educator Carl Orff, for the purpose of teaching children

Ostinato: a repeated musical phrase that is sung or played simultaneously with a more complex primary part

Paraphrase: a rendition of a phrase or text in words other than the original, often for the purpose of clarity

Pentatonic scale: consisting of five pitches only; the five black keys in one octave on the piano keyboard constitute a pentatonic scale

Piano: soft

Pizzicato: the technique of plucking the strings of a violin or other stringed instrument

Propers: the appointed parts of the Eucharist that vary according to the lectionary date, such as the collect, psalm, readings, and preface

Question and answer: consecutive musical phrases that constitute a complete musical sentence; a question phrase does not sound complete unless followed by an answer phrase, which often returns to the home key pitch (see #32 "Lord, I pray": the question phrase ends in measure four, the answer phrase completes the song)

Rallentando: becoming gradually slower

Repeat sign: a double bar line preceded (or followed) by two dots in the middle of the staff

Rote: learning music by repetition without the aid of printed music

RSV: the Revised Standard Version of the scriptures

Rubric: liturgical directions concerning the conduct of worship, originally printed in red (from the Latin, *ruber*), but now usually in italics or a contrasting typeface

Sanctuary: the area of the church building that includes the altar. In some non-liturgical churches the sanctuary is the entire worship space.

Sequence: a melodic phrase immediately repeated exactly but beginning on a different pitch

Slurred: musical notes of different pitch connected by a curved line, which means to move from one note to the next without articulating the beginning of subsequent note

Solfeggio: a system of reading pitch based on the use of syllables such as do, re, mi, fa, sol, la, ti, do

Staccato: short, separated; usually indicated by a dot above or below a note

Strophic: music that consists of several verses set to the same music, such as a hymn

Subdominant: the fourth degree or pitch in a DIATONIC scale, or the chord built on that pitch. The pitch F is the subdominant of the C major scale.

Syncopation: in music, the shifting of the natural accents on certain notes to normally unaccented notes. In 4/4 time the natural accents fall on beats one and three; syncopation might shift them to beat one and a half and to beat four.

Taizé: an ecumenical community of prayer in eastern France that popularized a style of short, repeated phrases of music originally in Latin to accommodate singing by the groups of international students making pilgrimage to the community. www.taize.fr.

Tempo: the speed of the underlying pulse of the music

Three-against-two: three even notes to be played or sung in the space of two primary pulses or beats

Through-composed: having a different melody for each verse so that one sings continuously through several verses rather than returning to the beginning for each verse as in a hymn

Timbre: the unique quality of a sound that distinguishes it from another; a flute has a different timbre from a clarinet

Tonic: the first degree or pitch in a DIATONIC scale, or the chord based on that pitch. The pitch C is the tonic of the C major scale.

Treble clef: often called the "G" clef; establishes the names of the five lines and four spaces on the musical staff from A through G; E is the name of the first line at the bottom; the first space is F; the second line is G; the second space is A; and so on

Index of Authors, Translators, and Sources

Index of Composers, Arrangers, and Sources

Accompaniment Index

Unaccompanied

*(Selections marked with * have a harmony part. All others are unison.)*

Gentle Jesus, risen Lord, 51
Gloria, gloria, gloria, 64
Glory to God, 5
Glory to God, 6
God ever-faithful, 29
God is here today, 4
God it was, 85
God of the sparrow God of the whale, 129
God the sculptor of the mountains, 130
God, when I came into this life, 123
Grant me a blessing, 148
Great work has God begun in you, 124
Here I Am, Lord, 77
His love is everlasting, 24
Holy, 154
Holy God, 17
Holy, holy, holy, 38
Holy, holy, holy Lord, 40
I am the church, 109
I say "Yes," Lord, 106
I thank you, Jesus, 10
I want Jesus to walk with me, 87
I will praise your name, 25
I, the Lord of sea and sky, 77
If you love me, 83
In love you summon, 125
In the bulb there is a flower, 86
In the night, in the day, 116
It rained on the earth forty days, 97
Jesus our brother, kind and good, 65
Jesus said, I am the door, 88
Let there be peace on earth, 151
Let us now depart in your peace, 53
Let us talents and tongues employ, 50
Longing for light, 59
Look up! 73
Lord, I pray, 32
Lord, my soul is thirsting, 148
Los magos que llegaron a Belén, 71
Loving Creator, 115
Loving Spirit, 111
May the God of hope, 54
May the Lord bless us, 56

May your loving spirit, 112
Mothering God, 142
My heart sings out with joyful praise, 60
Now it is evening, 159
O sing unto the Lord, 134
Oh, come, Lord Jesus, 157
Oh, how good is Christ the Lord, 103
Oh, qué bueno es Jesús, 103
Oh, the love of my Lord, 147
One more step along the world I go, 127
One ohana, 131
One, two, three, Jesus loves me, 144
Our Father in heaven, 42
Pan de Vida, 93
Peace among earth's peoples, 150
Peace before us, 152
Praise God for this holy ground, 135
Praise to God, 132
Praise to the Trinity, 116
Prepare ye the way, 63
Santo, 154
She sits like a bird, 110
Sing our God together, 101
Sing, O people, 101
Sleep, sleep, gently sleep, 66
Soplo de Dios viviente, 107
Stay awake, be ready, 62
Take, O take me as I am, 46
Taste and see, 136
Thank you for the gift of Jesus, 139
That Easter morn, 99
The light of Christ, 80
The magi who to Bethlehem did go, 71
The Servant Song, 94
The Virgin Mary had a baby boy, 67
To the God who cannot die, 106
We are a part of all creation, 131
We are all children of the Lord, 105
We are on our way, 96
We bring our children, 121
We see the Lord, 114
We sing of the saints, 118

We thank God, 137
We will lay our burden down, 78
What does it mean to follow Jesus? 89
What does the Lord require of you? 153
When Did We See You, 155
When in our music God is glorified, 140
Who are these eastern strangers? 72
You are my shepherd, 104
You are our God, 97
You have put on Christ, 122
Your word, 81

Steel drums

Halle, halle, hallelujah! 18
Let us talents and tongues employ, 50

Strings

All who hunger gather gladly, 52
Amen, amen, it shall be so! 74
Blest are the poor in spirit, 74
Cantemos al Señor, 134
Come now, O Prince of Peace, 82
Come now, you blessed, 155
Dios está aquí, 4
Forty days and forty nights, 84
Gloria, gloria, gloria, 64

Glory to God, 6
Glory to God, 7
God is here today, 4
God the sculptor of the mountains, 130
God, when I came into this life, 123
Holy, holy, holy Lord, 36
Holy, holy, holy Lord, 37
I am the world's true light, 75
Jesus Christ the apple tree, 149
Listen, my friends, 68
My heart sings out with joyful praise, 60
O sing unto the Lord, 134
Praise to God, 132
Prepare ye the way, 63
The tree of life, 149
We bring our children, 121
When Did We See You, 155
Yo soy la luz del mundo, 75
You have put on Christ, 122

Trumpet

Holy, 154
I am the world's true light, 75
Santo, 154
The King of glory comes, 90
Yo soy la luz del mundo, 75

Age Level Index

Harmony Index

Challenging rounds

I am the world's true light, 75
What does the Lord require of you? 153
Yo soy la luz del mundo, 75

Simple harmony parts

Allelu, alleluia, 21
Amen, amen, it shall be so! 74
Amen, siyakudumisa, 34
Amen, we praise your name, 34
Blest are the poor in spirit, 74
Come all you people, 2
Gloria, 11
Glory to God, 11
Grant me a Blessing, 148
Halle, halle, hallelujah! 18
Hallelujah, 19
Heaven and earth, 133
Holy, 154
Holy, holy, holy God, 16
I thank you, Jesus, 10
I want Jesus to walk with me, 87
Know that God is good, 31
Kyrie eleison, 15
Kyrie eleison, 30
Lord, in your mercy, 23
Lord, my soul is thirsting, 148
Loving Creator, 115
Mungu ni mwema, 31
O bless the Lord, 28
'Sanna, 91

Santo, 154
Send me, Lord, 35
Thuma mina, 35
Uyai mose, 2
What does the Lord require of you? 153
When in our music God is glorified, 140
Your kingdom come, O Lord, 27

Advanced parts

A new commandment, 92
Bendice, Señor, nuestro pan, 156
Brother, sister, let me serve you, 94
Christ has arisen, alleluia, 100
Come now, O Prince of Peace, 82
Come, Holy Spirit, descend on us, 108
From my birth, 126
God to enfold you, 146
Holy, holy, holy, 38
In love you summon, 125
In you our hearts find rest, 145
Kyrie eleison, 14
Let there be peace on earth, 151
Love is never ending, 98
O give thanks to the Lord, 138
O Lamb of God, 43
Sent by the Lord, 79
Sleep, sleep, gently sleep, 66
The Servant Song, 94
We give thanks unto you, 98
We will lay our burden down, 78

Scriptural Index

Genesis

1	Cantemos al Señor *O sing unto the Lord*, 134
12:1–2, 15:5, 17:19, 21:1–2	We are on our way, 96

Deuteronomy

8:3	Bendice, Señor, nuestro pan, 156

1 Samuel

3:1–18	I, the Lord of sea and sky, 77

Psalm

19	Heaven and earth, 133
19:1	Cantemos al Señor *O sing unto the Lord*, 134
23	The Lord, the Lord, the Lord is my shepherd, 102
23	You are my shepherd, 104
34	Taste and see, 136
47:1	Clap your hands, v. 1, 113
62	In you our hearts find rest, 145
96	Heaven and earth, 133
103:2	O bless the Lord, 28
106:1, 48	Give thanks to the Lord our God *Rendei graças ao Senhor*, 8
119:105	Look up! 73
136	We give thanks unto you, 98
136:1–9, 21–26	O give thanks to the Lord, 138
139	From my birth, 126
139	Everywhere I go, 143

Isaiah

6:1–3	We see the Lord, 114
6:3	Holy, holy, holy *Santo, santo, santo*, 26
6:1–8	I, the Lord of sea and sky, 77
40:3–4, 9	Prepare ye the way, 63

Jeremiah

10:12–13	Many and great, 128

Micah

6:6–8	What does the Lord require of you? 153

Liturgical Index

New Year's Eve

The Epiphany
January 6

Three Kings Festival

Season after The Epiphany

Ash Wednesday

Lent

Liturgical Index (continued)

Topical Index

Index of Tune Names

Index of First Lines and Popular Titles

First lines are in regular typeface.
The second language of the first line is in italic.
Popular titles are in **bold**.